NEGOTIATING
LINGUA
FRANCAS

Complexity Theories Approaches to the
Interrelationships between Saudis' Perceptions of
English and their Reported Practices of English

Dr. Shahinaz Bukhari

NEGOTIATING LINGUA FRANCAS
COMPLEXITY THEORIES APPROACHES TO THE INTERRELATIONSHIPS BETWEEN SAUDIS' PERCEPTIONS OF ENGLISH AND THEIR REPORTED PRACTICES OF ENGLISH

iUniverse books may be ordered through booksellers or by contacting:

iUniverse
1663 Liberty Drive
Bloomington, IN 47403
www.iuniverse.com
1-800-Authors (1-800-288-4677)

ISBN: 978-1-6632-0197-3 (sc)
ISBN: 978-1-6632-0199-7 (hc)
ISBN: 978-1-6632-0198-0 (e)

Library of Congress Control Number: 2020913475

Print information available on the last page.

iUniverse rev. date: 07/27/2020

ABSTRACT

The extensive use of English in Saudi Arabia has inspired some studies to describe so-called 'Saudi English'. While these fruitful contributions have documented the linguistic features of this phenomenon, they have not taken into account the other dimensions in communication that interact with the linguistic dimension. This partialist approach could be part of a wider trend in the field of linguistics, with some researchers seeking generalisable findings and treating emergent languages as fixed systems of forms that can be researched in isolation. To open investigations of English in Saudi Arabia to insights beyond reductionism and variationism, this exploratory study adapts a holistic approach and a position inspired by complexity theory. This study's large-scale survey and interviews aimed to explore Saudis' (in)tolerance towards misalignment with standard English and how their positions relate to their reported language practices, beliefs, attitudes, motives, identity management, and ideologies. The statistical tests display significant interrelationships among all these parts. Overall, the findings reveal that Saudis' positive attitude towards the spread of English is enhanced by their international endeavours and willingness to play the role of transcultural negotiators, albeit not at expense of their non-negotiable Islamic identification. Prioritising Arabic over English enhances participants' tendency to transfer impressions from Arabic as a lingua franca to perceptions of English as a lingua franca. Participants' appreciation of standard Arabic in pedagogical settings aligns with their appreciation of standard English in pedagogical settings. However, participants' contextual(ised) tolerance towards misalignment with standard and native English usages is developed by their experiences with lingua franca communications. In favour of Islamic Saudi Arabian identification, participants' reported use of English in locally informal settings matched, with varying degrees, the linguistic description of so-called 'Saudi English'. As empirical evidence of this study displays, the regularity of 'Saudi English' language patterns is a by-product of repeated practices with religious, sociocultural, sociolinguistic, and translingual justifications. In favour of contextual performativity and adaptation, participants' reported use of English in international, transcultural, and multi-religion settings indicates openness to negotiation. This sensitivity to change suggests inadequacy of the label 'Saudi English' and a need to go beyond variationist approaches when seeking to understand language practices and perceptions. This study calls for the provision of a pedagogical space to address linguistic, cultural, functional, and contextual diversities of transcultural communication in English.

Table of Contents

Table of Tables

Acknowledgements

I would like to thank King Abdulaziz University for providing me with a PhD scholarship. I express my gratitude to everyone who contributed to this thesis, including the participants. My thanks goes as well to the staff and students at the University of Southampton, particularly to the faculties of Modern Languages Department and Centre of Global Englishes. These individuals have been a constant inspiration and source of guidance throughout this project.

Thanks must also go to the statisticians whose suggestions helped in raising the quality of the statistical procedures I have conducted and to the editors for their editorial advice on phrasing and language. Their advice has been sought with the oversight of my main supervisor. No changes of intellectual content were made as a result of their recommendations.

My main supervisor, Dr. Robert Baird, has earned my deep-felt gratitude for all the faith he showed in my project and for all his efforts and suggestions during the completion of my PhD journey.

My deepest appreciation to my beloved parents, siblings, and friends, whose support and encouragements were always with me. Special thanks to my mother, who took care of my children when I needed time for myself to complete this thesis.

Lastly, I dedicate this thesis to my children (Faris, Leen, Jowan, and Yousef), who have always motivated me to carry on.

Abbreviations

ALF	Arabic as a Lingua Franca
EFL	English as a Foreign Language
ELF	English as a Lingua Franca
ELT	English Language Teaching
ENL	English as a Native/First Language
ESL	English as a Second Language
KSA	Kingdom of Saudi Arabia
L1	First Language
LF	Lingua Franca
SLA	Second Language Acquisition
StE	Standard English
WEs	World Englishes
(un)…	The brackets in words such as (un)conscious and (in)tolerance mean 'or'.
…/…	The front slash between two words (e.g., ethnic/tribal) means 'or'.

Chapter 1:   Introduction

1.1   Starting point

1.1.1   Questioning orthodox assumptions

With an a priori way of thinking, in 2013 I described Saudi students' outcomes of English as 'abysmal' in an empirical study I conducted with Bahanshal (see Bukhary and Bahanshal, 2013: 192). Our study examined boosting Saudi students' motivation to improve their English. In that study, I judged students' non-standard English negatively, but I had forgotten that my own English does not always conform to Standard English (StE). The goal was to transform students' English into 'correct' English in the eyes of mainstream orientations such as English as a foreign language (EFL), English as a second language (ESL), Second Language Acquisition (SLA), and English language teaching (ELT) models. Our findings revealed that Saudis are very eager to learn/use English for 'instrumental motives' (e.g., education and career), but they feel demotivated in English classes because formal teaching focuses on the correction of linguistic forms (especially grammar) and does not allow students to develop the skills necessary for real-life interactions. Students complained that teachers' overcorrection to produce StE and teachers' imposition of usages of English as a native/first language (ENL) demotivated students and blocked their language creativity. Our recommendations proposed a shift toward communicative skills with an underlying assumption that this shift should involve matching StE and ENL usages, interactive strategies, and the integration of English for Specific Purposes within general English courses.

At that time, I did not question the fundamental assumptions of the mainstream SLA/ESL/EFL/ELT models. For instance, I did not ask myself whether they suit today's globalisation of

English, whether conformity to StE or ENL usages guarantees success in international communication in English, whether users depart from StE or ENL usages for certain reasons, and whether the stabilised language models exist in real-life practices. In 2016, after taking a Global Englishes course at the University of Southampton, I started questioning these orthodox assumptions and looking beyond the surface of the linguistic forms. Thus, I revisited the data that Bahanshal and I had collected in our study. When I reinterpreted our participants' accounts, I came up with different conclusions (e.g., students' desire to add their own imprints on English, students' positive attitudes towards English in spite of teachers' insistence to the contrary, and the mismatch between the kind of English students need/love to learn/use and the kind of English they are taught). Because Bahanshal and I employed partialist approaches, our data were not rich enough to achieve an understanding of the whole. A holistic picture is what the present study aims to explore. With an a posteriori way of thinking, the present study aims to examine the voices of Saudis, who have not previously been given the chance to reveal how far they (in)tolerate misalignment with StE and/or ENL usages, when and why they adjust their English usage, what motivations, identifications, and ideologies are behind their judgements, how their positions relate to their reported use of English, and how their reported use of English relates to 'Saudi English' corpora and natural discourse studies (see Section 2.4).

1.1.2   Going beyond variationist perspectives

'Global Englishes' is used as an umbrella term to capture interests in understanding English beyond the narrow confines of ENL settings and in challenging the orthodoxy of ELT, ESL, SLA, and EFL (Galloway and Rose, 2015). According to the various schools of thought and/or times of publishing, scholars have associated different terms with these interests. I have avoided all paradigms and expressions which suggest an impression of stability, one bounded entity, and/or exclusion of ENL users such as English as an international language (e.g., McKay, 2002, 2003, 2009; Pennycook, 1994), English as a global language (e.g., Crystal, 1998), English as a world language (e.g., Mair, 2003), and lingua franca English (e.g., Canagarajah, 2007; Firth, 1996). I have chosen to adapt the expression 'English as a lingua franca' (ELF) because its paradigm acknowledges dynamism, complexity, translingual liquidity, and the transcultural nature of today's use of English within and across geographical borders (e.g., Baird, 2012, 2013; Baird and Baird, 2018; Baird, Baker, and Kitazawa, 2014; Baker, 2015a, 2015b; Cogo, 2015; Galloway, 2013; Galloway and Rose, 2013, 2014, 2015; Jenkins, 2015a, 2015b, 2017a, 2017b; Mauranen, 2012, 2013; Seidlhofer, 2010, 2011). Although early ELF researchers in the 2000s tried to examine the possibility of ELF codification (e.g., Kirpatrick, 2007a, 2007b), ELF theorisation, analysis, and data revealed diversity, dynamism, and complexity (see Section 2.3). It is important to state that I do not suggest that ELF is sui generis because diversity, dynamism, and complexity exist in any communication in any language use. My framework suggests that all lingua franca (LF) communications exhibit these characteristics more often than monolingual/monocultural communications do.

Due to notorious debates around birth-right native-ness and functional native-ness in applied linguistics, some ELF studies have replaced the expressions 'native' and 'non-native' with other expressions, such as 'Anglophone' and 'non-Anglophone' (e.g., Baker, 2015a). My adaptation of some expressions (e.g., native, non-native, and first language) does not indicate my full compliance with them (see Section 3.3.2). For ease of reading, I use them sometimes but not without questioning. For instance, I use the expressions 'native English users' and 'ENL users' when I refer to Kachruvian Inner Circle users, and I use the expressions 'non-native English users' and 'ELF users' when I refer to Kachruvian Outer Circle and Expanding Circle users (see Kachru's 1986 and 1992 models). However, I believe that ENL users become ELF users when they adjust ENL with interlocutors whose first language (L1) is not English. In some

Kachruvian Expanding Circle regions, the intranational use of English reflects the sociolinguistic realities of the regions; it contains intensity and depth in their formal, informal, and contextual features; and it possesses a body of nativised registers and styles which are developed and codified as localised Englishes. In such regions, some scholars argue for the emergence of 'new English varieties' (e.g., 'Asian Englishes' in Bolton [2008], 'Gulf English' in Fussell [2011], and 'Saudi English' in Al-Rawi [2012]). To construct a holistic picture, my study seeks further insights into the issues that are behind non-conformity with StE and ENL usages. It investigates holistically how the linguistic dimensions and cognitive dimensions interact with the other dimensions of communication, including time and context. Such an investigation needs to examine Saudis' accounts of when, why, how and how far they (dis)align their use of English with StE models, ENL usage, and 'Saudi English' variants.

1.1.3   Relevance of complexity theory to the present study

The present study does not investigate 'perception' itself. It investigates the interrelations and interactions of interconnected parts of perceived language use. By viewing language as a social practice, I treat conscious introspection, context, and time as intrinsic parts of language use. From this complexity theory-informed lens, the unit of study of this research consists of a nested web (webs within webs). To holistically explore the interactions among the parts of this web, I add cognitive, affective, conative, social, temporal, and contextual dimensions to the traditional conceptualisations of 'perception' and its interconnected parts (e.g., beliefs, attitudes, ideologies, motives, identifications, and experiences). With this transdisciplinary perspective, I conceptualise each part as a fluid process that is capable of change in response to change in other interrelated parts. I realise my complexity theory-informed perspectives on some notions such as 'action', 'language', 'perception', 'mind', and 'ideology' may not obtain the approval of some philosophers in the humanities, social sciences, and ELF fields. Of course, as argued by Van Dijk (1998: 1), these 'complex' notions are always controversial and 'seem to happily live in the fuzzy life'. Furthermore, I realise that many humanities and social science scholars have no liking for these complexity theory-informed approaches and perspectives on social phenomena, perception studies, and language use research. However, my overall orientation in the present project mirrors my position as an applied linguist who is attempting to mediate between the rigidity of theories and real-world problems. Bearing this position in mind, this section discusses the relevant insights of complexity theory.

Complexity theory originally emerged from research in the physical sciences, biology, and mathematics to investigate complex phenomena. It has been productive in psychology and social psychology. A complexity theory paradigm is an emerging research paradigm in social science studies when traditional paradigms cannot adequately explain a phenomenon (Cohen, Manion, and Morrison, 2013). Complexity theory was first prominently employed to applied linguistics research by Diane Larsen-Freeman (1997) as an alternative to the simplistic linear model of SLA. Larsen-Freeman (2011) and Baker (2015a) proposed a complexity theory approach to accommodate both psychological and social perspectives when investigating the relationships between language use and perception to consider the social and cognitive dimensions of these relationships. This is not to suggest adopting identical approaches of complexity theory research in natural sciences but to employ complexity theory as a useful heuristic to contribute to a more holistic understanding of characteristics of a whole. In this study, I adapt the complexity theory-informed research paradigm, which means that I employ complexity theory as a way of thinking rather than as a mathematical or computerised model. I also do not use a complexity theory approach to model systems or make predictions. I instead use it to offer a complex description of a complex unit of study. In other words, I adapt it as a philosophy in all the stages of the current study to explore the interrelationships without modelling them (starting from formulating research questions, designing theoretical frameworks, and making decisions on methodologies to the stages of analysis, interpretations, conclusions, and recommendations). As argued by Baker (2015a) and Baird and Baird (2018), we can use complexity theory as a perspective, not as an algorithmic model. Blommaert (2013) offered a relevant position:

'I use complexity theory as a perspective, not as a compulsory vocabulary or theoretical template. It offers me a freedom to imagine, not an obligation to submit' (Blommaert, 2013: 10).

According to Larsen-Freeman and Cameron (2012), the expressions 'complex system' and 'complex adaptive system' refer to a phenomenon (e.g., language use) that has certain specified characteristics (e.g., casual interactions of many agents, non-linearity, disproportionality, emergence, co-adaptation, and self-organisation). It is important to mention that the terms 'system' and 'complex' have special meanings as used in the context of complexity theory perspectives. The two words are coupled to refer to a web that has some properties of processes and some properties of systems. The term 'complex' does not merely mean 'complicated'. A complicated system is difficult to study, but its rules can be addressable, identifiable, manageable, and controlled. A complex system involves too many interdependent agents that adapt continuously to turbulent surroundings through its own logic of emergence and freedom that cannot be controlled. The term 'system' does not mean a fixed set of entities with closed boundaries and well-defined behaviours but instead refers to a phenomenon that consists of a nested web in which each web has properties that reflect its interconnected belonging to the whole. In this sense, this study dissolves the dichotomies of system–process, function–form, competence–performance, top down–bottom up, and deduction–induction. In a nested approach, there is no point in affirming that one part is shaped by another. All the parts essentially and crucially shape and influence each other.

The bidirectional, interdependent, and multi-level interactions can generate adaptive changes in the system's outcome and patterns. Therefore, Larsen-Freeman and Cameron (2012) pointed out that the behaviours of language patterns in the outcomes need to be investigated to gain a comprehensive understanding of the whole. In compliance with this complexity perspective, the present study examines whether Saudis' reported use displays any language patterns in relation with 'Saudi English' variants. If so, it is within my interest to examine the sensitivity of these language patterns to cognition (e.g., beliefs and attitudes), affection (e.g., motivations), social dimensions (e.g., experiences), contextual factors (e.g., formal and informal settings), ideologies, and identifications. Based on complex adaptive system approaches to language use, language patterns in a LF, if they exist, are highly sensitive to change due to the cultural, contextual, and functional diversities of the LF (see Section 2.4.3).

Social phenomena are not approached as complex adaptive systems unless they exhibit 'significant complexity features' (Cohen et al., 2013; Larsen-Freeman, 2011; Larsen-Freeman and Cameron, 2012; Schroder, Homer-Dixon, Maynard, Mildenberger, Milkoreit, Mock, Quilley, and Thagard, 2013). The 'significant complexity features' include: dynamic interactions, multiple agents, overlaps, multiplicity, non-linearity, non-predictability, emergence, co-adaptation, self-organisation, openness, and patterns in the outcome of the whole. In Chapter 2, I discuss the 'significant complexity features' exhibited by ELF phenomena. In Chapter 3, I discuss how I approach the relationship between language perception and language use in light of complex adaptive systems. In traditional theoretical frameworks, researchers aim to conceptualise concepts with fixed definitions and clear boundaries. In complexity theory-informed research, researchers aim to remove the boundaries between parts by focusing on their interconnected interactions rather than singling out each part out of the whole (Baird et al., 2014; Baker, 2015a; Larsen-Freeman, 2011). Because the present study adapts complexity theory-informed philosophy, its theoretical framework conceptualises parts in terms of characterising and analysing interactions with each other rather than in terms of fixed definitions with clear-cut boundaries. To reflect this way of thinking, I highlight the dynamic interactions of the parts rather than debates on their classical conceptualisations. For ease of reading, I divide the discussions into sections, but this separation does not imply singling out each part of the whole. This anti-routine and interactive method may disappoint readers whose philosophy prefers precise definitions and clear-cut structures. Transcending the familiar in complexity theory research may expose the research to disapprobation. This dissent from the familiar might be criticisable; the field of ELF itself is rejected and attacked by some scholars (e.g., O'Regan, 2014).

1.2 Complex research problem

1.2.1 English within the complexity of the Saudi context

Previous studies have described the linguistic features of so-called 'Saudi English' (see Section 2.4.2). Such a focus on the linguistic dimension underestimates how English in the Kingdom of Saudi Arabia (KSA) is loaded with historically complicated, politically problematic, religiously sensitive, culturally conflicted, and ideologically contradictory issues (see Elyas, 2011). This load affects Saudis' symbolic relationships, identity positioning, and idea formations across gender, ethnic/tribal, regional, and many other fault lines. Because of the dimensions of this load, government policies of foreign languages and ELT in the KSA have been amended several times between 1925 and today (Elyas, 2011; Elyas and Picard, 2012a, 2012b; Faruk, 2014). Although language and ELT policies in the KSA use the term 'foreign language' when referring to English, they also announce explicitly that English is a means for communication with the globe and that it should be used/learned/taught with a projection of the Saudi/Islamic identity and without linguistic or cultural bias nor resentment toward any nation (Elyas, 2011; Elyas and Badawood, 2017; Faruk, 2014).

However, ELT public school books almost never integrate reference to ENL cultures, and this position comes, as some Saudis believe, in favour of protecting youths from 'Western ideologies'. ELT university materials include some ENL cultural aspects with superficial modifications to images and words that are 'taboo' or 'alien' to Muslims (Ahmad and Ahmad, 2015; Ahmad and Shah, 2014; Al-Asmari and Khan, 2014; Hudson, 2011; Mahboob and Elyas, 2014; Mekheimer and Aldosari, 2011; Nouraldeen and Elyas, 2014; Osman, 2015). Such a modification of university ELT materials is described by Ahmad and Shah (2014) as a 'superficial' and 'cosmetic' attempt to 'neutralise' and 'Saudised' English (i.e., transform it into Saudi). Previous studies (e.g., Elyas, 2011; Elyas and Badawood, 2017) have reported that Saudi English users struggle to achieve their roles as guardians of Islamic identification, Saudi cultural values, and the Arabic language, as these roles sometimes contradict the demands of globalisation, intercultural settings, and non-Muslim lifestyles. The present study attempts to holistically determine where this struggle exists; where it does, I will explore the issues related to this struggle and consider how Saudis manage the struggle and their identity negotiation in relation to English use and contextual dimensions.

In addition, reports from the 2015–18 edition of Ethnologue, published by SIL International organisation, show that the number of non-native users of Arabic is larger than the number of native Arabic users. In discussing the future of ELF, Jenkins (2017a: 6) pointed out that some scholars 'have suggested as possible replacements as the primary global language, Mandarin Chinese, Arabic, and Spanish', and others have suggested that 'English may at some stage share its lingua franca role with other languages'. Some studies (e.g., Hudson, 2011; Nouraldeen and Elyas, 2014) have noted that the generous scholarships of Gulf countries to ENL countries support the spread of both Arabic and English and that many non-Arabs who work/live in Gulf countries end up speaking or understanding Arabic or some Islamic expressions. This suggests that Saudis do not completely abandon Arabic or Islamic usages when they communicate in English with non-Arabs. Moreover, it means that Saudis experience at least two lingua francas (Arabic and English).

The lingua francas of 2016 identified by the United Nations are English, Chinese, Arabic, Spanish, French and Russian. This acknowledgement indicates the status of Arabic as the first lingua franca in the Middle East and the third lingua franca in the world. Since 2007, UNESCO has recognised English as the official lingua franca used in the KSA to communicate with the yearly mass of international pilgrims from around the globe (UNESCO IBE, 2007 as cited in Al-Rawi, 2012). This recognition underestimates the fact that Saudis use ELF and Arabic as a lingua franca (ALF) with non-Arabs who work/live in the KSA and with the masses of international Muslims who come to the KSA to visit the two Holy Mosques in Makkah and Madinah or to perform pilgrimage, and the majority of these pilgrims and expatriates are non-native English users and Arabs (Al-Rawi, 2012; Nouraldeen and Elyas, 2014). Nouraldeen and Elyas (2014) noted that the Arabic Saudis use in ALF communications differs from the Arabic they use to communicate with Arabs. This implies that Saudis experience different lingua francas, different kinds of English, and different kinds of Arabic (e.g., Quranic Arabic, modern standard Arabic, different Saudi Arabic dialects, and different non-Saudi Arabic varieties).

This complexity of the Saudi context and its users creates a new avenue of research, as perceptions of English have rarely considered whether people are native users of other lingua francas themselves. In this study, Saudis are positioned to shed light on how English is perceived by those expected to be aware of LF communications in their L1. An investigation of Saudis' experiences and perceived language use can yield to exploring whether and how perceptions of different kinds of English relate to perceptions of different kinds of Arabic. Finding answers to these open and complex inquiries requires employing theoretical, methodological, and analytical frameworks that account for notions of complexity, translingualism, LF functions, and transcultural interactions. Through the practical application of complexity theory approaches, this study can expand on the conceptual foundations of English in the field of ELF and in the Saudi Arabian context.

1.2.2 Circle of blame

In the KSA, recent studies have documented the extensive use of English by Saudis in both formal and informal settings in international and intranational interactions with other Saudis and non-Saudis in many domains, including higher education, school education, work, conferences, publications, business, research projects, tourism, entertainment, family gatherings, internet, media, street signs, official bills, and everyday speech in hospitals, restaurants, shopping malls, companies, banks, airports, tourism agencies, post offices, supermarkets, shops, and other settings (Al-Asmari and Khan, 2014; Al-Rawi, 2012; Alshahrani and Al-Shehri, 2012; Al-Shurafa, 2009; Ebrahim and Awan, 2015; Elyas, 2014; Mahboob and Elyas, 2014; Nouraldeen and Elyas, 2014). These studies have also reported that Saudis use English most of the time when interacting with non-native English users who work/live in the KSA and who have brought with them a wide variety of Englishes, and these Englishes have influenced Saudis' English.

To prepare future generations to communicate with the globe, the KSA has set aside a large budget and made efforts to develop English courses, make ELT reforms, and provide Saudis with scholarships to ENL universities. However, it is reported that Saudis' English is unsatisfactory and that Saudi students encounter significant problems in StE-based exams at universities (see Alhawsawi, 2014; Al-Johani, 2009; Alrashidi and Phan, 2015; Al-Seghayer, 2014; Grami, 2012; Javid, Farooq, and Gulzar, 2012; Khan I., 2011; Khan M., 2015; Ur Rahman and Alhaisoni, 2013). Despite the many years of formal education and the expansion of English use in wider domains in the KSA, ELT/ESL/EFL/SAL studies have reported that Saudis still have 'weakness' in the 'four language skills', commit 'frustrating errors' in basic grammatical rules, and produce 'bad', 'weak', and 'poor' English (see Grami, 2012; Javid et al., 2012).

It is not only Saudi students who are judged negatively for their 'deviations' from StE but also ELT Saudi professionals, who are blamed for not conforming to StE and for codeswitching (see Alfahadi, 2012; Alhawsawi, 2014; Alrashidi and Phan, 2015; Javid et al., 2012). Saudi ELT professionals have been perceived as 'incompetent', and their use of English has been described as 'inappropriate' because it differs from StE and ENL usages. Such conclusions have been drawn based on the reports of Saudis' scores in StE-based exam boards such as Test of English as Foreign Language (TOEFL) and International English Language Testing System (IELTS). It is not only ELT Saudi teachers who misalign with StE and ENL usages but also ELT public school textbooks in the KSA. A linguistic analysis of these textbooks revealed that the grammatical rules are prescribed based on Standard British English, but the usages of these rules sometimes 'deviate' from StE and reflect a mixture of different Englishes and some localised English usages (Grami, 2012; Mahboob and Elyas, 2014; Nouraldeen and Elyas, 2014). The English variants appearing in these textbooks match English variants appearing in the real-life usage of Saudi students, teachers, authors, and well-educated professionals but with different frequencies and levels of proficiency (Al-Rawi, 2012; Mahboob and Elyas, 2014). From the aforementioned studies, I have found that some ELT stakeholders in the KSA blame one another, and sometimes themselves, for not conforming to StE. Other ELT-related dimensions, such as policies, school education, university systems, teaching materials, teaching methods, the delayed introduction of English, management systems, the number of hours of English classes per week, lack of language labs, lack of educational aids, assessment systems, and teacher education/development programmes, are also blamed.

Interestingly, reports of previous research, articles and newspapers suggested that the majority of Saudis are 'well aware' of their 'deviations' from StE, but they insist on repeating the same 'errors' again and again (e.g. Javid et al., 2012). Because I think that these repetitions of 'mistakes' and 'errors' may be (un)conscious or related to underlying sociocultural factors, I aim to explore whether Saudis intend to use some variants on purpose (and if so, why, when and how?). In other words, it is within my interest to explore whether Saudis support making certain kinds of educational decisions in relation to English and ELT. Furthermore, ELT in the KSA creates a new avenue of research for the present study, as Saudis are well-positioned to shed new light on how English in relation to ELT is perceived by those who have experienced both locally-oriented ELT (in schools) and British/American-oriented ELT (in universities). I will also examine Saudis' opinions about ELF-oriented approaches to ELT. Understanding Saudis' perceptions of English and ELT from this perspective raises awareness of their needs. Based on their needs, the present study offers pedagogical implementations that can bridge the gap between theory and practice. It is important to clarify that an ELF-oriented approach to ELT does not mean teaching ELF or replacing models. Inspired by Galloway and Rose's (2014, 2015) ideas about a Global Englishes-oriented approach to ELT, an ELF-oriented approach raises students' awareness and tolerance of linguistic, cultural, functional, and contextual diversities of the globalisation of English; it provides opportunities to use English in real-life settings; and it allows students to reflect critically on their experiences of English.

1.3 Literature gap

As discussed by Barcelos (2003), mainstream SLA/ESL/EFL/ELT studies, which investigate the relationship between language perceptions and practices, tend to describe both perceptions and outcomes as obstacles when they do not match the hypothesised 'ideal' ones. Based on this deficit perspective, pedagogical interventions are suggested to transform language users' perceptions, outcomes, and practices to become 'good' and 'successful' in the eyes of mainstream models. My project, from an ELF standpoint and complexity theory-informed perspective, views language perceptions and language practices as experience-based, socially constituted and conditioned, interactively sustained, and contextually bounded because they are interrelated with their own ecology. Many fruitful ELF studies on perception relate language users' views with their practices, but most approach these issues with orientations other than complexity theory approaches. Chapter 2 acknowledges useful contributions of relevant studies, discusses their limitations, and highlights how the present study covers their shortcomings. This is not to suggest the superiority of complexity theory orientation over others but to suggest exploring ELF issues with more contextually grounded, dynamic, and open orientations. As noticed by Baker (2015a), complexity theory has not yet been explored extensively in social sciences, or more specifically, applied linguistics and ELF studies. In the ELF field, Seidlhofer (2011) and Mauranen (2012) suggested approaching ELF communication as a complex system, but they have not expanded on this suggestion. Baird et al. (2014) and Baker (2015a) proposed approaching ELF communication in light of complexity theory perspectives and suggested approaching the relationship between ELF practices and perceptions in light of complex adaptive systems, but they, like Seidlhofer (2011) and Mauranen (2012), have not explored this suggestion in detail.

While reviewing literature on Saudis' perceptions and/or use of English in relation to globalisation, I found a few World Englishes (WEs)-oriented studies and a scarcity of ELF-oriented studies. Previous studies in the Saudi context have indicated that little research has been conducted to address how English and ELT in the KSA can respond successfully to the latest controversial issues of pedagogy that have emerged due to the globalisation of English (Abdalla, 2008; Al Asmari, 2014; Al-Asmari and Khan, 2014; Alharbi, 2016; Elyas, 2015; Elyas and

Picard, 2012a; Onsman, 2012). At the time of writing, I found only three articles on ELF and two ELF empirical studies in the Saudi context, and all four works complain of the scarcity of ELF studies in the Saudi context. The articles by Abdalla (2008) and Al-Asmari and Khan (2014) stated that ELF is not recognised nor encouraged in the KSA. Onsman's (2012: 477) article criticised 'perceptions of mistrust by and towards non-Saudis', encouraged multilingualism in education, and suggested the disassociation of English from ENL models and the adoption of ELF in the KSA. Al-Asmari and Khan's (2014) article suggested that the younger Saudi generations may be interested in going beyond the narrow confines of standard British/American models and in broadening ELT cultural components beyond Saudi and ENL cultures. Al Asmari's (2014) quantitative study investigated ELT teachers' perceptions of ELF-oriented ELT at a Saudi university, and Alharbi's (2016) PhD qualitative methodology investigated business ELF pragmatics at a Saudi multinational corporation. Both studies employed partialist approaches, were conducted on a relatively small scale, and had a considerable number of non-Saudi and non-Arabic participants.

Through WEs-oriented approaches and variationist perspectives, some studies have described Saudis' observed usages and linguacultural markers of what has been dubbed 'Saudi English' (see Section 2.4.2). Despite the fruitful contributions of these studies, I disagree with their WEs-oriented approaches because I underscore the dynamic nature of LF interactions within/ through/across boundaries. Through a complexity theory lens, I believe that a corpus cannot explore the dynamics of language use because it consists of a static set of attested language patterns, and I believe that an actual discourse cannot explore how a conscious introspection, which is considered part of the complex system in language use, interacts with the other parts. To fill the literature gap, I employ complexity theory to go beyond mere comparisons between ELF variants and StE models or attitudes towards ELF variants and ENL usages. To gain a holistic understanding, I examine on a relatively large scale the interrelationships between Saudis' observed usages of English (which were described by previous studies) and perceived usages (which the present study investigates).

1.4 Research purposes, questions, objectives, and significance

This project is a mixed-method, sequential, exploratory study with a qualitative phase (interviews) building on and helping to explain the initial mixed-method survey on a relatively large scale. This study offers a holistic description of how the linguistic dimension relates to the cognitive, affective, social, contextual, and temporal dimensions of perceived language use in relation to the experiences of Saudi English users in the Global Englishes era. To explore the interrelationships, I see the unit of study of my project as a nested web. This view mirrors how I posed my research questions (questions within questions):

> RQ1. How, and to what extent, do Saudis report (in)tolerance towards misalignment with StE models?
>
> RQ2. How, and to what extent, do Saudis' judgements of (in)tolerance relate to their:
>
> a. beliefs and attitudes towards their own English, the global spread of English, and English associations with natives and non-natives;
> b. motives for using/learning English;
> c. identifications and feelings of belongings;
> d. contextual factors?

In the first stage, a survey (with open and closed items) addresses RQ1 and RQ2. In the second stage, individual follow-up interviews investigate participants' justifications for their survey responses. To understand how unconscious usages of English relate to reported practices of English, data from 'Saudi English' corpora and natural discourse are used in the survey and interviews. In addition, it is within the interpret of the present study to comment on the differences and similarities between what participants say (reported practices, experiences, and perceptions) and how they say it (observed use of English in written and oral responses). The present study's complexity theory-inspired questions, unit of study, and theoretical, methodological, and analytical frameworks are designed to explore what constitutes 'good' English in the eyes of Saudis and how their outlooks relate to their experiences (with ELF, ALF, and ELT), time dimensions (e.g., temporal motives), identity management and negotiation (e.g., Islamic identification, professional identity, transcultural identity, and L1 linguacultural identity), and contextual settings (e.g., local, international, pedagogical, and non-pedagogical).

Complexity theory is not necessary to appreciate the complexity of the relationships among these parts. Some complexity theory considerations (see Section 1.1.3) are based on other theoretical frameworks such as ethnography, critical theory, and sociocultural theory, which appreciate complexity and do not view constructs as stable but socially created. However, the complexity theory framework allows for the forwarding of a narrative that opens a space for the appreciation of the complex relationships between language perceptions and practices. In ELF research, the narrative has focused on simplistic accounts and/or how ELF users 'co-operate'. This treatment suggests that there is a group of 'ELF speakers' that always co-operate. The treatment does not allow for the appreciation of who people are and what they actually do in practice. A complexity theory focus guides this project to examine language, people, thinking, and practices as complex. This treatment reflects the reality of language use and users' thinking and practices. The present project's contribution, which uses a complexity theory lens, provides a narrative that frees itself from common narratives in language research, teaching, and applications that look for a uniform narrative and/or tend to talk about people in groups, languages as varieties, and/or perceptions as being 'sable thinking' of 'stable forms' of language. To change these narratives, complexity theory and ELF frameworks are useful for this project to examine English that Saudis perceive and experience because these frameworks aid in understanding the complexity of the language and deconstructing narratives. These issues may be considered in a number of different forms without complexity theory and embedded in the way that people talk about research and/or language of groups of people or language performances broken down into small elements and treated with complexity theory. It is possible to appreciate complexity without complexity theory framework, but the difference is in the narrative, the way in which people talk about language, and treatment of language thinking and practices in large-scale studies rather than criticising the field as an object. This framework offers opportunities to treat people, language, and narratives with a more realistic and practice-based focus that looks at what language really is, and who these people really are, rather than measuring or summarising their existence.

To construct a holistic picture based on complexity theory approaches, the present study moves beyond its own disciplinary boundaries and undertakes a transdisciplinary orientation by borrowing insights from natural sciences, linguistics, sociolinguistics, cognitive linguistics, psychology, and social psychology. This transdisciplinary orientation can bring new insights that are translated across fields. This complexity framework can shed new light onto English usage in the KSA and will highlight the voices I want ELF researchers to listen to in a new way. Understanding the participants' perceptions of their practices and experiences (i.e., their own realities) in their own words can offer awareness from those in ELF contexts for future research, displaying the gap between theory and practice (Baird, 2013).

As an applied linguist, I take users' views seriously as a valuable source for identifying their English language-related problems and for suggesting adequate solutions that align with their own contexts. By acknowledging the significance of language users' views, some ELF scholars have argued that the voices and accounts of ELF users should be heard and taken seriously, rather than assumed, in order to develop implementations that aid in solving users' language-related problems (Dewey, 2014; Wang and Jenkins, 2016). Language users' perceptions can represent the starting point for research into linguistic theory and develop the theoretical framework in linguistics and applied linguistics. The present study's findings, conclusions, and recommendations can provide opportunities for new understandings and actions. The present study's implications and implementations can contribute to the future development of pedagogy and provide immense benefits for ELT stakeholders, including researchers, teacher-educators, trainers, institutions, publishers, and policy makers. Bearing this in mind, the present study is not free from the pressure to prove its validity for implementation by suggesting practical solutions for Saudis' English-related problems.

1.5   Structure of the thesis

This thesis is divided into seven chapters. Chapter 2 reconceptualises language in general and today's English practices in particular based on complexity theory approaches. It also discusses how and why I approach English reported practices in the light of LF approaches and complex adaptive phenomena. Chapter 3 discusses complexity theory approaches to perceptions of English in the Global Englishes Era. Chapter 4 discusses the present study's methodology in relation to the complexity theory research paradigm. Chapter 5 presents the results, analysis, and findings of the survey. Chapter 6 presents the results, analysis, and findings of the interviews. Chapter 7 offers a summary and a conclusion by providing an overview of the answers to the research questions. It also discusses the limitations and implications of the present study and presents suggestions for future research alongside implementations for pedagogy.

Chapter 2: Complexity theory approach to practices of English

2.1 Introduction

This chapter questions the stability of any language use, especially a LF use (not just ELF use). It starts with conceptualisations of ELF within contact language, usage-based, emergent grammar, multilingualism, translingualism, accommodation, and communication frameworks. The discussion suggests that what appears in ELF is not sui generis, but it is the manifestation of the scope and scale of language evolution and language contact under the agency of ELF users. Mauranen (2012: 29) describes ELF as 'a site of an unusually complex contact'. This complex evolution justifies why some scholars describe ELF communications as 'phenomena' (e.g., Cogo, 2015; Galloway and Rose, 2015). This chapter highlights the 'significant complexity features' that explain how and why I approach English (reported) use, sensitivity, and patterns in the light of complex adaptive phenomena. It concludes by questioning the existence of a Saudi static identifiable 'variety' of English.

2.2 Definitions, conceptualisations, and approaches

2.2.1 Definitions within language contact and communication perspectives

The origin of the expression 'lingua franca' comes from the Arabic expression 'lisan-al-farang' (House, 2003; Jenkins, 2013). During the Middle Ages, Arabs invented the term 'lisan-al-farang' to refer to the pidgin language developed spontaneously out of contact with people from different parts of the Mediterranean (Goebl, 1997; Kahane and Kahane, 1976).

The expression 'lingua franca' means in English 'Contact Vernacular' (Kahane and Kahane, 1976). Firth (1996: 240) defines ELF as a 'contact language between persons who neither share a common native tongue nor a common national culture and for who English is the chosen language of communication'. Both Firth (1996) and House (2002) exclude ENL users from ELF contexts. McKay (2002, 2003, 2009) excludes ENL users from ELF interactions and uses the expression 'English as an international language' when ENL users are involved. However, I do not agree on this narrow sense of ELF; I do not agree on excluding ENL users from ELF communications; and I do not exclude ELF interactions among users who share an L1.

ELF has been variously described as 'English when it is used as a contact language between people from different first languages' (Jenkins, 2013:24), 'English that functions as a lingua franca' (Seidlhofer, 2011:11), and 'second-order language contact between similects arising from first-order contacts between English and a good proportion of the world's other languages' (Mauranen, 2012: 243). Mauranen (2013) describes ELF as a 'similect contact' which has some features of 'dialect contact' such as simplification, complexification, and re-allocation because different languages, varieties, and lects are in contact with English, and these contact similects are in contact with each other. The concept of 'similect contact' emphasises hybrid cross-linguistic transfer, which highlights the discrepancy between ENL monolingual contexts and ELF multilingual contexts (Ishikawa, 2017).

Based on ELF extended theorisation, ELF is defined by Jenkins (2015a: 73) as 'multilingual communication in which English is available as a contact language of choice, but is not necessarily chosen' and where other languages or other lingua francas may be present. This definition reflects a communication perspective on ELF within a multilingualism framework, and it does not exclude ELF interactions among users who share an L1. With a complexity lens, I use the expression 'ELF' in the present study to mean:

'communication involving a number of interrelated complex systems that may include an individual's mental representations of language (Hall 2013), language as a social system (Sealey and Carter 2004), communicative strategies (Firth 2009), or even perhaps English itself (Larsen-Freeman 2011)' (Baird et al., 2014: 183).

2.2.2 Conceptualisations within usage-base, language contact, emergent grammar, multilingualism, and accommodation frameworks

Langacker's (1987) usage-based theories view language as an inventory of linguistic constructions accumulated in the repeated process of using the language by users in order to communicate. In the case of English, the large number of users repeating some usages and transferring them to one another and to younger generations contribute to linguistic changes and variants in all Kachruvian Circles (MacKenzie, 2015). When particular languages interact (not just contact) with each other extensively, they influence each other's structures (see Section 2.3.1). Therefore, Mauranen (2012) suggests that ENL may have traces of ELF variants in the future. The gradual changes in any language, particularly when it is used as a LF, result undoubtedly from language contact and pidginisation with other languages and/or varieties (e.g., Shakespeare's English and Quranic Arabic). These changes do not only involve simplifications and reductions, but they also involve complexification, enrichment, and admixture (Mauranen, 2013). These characteristics result from hybrid cross-linguistic transfer. Based on the idea of language change resulting from language contact, Trudgill (2011) argues that any high-contact language is likely to change gradually, especially when it is used by multilinguals who have learned it after Lenneberg's (1967) critical age of language acquisition (13 years old, which is controversial). In the case of Saudi context, some studies have criticised Saudis for not producing native-like English and blamed public education for introducing English to Saudi students in post-adolescence (see Section 1.2.2). As described by Trudgill (2011), post-adolescent learners tend to regularise irregularities (e.g., 'feeled' instead of 'felt'), replace synthetic structures (i.e., prescriptive rules about how language should be used) with analytic structures (i.e., observed real-life usages) to increase transparency (e.g., dropping the third person singular –s inflection), and pidginise usages (e.g., transferring L1 functions to other languages). As previous studies have documented these tendencies in Saudis' English outcome (see Section 2.4.2), it is within my interest to investigate Saudis' views on these usages.

Halliday's (1975) functional grammar suggests that static semantic functions are encoded to construct meaning making (i.e., forms follow functions). Therefore, Halliday's (1997) sociolinguistic perspective argues that a language includes 'an open-ended set of options', and any specific choice made by a language user is justified by its social context. Widdowson's (2012) discussion implies that the difference between functional grammar and ELF use is that the latter is (re)developed and (re) motivated by ongoing contextual functions. Hopper's (1988) account of emergent grammar proposes that grammar is a by-product of socially-shared sedimented usages from which identifiable patterns emerge. In this account of language, linguistic patterns are renegotiated in speech, and grammar is open to change depending on the contexts and interlocutors. These accounts suggest that ELF variants are natural results of expanding repertoires of communicative contests, and that these repertoires will never totalise around particular users/ regions, hence why ENL users are included in conceptualisation of ELF and why national-based conceptualisations can be problematic for ELF research. In order not to focus on function at the expense of forms, some ELF scholars (e.g., Seidlhofer, 2011) reject emergentist approaches and suggest the existence of underlying abstract sets of rules that ELF users exploit and make reference to when using ELF. From emergentist and complexity perspectives, Ishikawa (2015: 40) argues that 'form and function are not a priori; but emerge and operate interdependently during communication acts'. Therefore, emergentist approaches question the necessity of positioning an underlying structure that can be exploited. From a complexity theory perspective, regularity of patterns is an outcome of repeated engagements with shared practices in flux (Baird et al., 2014; Larsen-Freeman and Cameron, 2012).

As described by communication accommodation theories (e.g., Giles, 2009), interlocutors adjust their linguistic outcomes (e.g., accent, grammar, phraseology, echoing, borrowing, and codeswitching), and paralinguistic behaviours (e.g., pitch, intonation, inflection, and gestures) to accommodate to each other's verbal and non-verbal behaviours (see Sections 3.3.4). Accommodation theories help in understanding reasons why interlocutors emphasise or reduce each other's differences through employing verbal and non-verbal strategies (Cogo, 2015; Dewey, 2011). According to accommodation theories, 'convergence' refers to the strategies that interlocutors use to approximate each other's communicative behaviours. Convergence suggests that interlocutors have desires to fulfil identity expectations and gain social approval. By contrast, 'divergence' refers to the communicative strategies that interlocutors use to accentuate each other's differences (non-accommodation). Divergence suggests that interlocutors have the desire to signal individual identity, distance, and/or disapproval. Accommodation processes among multilinguals (e.g., ELF users) can be clearer than accommodation processes among users who share L1, because the former contains more variations than the latter. If interlocutors have the will to coverage, they 'soft assemble using their language resources on a given occasion and then interact and adapt to each other, the state space of both their language resources changes as a result of co-adaptation' (Larsen-Freeman and Cameron, 2012: 84). In this sense, language forms a part of people's symbolic interactions, through which they do or do not accommodate each other, whilst also wishing to reach particular goals (see Sections 3.3.4) and to be identified in particular ways (see Sections 3.3.5). Through investigation of contextual reflections on experiences, the present study can understand how Saudis perceive adjustment, convergence, and divergence in relation to others with whom they communicate.

2.2.3   Approaching ELF use as a complex social practice

Jenkins (2015a) categorises the development of ELF field as a research inquiry into two phases 'ELF 1' (i.e., modernist and variationist perspectives) and 'ELF 2' (i.e., appreciation of linguistic creativity, fluidity, social situated-ness, and tendency to hybridity), and then, she proposes a potential third phase, 'ELF 3' (i.e., taking multilingualism, interculturality, and emergence into consideration). During the ELF 2 phase, House (2003) and Seidlhofer (2009a, 2009b) suggested that the notion of a 'community of practice' fits ELF settings more than the traditional notion of a 'speech community' because ELF contexts gather interlocutors from diverse social and linguistic backgrounds as equal members in a community of practice with 'shared repertoires' for a specific reason with mutual engagements and jointly negotiated enterprises. They argued that the traditional concept of a 'speech community' does not suite the global use of English because this concept is linked with locality, physical proximity, and having mutual cultural references and linguistic features in a specific geographic community. Although the notion of a 'community of practice' emphasises connectivity and socially shared practices, the term 'community' needs to be treated with caution because it may reify connections where they are loose or may dislocate one community in an analysis from other communities that might be more relevant for the behaviours, practices, or perceptions involved (Baird, 2012). The unrealistic idea of the existence of homogenous communities 'sharing the same language and idioms and references and allusions is increasingly a fiction' (MacKenzie, 2014: 101). Some scholars criticise the concepts of an English 'native community' and an 'ELF community' as these concepts suggest identical homogeneity of backgrounds, usages, communicative strategies, and linguistic competence (Baird et al., 2014; Davis, 2003; MacKenzie, 2014).

Inspired by the proposals of Canagarajah (2012) and Jenkins (2015a), I view ELF use as a dynamic social practice in contact zones with translingual and transcultural resources in flux. The idea of 'social practice' goes beyond mere performance and embodies the locale of semiotic meanings, contextual(ised) performativity, social actions, and relations (Baird et al., 2014; Baird and Baird, 2018). The concept of 'contact zones' associates language use with timescales (e.g., transient interactions and temporal purposes). The notion of 'translingualism' conceives English practices in a hybrid way that resembles the complex vision of globalisation and emphasises the mutual influence of all available languages on users' English and their other languages. The 'transculturalism' concept suggests a wide pluralistic view of multi-competence and implies that ELF settings involve interactions occurring through and across cultures. The idea of 'resources in flux' suggests that interlocutors' resources and repertoires are influenced and adjusted by one another. Inspired by these perspectives, this study treats context, timescales, and conscious introspection as intrinsic parts of (reported) language use.

2.3 ELF phenomena in relation to complex adaptive systems

As discussed in Section 1.1.3, a social phenomenon cannot be approached as a complex adaptive system unless it exhibits 'significant complexity features'. This section discusses how ELF phenomena fulfil the 'significant complexity features' of complex adaptive systems. The discussion draws attention to the complex nature of any language use in general and ELF in particular.

2.3.1 Linguistic conformity vs translanguaging

Linguistics studies reveal that ENL users do not conform to one stable model and their uses of English are different from the constructed grammars prescribed in language textbooks

(Jenkins, 2015a; MacKenzie, 2014; Matras, 2009; Trudgill, 2002). Medgyes (1994) and Crystal (1998) highlight the fact that the number of British people who speak with Received Pronunciation is limited. Trudgill (2002) asserts that more than 85% of ENL users use non-standard usages in spoken discourses. This fact means that linguistic conformity to StE models is not widely produced, but these models are still viewed as 'prestigious' or 'correct' 'norms'. In the light of what has been discussed in Section 2.2 about real-life language usages, ELF scholars move beyond conformity to any fixed rule-based language models. This move suggests that traditional models of language have already failed to describe linguistic realities, and that is before we consider the translingual, transcultural, and heteronormative nature of ELF interactions. In LF interactions, LF users exploit resources to produce language constructions that can fulfil the target functions (Cogo, 2015; Dewey, 2014; Seidlhofer, 2011; Mauranen, 2013). From a LF standpoint, some ELF variants can be viewed as a cumulative by-product of natural development (see Section 2.2.2), communication situations (see Section 2.2.3), transcultural awareness (see Sections 2.3.4), contextual co-adaptation (see Section 2.3.2), identity-processed languaging (see Section 2.3.5), situated performativity competence (see Section 2.3.3), and translanguaging (as discussed in this section). I use the term 'translingualism' when I refer to phenomena relevant to more than one language and I use the term 'translanguaging' when I refer to a practice-based process that 'involves dynamic and functionally integrated use of different languages and language varieties, but more importantly a process of knowledge construction that goes beyond language(s)' (see Wei, 2017: 15).

Composing one's own language constructions and expressions that can fulfil the target functions indicates energy, proficiency, and/or creativity (Dewey, 2014). From a complexity theory standpoint, language learning 'is a matter not only of learning conventions, but also of innovation, of creation as much or than reproduction' (Larsen-Freeman and Cameron, 2012: 10), and language mastery is evaluated by the ability to compose infinite numbers of novel and meaningful constructions (and each construct is an open network of constructions), not by the ability to reproduce sedimented and ready-made language usages. The more ready-made ENL expressions and constructions that ELF users use, the less analytic processing they complete (MacKenzie, 2014). Dewey (2014) suggests that as ELF users become more proficient in English, they exploit more resources in different ways to meet specific communicative demands and achieve contextual functions. This is not to suggest that all ELF variants or users are innovative, but to take into consideration that an ELF user may use English in a different (but not necessarily deficit or creative) way.

The notions of 'multilingualism' and 'tranculturalism' suggest that ELF users can deactivate one resource, but this deactivation may not be total. They also showcase the fluidity of linguistic and cultural hybridity in ELF use, and imply that languages and cultures interact (not just contact) with one another. Herdina and Jessner's (2002) dynamic model of multilingualism describes languages' interactions as 'liquids' which, when mixed, produce a new liquid whose properties are different from the main languages. In this sense, language proficiency relates to 'the way different languages constitute an integrated competence' (Jenkins, 2017b: 5). ELF users may intertwine, intentionally or unintentionally, other languages' components with each other (i.e., cross-linguistic influence) and exploit multiple linguistic and cultural resources. It is important, here, to mention that I do not claim that all ELF users fuse languages. For instance, in some cases, ELF users may conform to StE models more than ENL users do.

Through taking these perspectives into consideration, some ELF variants have been described by ELF scholars in terms such as legitimate 'borrowings', purposeful 'code-switching', 'multi-communicative styles', 'intentional transfer', 'coining', and 'analogy'. This is because some deficit notions such as 'deviations', 'interference', 'fossilisation', 'intrusions', 'lexical gaps', 'incorrect semantic extensions', 'incorrect calquing', 'negative collocational transfer', 'negative subcategorising transfer', and 'interlanguage' do not suit some ELF variants. Regarding this, MacKenzie (2014: 140-155) describes ELF perspectives as 'angelic accounts' which tend to 'interpret evidence optimistically'. His criticism is right sometimes as some ELF studies tend to interpret every non-standard use positively. To clarify my position, it is important to state that I do not claim that there are no errors in ELF use. In some cases, misalignments are errors resulting from low language proficiency. With caution, the present study adapts Kachru's (1992) distinction between errors and variants (see Section 2.3.2). Without caution, the reported English, and may be Arabic, that Saudis have experienced, practised, valued, perceived, and talked about might be misunderstood or treated differently.

2.3.2 Correctness vs contextual co-adaptation

Based on Kachru's (1992) distinction between errors and variants, WEs research identifies errors as divergent usages from StE and ENL usages which do not have any sociolinguistic or sociocultural justifications in research. Variants are identified as different usages for which research could document their sociolinguistic explanations, sociocultural justifications, pragmatic dimensions, and exploitation of linguistic resources to meet specific communicative demands. From a variationist perspective, Kirkpatrick (2007b) suggests codification of a local ELF benchmark, as exemplified by the use of local proficient users of ELF to provide an attainable target model for local users/learners. This idea of codification is rejected by many ELF scholars (Baker, 2015a; Baird et al., 2014; Baird and Baird, 2018) because its reductionist orientation underestimates the complex nature of language use and communication, simplifies ELF use to intranational usages, neglects ELF use in intercultural settings, suggests the denial of the indefinite ways of constructing language acts, and implies stabilising static rules systems which conflict with the inconsistency of linguistic realities. Codification of a LF use ignores the fact that LF patterns negotiate their (super) diversity, (re)adjust their practices, and co-adapt with their other interactive parts, including the contexts. From a complexity theory point of view, the context is coupled with the individual in a process of co-adaptation that affects behaviours, including linguistic choices (Larsen-Freeman and Cameron, 2012). In this sense, the context of language use (with its language resources) is not external to the language users (and their language resources). Complexity theory approaches treat the context as an intrinsic part of language use and experiences. Thus, a-contextual judgments on language are rejected by complexity advocates.

Taking contextual language judgments into consideration, ELF research replaces the principle of 'doing the right things' with the principle of 'doing things right' in favour of appropriateness of convergence in transcultural interactions. Mauranen (2013) argues that if 'good' equals 'native-like' in the eyes of traditional perspectives, 'good' equals 'appropriate' from an ELF standpoint. Jenkins (2013: 38) argues that 'it is the skill of converging appropriately that constitutes "correctness" in ELF'. ELF field questions notions of linguistic accuracy and replaces them with other notions such as accommodation, intelligibility, appropriateness, and effectiveness (Cogo, 2015; Jenkins, 2013). This replacement draws attention to pragmatic competency dimensions such as discourse strategies, initiating and changing topics, carrying out weight in balancing turn-at-talking, providing suitable responses, using a reasonable rate of speech and pauses, reflective echoing, using functions of repairs, and adjusting accents, lexis, phraseology, grammar and other aspects of speech (Baker, 2011, 2015a, 2015b; Bjorkman, 2008a, 2008b, 2013; Mauranen, 2006, 2012). From a complexity theory standpoint, language judgments are not merely made based on linguistic accuracy, semantics, and intelligibility. Complexity-oriented language judgments consider all problem-solving approaches to achieve contextual functions in communications. Complexity-informed language judgement treats openly the notion 'problem-solving' with its multiple dimensions such as appropriateness, effectiveness, meaning making, and contextual performativity. Through these complexity theory perspectives, the present study contributes to understanding how language adjustments and judgments work in Saudis' visions of the world and what is likely to be useful in similar situations.

2.3.3   ENL linguistic competence vs situated performativity

Based on Chomskyan accounts of language, competence is defined as the 'perfect knowledge' of a language possessed by 'ideal' native speakers of a 'completely homogeneous speech community' (Chomsky, 1965: 3 as cited in Baker, 2015a). This idealised abstraction of Chomskyan accounts has been controversial in linguistics and applied linguistics research. Previous studies in Linguistics have heated debates about who might be the 'ideal' ENL user as ENL users do not conform to one model within the same 'speech community' (Crystal, 1998; Jenkins, 2015a, Larsen-Freeman and Cameron, 2012; MacKenzie, 2014, Matras, 2009; Medgyes, 1994; Trudgill, 2002). Baker (2015a) criticises the restriction of Chmoskyan accounts to the knowledge of linguistic structures (i.e., forms), their irrelevance to actual uses (i.e., performances, functions, and practices), their association of competence with an 'ideal' native speaker, their assumption of absolute homogeneity within a speech community, and their omission of social and communicative dimensions. Blommaert (2010) argues that no one possesses complete knowledge of a language, and it seems more realistic to conceive competence in terms of repertoires and resources of linguistic, communicative, and pragmatic strategies. From a complexity theory perspective, competence is coupled with performance in a process of co-adaptation with each other and with other parts (Larsen-Freeman and Cameron, 2012). Co-adaptation of language resources with each other and with other parts (including context and timescales) affects language behaviours.

Theoretical, empirical, and corpora studies reveal that conformity to ENL and StE usages does not guarantee intelligibility or success in ELF settings (Cogo, 2010, 2015; Cogo and Dewey, 2012; Crystal, 1998; Dewey, 2014; Galloway, 2013; Galloway and Rose, 2013, 2014, 2015; Jenkins, 2006b, 2007, 2009b, 2014, 2015a; Mauranen, 2012, 2013; Phillipson, 2013; Seidlhofer, 2011). These studies also assert that ENL linguistic competence does not guarantee communicative competence, appropriateness, or success in ELF communication. Through widening the dimensions of competence in communications, ELF studies break the exclusive connection between ENL competence and success, and challenge the myth of ENL exclusive relevance to communicative effectiveness in ELF contexts. They assure that success in ELF communication is reached through the flexible use of English, appropriateness of communicative strategies, and effectiveness of achieving contextual functions. From a complexity-informed perspective on language, this is true beyond ELF communication, as competence in communication is based on adjustment and alignment in general, even among people sharing an L1 as they may have different language practices, dialects, or social positions.

To widen the dimensions of competence, Seidlhofer (2011) and Widdowson (2012) suggest conceiving competence in ELF communication with notions of feasibility, appropriateness, contextual performativity, and resource exploitation for meaning making. For instance, Cook's works on multilingualism (e.g., 1992, 2008) propose 'multi-competence' in which representations from different languages and cultures interact. With a practice-based approach, Canagarajah's (2012) notions of translingual practices, integrated proficiency, and performative competence emphasise awareness and exploitation of linguistic, cultural, and functional diversities. Instead of linking competence with specific languages and pre-established norms, competence is interpreted in relation to the ability to employ a diverse repertoire of language resources appropriately to achieve mutual understanding and contextual function (see Section 2.3.2). Canagarajah (2009) and Jenkins (2017b) propose the idea of 'integrated competence' for ELF communication as a part of one's social practices, in which all contributing parts have equal statuses.

To go beyond the notion of 'intelligibility', a body of ELF empirical and corpora studies have investigated interactional competences in exploitation of plurilingual resources and achieving different degrees of mutual understanding, starting from intelligibility to comprehensibility, and to interpretability (Bjorkman, 2013; Cogo and Dewey, 2012; Jenkins, 2007; Mauranen, 2006, 2013; Seidlhofer, 2003). These studies reveal that ELF users employ different problem-solving strategies to achieve success in communication (e.g., clarifications, comprehension checks, co-construction of expressions, lexical suggestions, gauging interlocutors' linguistic repertoire, and negotiation of non-understanding, to name a few). From a complexity-informed perspective, 'competence' is coupled with 'contextual performativity' in a process of co-adaptation with each other to achieve situated-success in communication. By exploring Saudis' experiences with English communication in relation to exploitation of multilingual and multicultural resources, the present study can understand how their multiple resources co-adapt with each other and with their surroundings to achieve situated-success in communication.

2.3.4 ENL cultural knowledge vs transcultural awareness

Hymes's (1971) communicative competence expands Chomskyan's accounts of competence to include social knowledge and context. Canale and Swain (1980) and Canale (1983) expanded Hymes's (1971) model to include four areas: language competence, sociolinguistic competence, strategic competence, and discourse competence. Both models have been criticised for their some limitations, such as giving priority to linguistic competence and representing ENL usages as the only 'right' and 'ideal' forms of communication (Baker, 2011, 2012a, 2012b, 2015a, 2015b; Brumfit, 2001; Kramsch,

2009; Larsen-Freeman and Anderson, 2013; Widdowson, 2012). To move beyond linguistic dimensions and mono-cultural perspectives, intercultural competence is adapted with different approaches by some scholars (e.g., Fantini, 2007). Intercultural competence is defined by Fantini (2007: 9 as cited in Baker, 2015a: 146) as a complex series 'of abilities needed to perform effectively and appropriately when interacting with others who are linguistically and culturally different from oneself'. Osman (2015) suggests that the omission of 'communicative' from 'intercultural competence' implies emphasis on dimensions other than linguistic knowledge. Baker (2015a) refers to five broad dimensions of most intercultural competence models: motivation, knowledge, skills, context, and outcome. As criticised by Baker (2015a), intercultural competence does not give enough attention to linguistic, affective, and ideological aspects, which are inevitable in intercultural situations.

To address some shortcomings of communicative competence and intercultural competence, Byram's (1997) intercultural communicative competence gives a space for comparison of the national culture with ENL cultures within five areas: attitude, knowledge, skills of interpreting and relating, skills of discovery and interaction, and critical cultural awareness. This model replaces ENL competence with intercultural users' multi-competence. As justified by Byram (1997: 11 as cited in Baker, 2015a: 149), the purposes of this replacement are two-fold: Firstly, 'It is the problem of creating an impossible target and consequently inevitable failure... even were it possible, it would create the wrong kind of competence'; Secondly, few learners/users may desire to become a member of a target nation with its cultural identity. However, Byram's (1997) recommendations for ELF users/learners suggest reliance on British or American usages due to their dominance. This recommendation seems problematic in ELF use where there is no one target culture in particular (Baker, 2015a).

Baker (2011, 2015a, 2015b) criticises both communicative competence and intercultural communicative competence for their national-based correlation of English with Anglophone nations. This correlation neglects the increasing shift in motivation to grasp English from integrative into instrumental motives to communicate with anyone who can use English (Al Asmari, 2014; Canagarajah, 2015), marginalises diverse cultural groupings (Baker, 2015a), and ignores the competences needed for successful transcultural communication in the absence of a target national community (Baker, 2015b). Based on complexity theory and emergentism frameworks, Baker (2009, 2011, 2012a, 2012b, 2015a, 2015b) proposes the notions of intercultural awareness to suit the dynamism of the complex and emergent nature of ELF interactions. To connect insights from intercultural awareness and intercultural communicative competence with ELF perspectives on competence, Baker (2015a: 163) omits the term 'competence', suggests replacing the term 'intercultural' with 'transcultural', and defines intercultural/transcultural awareness as 'a conscious understanding of the role culturally based forms, practices and frames of reference can have in intercultural communication, and an ability to put these conceptions into practice in a flexible and context specific manner in communication'. Omission of the term 'competence' implies resolving the competence/performance distinction and reflects emergentist perspectives of interdependence.

In addition, Baker's (2015a) proposal addresses ideological aspects as potential issues in transcultural situations. With a holistic approach, Bakers' transcultural awareness approach includes knowledge, skills, and practices that are necessary for the success of ELF interactions. Baker (2015a) suggests a list of twelve dimensions, divided into three sequential levels. The first level addresses: a conscious understanding of one's own linguaculture (see Section 2.3.5); how one's own linguaculture influences behaviours, beliefs, values, and communication; and the ability to compare one's own linguaculture with others' linguacultures and practices. The second level addresses complex understandings of diverse groups, how to make predications for possible misunderstandings, and the ability to mediate between specific cultural practices and frames of reference. The third level involves the complex interrelationships between language, culture, and communication. It addresses the ability to negotiate between different frames of reference and communicative practices beyond national levels.

In the light of complexity theory perspectives, emphasis is given to the ability to accommodate and cope appropriately, effectively, and successfully in a way that reflects understanding of actions, feelings, thoughts, similarities, and differences without prejudice to any race, religion, or class. ENL cultures do include racial, religious, and class-based divisions, which are sometimes overlooked when dividing these broad categories of users and their cultures. In this sense, being an ENL user, having knowledge about ENL cultures, and achieving ENL competence do not guarantee success in undertaking the role of a transcultural mediator. It is within the interest of the present study to explore Saudis' perceptions of a transcultural mediator in ELF settings and their preferences for ELT linguistic, communicative, and cultural dimensions.

2.3.5 Identity- free language vs identity-processed languaging

Traditionally, ENL users are regarded as birth-right natives, custodians of ENL, and the only agents who have the authority to influence it. Based on Schneider's (2007) 'identity-driven process of linguistics convergence' and Kachru's (1992) model, Kachruvian Outer Circle users influence their own Englishes in a way that reflects their images of themselves, the others, and relationships between ENL users and non-native English users, ENL users and English, and non-native English users and English. When ELF users view English as a positive resource, not a threat, they exploit it excessively to expand their interactional choices. When they see themselves as agents, they confidently add their own local flavour to their usages of English in a way that mirrors their L1 linguacultural backgrounds (e.g., borrowings and translanguaging). When they consider themselves as functional native users of their own English, they give themselves the authority to be legitimate 'norm-developers' for their own Englishes. Accordingly, their linguistic outcomes function as markers of their identities and as indicators of relationships between ENL users and ELF users, ENL users and English, and ELF users and English (Wang, 2012). These relationships may represent the 'ownership of English'. The notion of 'ownership' here means the authority to change and adapt the use of English (Brumfit, 2001).

These models seem fruitful to understand how ELF users align with or distance themselves from StE and ENL usages, and how translinguals' multiple memberships result in moving languages and cultures across each other. Still, these models are based on national perspectives which do not suit the fluidity of ELF use and translinguals' multiple resources, which go beyond geographical boundaries. This fluidity inspired ELF studies to investigate what forms of culture and membership actually go with ELF use. The discussion of ELF variants in terms of linguacultural resources results in decentring the authority over English from ENL users to the (super) diversity of ELF contexts (Wang, 2012, 2015a). The well-documented growth of ELF has led to a shift from viewing ELF users as 'eternal learners', 'failures', 'foreigners', 'passive receivers' of ENL usages, and 'outsiders' into eligible 'users', equal 'member', competent 'transilingual users', active 'agents', and 'transcultural mediators' who can exploit resources confidently, freely, and creatively (Bayyurt and Akcan, 2015; Bjorkman, 2013; Cavalheiro, 2015; Jenkins, 2006c, 2011, 2015a, 2015b; Jenkins, Cogo, and Dewey, 2011; Mauranen, 2013; Seidlhofer, 2009a, 2009b; Wang, 2012, 2015a; Wang and Jenkins, 2016).

In the light of this, many ELF researchers associate the authority to adjust English with those who use it, regardless of their L1 (Cogo, 2010; Galloway, 2013; Galloway and Rose, 2013, 2014, 2015; Seidlhofer, 2011; Wang, 2012, 2015a; Wang and Jenkins, 2016).Therefore, Seidlhofer (2011) describes ELF as 'a common property'. On the same lines, Cogo (2010), Wang (2015a), and Wang and Jenkins (2016) suggest that ELF is no one's native language and no longer under the authority or influence of ENL users. Jenkins et al. (2011) point out that ELF users treat ELF as a shared communicative resource while enjoying freedom from conforming to ENL usages to promote intelligibility, project linguacultural identity, and perform solidarity. However, it is rare for languages to really belong to groups or fit into neat models, with some educational and elitist descriptions of 'proper language use' being exceptions to a general trend of adaptation and ownership in practice/use.

House (2003, 2010, 2014), on the other hand, distinguishes between 'language for identification' and 'language for communication'. According to her perspectives, 'language for identification' refers to individuals' L1 and additional languages that are acquired to integrate and be identified with their native 'speech community'. She describes 'language for communication' as a culture- and identity- free lingua franca. However, the notions of culture- and identity- free languages have been questioned and challenged by a body of studies (Baker, 2011, 2015a, 2015b; Cavalheiro, 2015; Jenkins, 2011, 2013, 2015a, 2015b; Seidlhofer, 2010; Mauranen, 2012, 2013; Wang 2012). From a complexity view on ELF interactions, Baker (2015a: 83) argues that Reisager's (2006) language-culture nexus (i.e., linguaculture: the link between language and culture) has become a complex network of networks with 'a multitude of flows in complex multidimensional layers' in ELF interactions. In communication through any lingua franca, both native language users and non-native language users adjust the language use, and this adjustment is influenced by lingucultures of interlocutors. This adjustment is not an identity-free form of communication because it is influenced by its users, settings, purposes, available choices, and other dimensions, none of which is culturally neutral (Baker, 2011, 2015a, 2015b).

Interestingly, MacKenzie (2014: 115,116) questions ELF users' willingness to converge if they choose to project their L1 linguacultural identity which signals distance from the interlocutors who have different linguacultural backgrounds. He argues that such a projection reflects a 'monolingual-plus-ELF concept of identity'. When taking into consideration that a person can have multi-identities, hybrid identity, or transcultural identity, we can understand that the double-belonging involves converging with linguacultural behaviours of other interlocutors without complete divergence from one's L1 linguacultural behaviours. As discussed in Section 3.3.5, complexity theory approaches consider multi-layered dimensions of identity management as a contextual process of identification which is (re)established, (re)adjusted, (de)activated, (de)personalized, (de)motivated, and (re)negotiated simultaneously depending on context. Through this complexity informed approach to identification, the present study explores how Saudis identify themselves in relation to English and other users of English, and how they perceive relationships between ENL users and ELF users, ENL users and English, and ELF users and English.

2.4   Language patterns in ELF

2.4.1   Relevance of language patterns to the present study

As this study investigates interactions among parts of reported use of language contact, it takes into consideration that the linguistic outcome of interactions is an inseparable part of the whole (see Section 2.5). Bearing this mind, this section discusses previous studies on 'Saudi English' outcome. The discussion then questions the existence of a Saudi static identifiable 'variety' of English, the stability of 'Saudi English' outcome, and the adequacy of the label 'Saudi English'.

2.4.2   'Saudi English' variants

With a WEs-oriented position, previous studies have used different labels for the description of the linguistic features of Saudis' English such as 'Arabinglish', 'Arabicised English', 'Saudinglish', 'Saudi English', and 'Saudisation English'.

Al-Shurafa (2009) has used the term 'Arabicised English' to describe the common linguistic marks of 'Arabicisation of English'. She analysed syntactic features of English used by educated Arabs, from the Middle East (including Saudi Arabia), who have a good command of English. She has reported that 'Arabicised English' consists of 35.6% of complex clauses, over 45% of simple clauses, and 18.8% of unfinished verbal clauses. The most common marks are: 1) free mobility of adverbs, adverbials, and prepositional phrases because English has a strong overt syntactic movement at the surface structure while Arabic works at the logical form level; 2) generous use of the connector 'and' because it is a desirable connector in Arabic as a necessity to complement and connect words and ideas; 3) frequent use of the degree modifier 'very', expressive adjectives, and the first singular person, which reflects cultural qualities of stressing emotions, courtesy, and gratitude; 4) a high usage of the expletive 'it' in order to confirm the already stated facts; and 5) tendency to emphasise through repetition and/or unnecessary explanation. She highlighted the similarities between of 'Arabicised English' and 'Indian English' in terms of polite, formal, conservative, and emphatic styles of courtesy. Her study has contributed to filling a literature gap in the Saudi context, but it has provided a partial understanding as it has focused only on the syntactic differences between StE models and 'Arabicised English' variants. As she admitted this shortcoming, she has called for further investigations on these patterns. The present study attempts to provide a holistic understanding of this contact phenomena.

Fussell's (2011) study, which included Saudis, has used the term 'Gulf English' to suggest legitimisation of 'Gulf English'. His analysis displays the existence of regularised linguistic patterns, which are: 1) use of the dummy object, which is a feature of Standard Modern Arabic; 2) a preference for the masculine form, which reflects male-dominant culture; 3) a preference for the gerund form following 'for' in subordinate purposive clauses, which results from literal translation of such clauses in Standard Modern Arabic; 4) tendency to use some 'Indian English' usages such as the use of 'would' for future tenses, past perfect tense in place of present perfect tense, 'do' before a main verb, stress on the first syllable of a word, unaspirated /d/ for word-initial /t/, and /g/ sound for the word-initial /k/. These tendencies are imported to Gulf citizens from Indian expatriates, especially from the close contact of Gulf children with their Indian caretakers; 5) adding the plural morpheme '-s' to uncountable nouns, using uncountable nouns with the article 'a', and using progressive forms of stative verbs, which are imported from Kachruvian Outer Circle expatriates; 6) producing a mix of British, American, Indian and Arabic-accented pronunciation such as producing a /g/ sound in place of /dʒ/ due to the absence of /dʒ/ in some Arabic dialects and producing the vowels /i/, /a/, and /a:/ in place of /i:/, /æ/, and /a:/ uses which reflect the sociolinguistic contact between Gulf citizens and expatriates; 7) the frequent use of 'gonna', which reflects the amount of exposure to American forms of entertainment such as movies and gaming; 8) popularity of particular borrowings such as 'Niqaab' (i.e., a female face cover) and 'haram' (i.e., a forbidden behaviour in Islam), that refer to the local semantic domains; 9) using locally produced lexical items such as 'young adults' and localised verb forms such as 'to Emiratise', which indicates creative use of English; 10) omitting vowels in English abbreviations in the same way Arabic abbreviations are formed, such as local media's use of 'tmw' for 'tomorrow'; 11) using locally-invented abbreviations of officials' positions such as 'HH' for 'His/Her Highness'; and 12) code-switching for Islamic expressions such as 'Inshallah' to project Islamic identification. Fussell's (2011) analysis provided sociolinguistic/sociocultural justifications for 'Gulf English' variants. However, it has not considered the changeable nature of these patterns in response to any change in contextual (e.g., functions of interactions), sociocultural (e.g., length and intensity of contact), or psychological factors (e.g., beliefs, attitudes, and motivations). The present study attempts to address this changeability issue.

Al-Rawi (2012) has used the terms 'Saudi English' and 'Non-Standard Speech of Saudis' to describe Saudis' outcome of English. She compared and contrasted the English used by three groups: well-educated professionals, university students, and high school students. Her findings demonstrates that: 1) the students' tendency is higher than the professionals' tendency to drop the present tense of 'be'. This tendency occurs because the present tense in Arabic has a zero copula, but the past tense in Arabic has a fully realised copula; 2) the students' tendency is higher than the professionals' tendency to overuse the article 'the'. This tendency occurs because articles in Arabic have additional functions which are not available in English; 3) all groups, equally, tend to drop the article 'a/an' as the zero article in Arabic indicates indefiniteness; and 4) all groups, equally, tend to delete the third person singular -s. It was anticipated to find the presence of –s with singular and plural subjects because Standard Arabic has a default third person singular morpheme whether the subject is singular or plural. However, her results did not find the tendency to use the third person singular –s, and she concluded that the absence of this tendency might be the effect of the use of non-Standard Arabic (i.e., Amiyah). In this sense, Saudis, who live in the heart of the Arab world, do not use Standard Arabic for communication. Hence, it seems much more likely for them, and for other Arabs, not to follow StE models. Her study concluded that 'Saudi English' is heavily influenced by the substrate Arabic language, Saudis' interactions from an early age with different varieties of English, and the predominance of locally qualified English teachers. Although her study discussed the sociolinguistic/sociocultural justifications for 'angloversal' patterns in 'Saudi English', it implies that these patterns are stable and neglects the sensitivity of these patterns to any change in modes of communication (e.g., international and intranational), contextual factors (e.g., formal and informal purposes), and psychological factors (e.g., identification and ideologies). The present study attempts to cover these shortcomings.

Mahboob and Elyas (2014) used the terms 'Saudi English' and 'Saudisation of English' to describe variants in a Saudi ELT school textbook. Their linguistic analysis demonstrates five syntactic features that are different from StE models: 1) use of tense markers; 2) use of articles; 3) marking subject-verb agreement; 4) noun countability (singular/plural -s); and 5) use of the masculine pronouns as generic pronouns. The researchers suggested that 'If we agree that textbooks project a locally accepted variety of a language (as it is an instrument of corpus planning), then the variations and features described above may be considered features of English found in Saudi English' (p: 138). They also suggested that these variants are 'rule-governed', rather than 'random errors'. They concluded that 'English in Saudi Arabia is in the process of being nativised and that this Saudi English reflects recognisably local cultural, religious and social values and beliefs' (p: 128). The present study questions these suggestions and conclusions, as discussed in the coming section.

2.4.3 Sensitivity of language patterns to change

The complexity theory lens proposes that language patterns come into existence (i.e., emerge) without specific (upward or downward) plans. It also suggests that language patterns are aggregate outcomes from repetitions in discourse including linguistic forms, but not reducible to them. In the light of this, repetitions of some ELF variants are practised for reasons (e.g., acceptance, easiness, or status of their use), and they emerge in flux as they adjust and co-adapt with other cognitive, affective, social, and contextual dimensions. In the light of this,

'emergentism do not deny that with the need to communicate meaning (function) comes the knowledge of linguistic structures (forms). However, it does question the necessity of positing an underlying set of abstract rules to account for these structures. Emergentism suggests that any regular patterns of language use that can be described emerge from the aggregated or sedimented use of many individuals whose use of language is likely to be considerably more variable than these sedimented patterns' (Baird et al., 2014: 182).

This emergentist perspective on ELF rejects top-down and bottom-up principles of creating a monological ELF model as a new static identifiable form or 'variety' of English. As patterns are open to negotiation and change, their existence does not suggest their stability. This sensitivity to change applies to any language use, but at different rates and levels (Beckner, Blythe, Bybee, Christiansen, Croft, Ellis, Holland, Ke, Larsen-Freeman, and Schoenemann, 2009). When the change happens very slowly (i.e., emergent stabilities), 'it seems to humans not to be in process at all' (Larsen-Freeman and Cameron, 2012: 80). In a LF use, language patterns change fast in a noticeable way due to the linguistic, cultural, functional, and contextual (super) diversities of LF communications. If language patterns exists in the present study's data, it is within my interest to examine their sensitivity to change. In addition, the present study investigates Saudis' experiences with shared usages of English and 'Saudi English' variants to understand their relevance to the social psychological parts, which are discussed in the next chapter.

2.5 Summary:

In summarising this chapter, it discusses why investigation of language contact issues requires considering two main parts: the context in which languages interact through users; and language outcomes of this interaction. Through viewing language outcomes as social practices, the chapter discusses the necessity of approaching language practices in the light of two main parts: the 'linguistic inter-influence' of contact phenomena (e.g., syntax, morphology, and lexicon); and social/cultural psychological relationships between languages (e.g. power relations and motives of use). The discussion highlights how ELF theorisations, analysis, and data exhibit the 'significant complexity features' of complex adaptive phenomena such as requiring transdisciplinary frameworks (e.g., social psychology and applied linguistics), hosting meta-paradigmatic approaches (e.g., integration of multiple perspectives), giving rise to patterns and regularities (e.g., language patterns), and emergence of (unpredicted) behaviours as a result of open-ended interactions among the parts (e.g., inappropriateness of treating ELF use as a 'variety' with fixed grammatical rules even when it exhibits regular linguistic patterns because openness implies consistent evolvement of unpredicted structures as a response to any small change). In the light of complex adaptive phenomena, the chapter questions the stability of language use in general and ELF in particular. As this study investigates interactions among parts of perceived language use, it takes into consideration that the linguistic outcomes of the interactions is an inseparable part of the whole. Therefore, the chapter reviews the literature on 'Saudi English' outcomes and concludes by questioning the existence of a Saudi static identifiable 'variety' of English and the adequacy of the label 'Saudi English'. The discussion in this chapter helps me to interpret the differences and similarities between what participants say (reported practices, experiences, and perceptions) and how they say it (observed use of English in written and oral responses). The next chapter discusses the social psychological parts of language practices such as cognition (e.g., beliefs and attitudes), affection (e.g., motivations), ideologies, and identifications.

Chapter 3:   Complexity theory approach to perceptions of English

3.1   Introduction

Extreme cognitive approaches treat the cognitive constructs as static entities with clear boundaries. This way of treatment pays little or no attention to the interactions between social beings' thinking and practices. To cover this shortcoming, Wesely (2012) suggests employing complexity approaches to the relationship between language perceptions and practices. In the light of complexity theory approaches, this chapter starts with conceptualising 'perception' as a dynamic contextual(ised) process. This conceptualisation suggests that the way of thinking has cognitive, affective, conative, social, and contextual dimensions in motion. The chapter then discusses interactions among these dimensions in terms of: travelling of beliefs and attitudes in disguise; common sense and 'nativespeakerism' in non-linear relations; negotiation of multiple ideologies; multilinguals' (temporal) motives; and multiple memberships and identity management. The interactive method of discussion dissolves boundaries, highlights characterising and accounting for overlaps, and draws attention to non-linearity of interrelationships.

3.2   Conceptualisation of 'perception'

In applied linguistics, the expression 'views' is used as a generic cover for all other related cognitive constructs in language users' minds (e.g., ideas, beliefs, attitudes, opinions, and perceptions). As discussed by Woods (1996), conceptual separation of cognitive constructs (e.g., beliefs and attitudes) in theoretical discussion seems possible, but it seems almost impossible, especially for non-psychologists, to reach a clear distinction in empirical data. In this sense, some scholars distinguish the core characteristics of each construct, but acknowledge their overlaps (e.g., Pajares, 1992). In ELF field, different scholars use different terms to investigate language users' cognitive lives depending on their research orientations. The most common cognitive terms in ELF studies are: 'attitudes' (e.g., Jenkins, 2007; Kaur, 2014), 'perceptions' (e.g., Baird, 2013; Wang, 2012), and 'conceptualisation' (e.g., Kitazawa, 2013). The expression 'folk-perception' is used in folk-linguistic studies to refer to non-linguists' understandings of language and its relevant aspects. It is used as an umbrella term to cover a wide range of cognitive concepts such as beliefs, opinions, ideas, and ideologies. I avoided folk-linguistics approaches because they pay little or no attention to the attitudinal dimensions of perceptions (see Preston, 1989, 1994, 2004, 2011).

Inspired by social psychology and cognitive linguistics, I use the expression 'perception' to refer to a contextual(ised) process of interactions between human sensory systems and the mind (cognition and affection) to form representations (conation) of understandings and ways of thinking (Evans, 2007). Hurley's (2002) perception-in-action theory suggests that a perception influences and is influenced by actions and reactions in a deeply interdependent way. This conceptualisation suggests that language perception includes a combination of interconnected dimensions with conscious and unconscious layers. For instance, people are aware of their beliefs and actions, but they may not necessarily be aware of their presuppositions, their assumptions, the nature of their beliefs, their attitudinal reactions, or the nature of the outcomes of their actions. Bearing this in mind, I attempt to understand multiple layers of perceptions ranging from implicit indicators (e.g., underlying assumptions) to explicit discourse (e.g., vocalised comments on language), and from consciousness (e.g., language beliefs) to unconsciousness (e.g., language attitude). Having said that, the following section discusses how these dimensions interact with one another in an emergent way.

3.3 Characterising dimensions and analysing overlaps

3.3.1 Travelling of beliefs and attitudes in disguise

There is some agreement on the core characteristics of 'belief' as a combination of a specific proposition and a commitment towards what is held to be true or false, which can be explicit or implicit (Pajares, 1992). Acknowledging the judgmental dimensions of beliefs in notions other than true and false, Pajares (1992: 309) argues that beliefs can 'travel in disguise and often under alias – attitudes, values, judgements, axioms, opinions, ideology, perceptions, conceptions, conceptual systems, preconceptions, dispositions, implicit theories, explicit theories, personal theories, internal mental processes, action strategies, rules of practice, practical principles, repertoires of understanding, and social strategy', to name but a few that can be found in the literature. The concept of 'belief' seems to be a very crucial aspect for language studies because its judgmental function has implications for language perceptions and practices. When a pattern of beliefs serves as a 'foundational' and 'axiomatic' frame of reference for perceptions and practices, this pattern is conceptualised as a 'belief system' such as religious, ideological, and political belief systems (Van Dijk, 1998).

The 'attitude' concept can be described as the evaluative function of beliefs in notions other than true and false. Although no consensus has been reached on conceptualisations of 'attitude', there is wide agreement on its high level of implicitness and on its evaluative function in conscious actions and unconscious reactions (Kallstrom and Lindberg, 2011). According to Wenden (1999), the construct of 'attitude' is composed of cognitive variables (beliefs and opinions), affective variables (emotions and motivation), and behavioural variables (conscious actions and unconscious reactions). Ryan, Ellen, Howard-Giles, and Richard (1982: 7 as cited in Kallstrom and Lindberg, 2011:11) define language attitude as 'any affective, cognitive or behavioural index of evaluative reactions toward different language varieties or their speakers'. When people believe that there is only one ideal, stable, correct, right, appropriate, or prestigious way of language use, the other ways of language usages are viewed as bad, wrong, and inadequate (Jenkins, 2009b; Kitazawa, 2013; Kroskrity, 2004; Lonsmann, 2011).

Although many linguists have been arguing that language use is always in negotiation, some studies reveal that some language users still have some types of perceptions which last longer as relatively stable presuppositions, such as the idea of language standardisation (e.g., Dow, Niedzielski, and Preston, 2000; Kitzawa, 2013). For instance, some users describe misalignments with StE or ENL usages as 'inferior', 'devalued', 'reduced', 'simplified', 'incomplete', 'broken', 'corrupted', 'incorrect', 'unpleasant', 'vulgar', 'distorted', or 'less prestigious' (see Hassan, 2009; Jenkins, 2007, 2009b; Kaur, 2014; Kitazawa, 2013). Views may last for a long time when they are enhanced by repeated practices and/or discourse of authority, education, and/or media. This issue has been discussed the literature. For instance, Hassan (2009) argues that:

'dominant institutions, such as the media, the educational system, and corporate sector, claim the voice of authority and impose artificial ideas on the masses which internalise them as common sense notions' (Hassan, 2009: 239-240).

Findings of the relevant studies suggest the interconnectedness of the negative attitudes towards ELF usages with different factors such as: viewing English as a stable entity and StE ideology (Wang, 2013); unrealistic craze for ENL usages (Seidlhofer, 2004, Wang, 2012, 2013, 2015a; Wang and Jenkins, 2016); entrenched fascination with ENL prestigious status gained from the social dominance of ENL nations (Grill, 2010; Wang, 2015b); convictions in the necessity of StE or ENL usages for intelligibility (Seidlhofer, 2006; Wang, 2013,

2015a, 2015b; Wang and Jenkins, 2016); non-recognition of the wide worldview of English/Englishes (Cavalheiro, 2015; Jenkins, 2009a); and lack of ELF experiences and/or knowledge about ELF/WEs concepts (Bayyurt and Altinmakas, 2012; Wang and Jenkins, 2016). The present study benefits from a complexity theory viewpoint to investigate the relevance of these factors to perception.

3.3.2 Common sense and 'nativespeakerism' in non-linear relations

Some ELF data reveal not only cognitive notions (e.g., beliefs and attitudes), but also socially-shared presuppositions (e.g., some people think that being an ENL user guarantees success in ELF interactions). The present study takes into consideration that these taken-for-granted meanings do not necessarily serve ideological positions; they may mirror habitual ways of thinking and unquestioned understandings (i.e., common sense) with different variations. It also takes into consideration that common-sense meanings can be negotiated and socially elicited or deemphasised. According to Verschueren's (2012) socio-cognitive orientation, the notion of 'commonsensicality' implies explicitness, consciousness, and awareness of an agreement on a shared outlook. Although Verschueren associates 'commonsensicality' with ideologies, I do not agree with this association because I believe, as proposed by Van Dijk's (1998, 2006) multidisciplinary theorisation of ideology, common sense does not necessarily have a catalyst behind its logic and practices (see Section 3.3.3).

Some common-sense meanings about language use rely on the straightforward logic of 'nativespeakerism'. Holliday (2006: 385) defines 'nativespeakerism' as 'a pervasive ideology within ELT, characterised by the belief that "native-speaker" teachers represent a "Western culture" from which spring the ideals both of the English language and of English language teaching methodology'. I do not agree that 'nativespeakerism' has necessarily an ideological outlook; it may represent a normative or straightforward way of thinking. However, I refer to Holliday's perspectives to highlight the multi-layered dimensions of perception.

'The impact of native-speakerism can be seen in many aspects of professional life, from employment policy to the presentation of language. An underlying theme is the "othering" of students and colleagues from outside the English-speaking West according to essentialist regional or religious cultural stereotypes, especially when they have difficulty with the specific types of active, collaborative, and self-directed "learner-centred" teaching–learning techniques that have frequently been constructed and packaged as superior within the English speaking West' (Holliday, 2006: 385).

Based on nativespeakerism's simple logic, it is assumed that: biological native-ness is the only authentic source and naturalist benchmark for language use/teaching; all native users of a language are innately better users of that language than its non-native users; all native usages of a language are standard models of that language; and native-like usages guarantee success of using, teaching, and communication. The simple understanding of 'nativespeakersim' enhances assumptions of language users and researchers. The present study, in line with Davis (2003) and Baird (2013), questions the straightforward treatments of the 'nativespeakerism' concept with its relevant notions such as 'native language', 'mother tongue', 'home language', 'L1', and 'dominant language'. The person may have multiple native languages. Functional native-ness can be taken into considerations. The role of the mother, in a 'mother tongue', can be taken/shared by other adults who may use a different language from that of the mother. The mother herself, or the adults who take or share in this role, may use more than one language. The language at home can be a mix of languages, and/or it can be different from the language of the public environment but it is also a home language for some users. A child may learn more than one language at the same time, and none of them is learned before the other. In this case, the child has more than one first/native language. One can have multiple dominant languages; each language is dominant in a particular domain. In addition, one's L1, mother tongue, home language, or dominant language may change over time. In this sense, language native-ness, if it exists, depends on context.

Bearing this in mind, my investigation takes into consideration non-linear relations in the participants' understandings of English use and users. Before coming up with interpretations and assuming linear relations, the present study investigates the meanings of 'nativespeakerism', 'native user', and 'first language' in the participants' versions of the world. This is because I believe that taken-for-granted assumptions do not necessarily represent hidden/implanted/transmitted ideological positions. I believe, as argued by Baker (2015a), that the ideology does not necessarily always exist; they are not always imposed; they are sometimes adapted voluntarily by choice of some people for different motives. Having said that, I turn to discuss language ideology, and then motivation.

3.3.3 Negotiation of multiple or contradictory ideologies

Viewing language as a social practice implies its sensitivity to socially shared frames of reference (e.g., religious belief systems and ideologies). Thus, I believe, as argued by Garrett, Coupland, and Williams (2003), that language usages and perceptions are sensitive to social and ideological meanings. Woolard (1998: 3) defines language ideologies as 'representations, whether explicit or implicit, that construe the intersection of language and human beings in a social world'. I do not agree with this definition because it suggests that language ideologies are forms of shared sets of social representations before they operate as cognitive functions. Inspired by Van Dijk's (1998, 2006) multidisciplinary theorisation of ideology, I conceptualise language ideology as a socially/socioculturally biased cognitive frame of reference for perceptions and practices in favour of a particular catalyst. In this sense, an ideological outlook serves as an axiomatic foundation for perceptions to give rise to meanings, interpretations, representations, and judgments about the nature of the language and its status, usages, practices, and users. I associate ideology with a collective interest which can be rejected by other collectives with opposing interests. It is important to mention here that I do not restrict the notions of ideology to evil, fallacy, or hegemony. I also understand that ideologies are not necessarily transmitted or imposed; they might be tangled up in and performed through practices, social habits, or rituals; they might be chosen by individuals' through free will (or choice) for different reasons and motives. In addition, I understand that actual language behaviours may not always be consistent with explicitly proclaimed language ideologies.

The most prevalent language ideology in ELF data is StE ideology (Jenkins, 2009b). A StE ideology represents a set of beliefs about a standardised abstract set of English models including lexical, grammatical, and phonological components (Jenkins, 2007; Milroy, 1999). Milroy and Milroy (1985: 23) state that language standardisation is 'an idea in the mind rather than a reality ... to which actual usage may conform to a greater or lesser extent'. Siedlhofer (2011) and Wang (2015a) link StE ideology with an 'old-fashioned' outlook, which views the language as a stable entity based on stabilised forms of a confined territory. As 'consumers' of the mainstream 'ELT industry' and ENL media, including the Hollywood industry, ELF users may have an attachment to StE and/or ENL usages (Hassan, 2009; Jenkins, 2007; Kaur, 2014). Hassan (2009: 239-240) suggests that 'the educational system can be especially effective in maintaining dominant linguistic ideologies and delegitimising the status of dialects'.

In some ELF studies, there is a common tendency to interpret users' unquestioned assumptions in terms of misguided thinking promoted or transmitted by StE and/or ENL ideology to serve its own interests (see Cogo, 2010; Jenkins, 2007;

Seidlhofer, 2011). This tendency has been questioned and criticised in the literature. For instance, MacKenzie (2014: 140-155) thinks that engagement of ELF research with the critics of StE ideology or ENL ideology aims at 'demonisation of ENL' nations. Sewell (2013) thinks that the field of ELF serves a hegemonic 'bottom-up ideology' in favour of an 'ELF variety'. O'Regan (2014) describes ELF research as an 'ELF movement ideology'. In defence of ELF work, ELF scholars assert that epistemological intolerance and imposing one's own frame of reference on others reveals ideologically informed positions (Baker and Jenkins, 2015; Baker, Jenkins, and Baird, 2014; Ishikawa, 2015; Widdowson, 2015).

'In categorising ELF as a movement in these terms, O'Regan then proceeds to castigate ELF researchers on his terms as heretics, apostates, offenders against the true faith. So what really seems to offend O'Regan and motivates his attack is not that ELF research is guilty of hypostasy but that the ELF movement is guilty of apostasy, a denial of the revealed truth of things...And of course disciples of different beliefs, defenders of other faiths, make similar claims that they have privileged access to the truth of things, pillory the heretics, and seek to rally non-believers to their cause' (Widdowson, 2015: 126).

In contrast to the doubts of MacKenzie, Swell, and O'Regan, the ELF paradigm aims to: raise awareness of today's sociolinguistic realities and tolerance to linguistic, cultural, functional, and contextual diversities; promote a sense of global citizenship and transculturality; and consider additional choices without excluding ENL usages and users (Dewey, 2012, 2014; Sifakis, 2007, 2009, 2014a, 2014b; Sifakis and Bayyurt, 2015; Wang, 2012, 2013, 2015a, 2015b; Wang and Jenkins, 2016). However, doubts about ELF research have arisen because it, sometimes, makes a-contextual conclusions by drawing straightforward lines between perceptions of ELF and ENL ideology (Baird et al., 2014). Coming up with such linear relationships sounds problematic and limited for many reasons. For instance, there might be a preference for StE or ENL usages for particular motives other than carrying StE or ENL ideologies. Bearing this in mind, the present study investigates what factors are behind participants' preferences, rather than drawing a linear relationship between perceptions and StE or ENL ideologies.

Through a complexity theory lens, the present study does not limit its investigation within the boundaries of StE and ENL ideologies. It takes into consideration that other (unexpected) ideologies, beliefs, and/or agendas may be interconnected with perceptions and practices of English. As a result of multiplicity of conflicts in contact language situations, ideologies may include parts that are internally contradictory and may conflict with other core social beliefs and related agendas. Within multilingual settings in the Middle East and North Africa, Hassan (2009) refers to the dominance of the 'standard language ideology', 'divine language ideology', and 'pro-multilingualism ideology' which are stemmed from the Islamic beliefs and values in teaching, learning, and using.

'The belief that Arabic is a superior language by virtue of its association with the language of God makes this ideology the most potent in symbolic domination... Thus many said that it would be beneficial to learn a new language or that It would be (from a religious view) mustahabb (favoured) to learn a new language' (Hassan, 2009: 240-242).

If multiple or contradictory ideologies, religious beliefs, core values, or agendas exist in the data of the present study, it is within my interest to investigate how they interact and negotiate with one another and with the other dimensions of perception be delving into participants' experiences in relation to these issues.

3.3.4 Multilinguals' (temporal) motivations

'Motivation' refers to a willingness to take actions (including achievement, persistence, and resistance), which are expected to satisfy needs, desires, wishes, and goals (Dornyei, 2001;

Thagard, 2015). According to Gardner's motivation models (e.g., 1983, 2006), there are two motivational orientations for using/learning languages. 'Integrative motivation' refers to a willingness to integrate with the society of the target language, while 'instrumental motivation' refers to a willingness to gain benefits from obtaining language proficiency (e.g., passing exams or having a job). Cooper and Fishman (1977) integrate 'developmental motivation' as a third orientation that includes desires to do personal activities in the target language (e.g., entertainment, hobbies, and tourism). Guerra (2005) places motivations for using/learning languages into five categories: assimilative, integrative, instrumental, personal, and international use. 'Assimilative motivation' is associated with the longing to become a member of ENL nations through persistent contact. 'Integrative motivation', which does not necessitate extended contact, is associated with interaction with ENL users. 'Instrumental motivation' is associated with the aspiration to achieve practical goals (e.g., exams and jobs). 'Personal motivation' is related to one's own desires (e.g., hobbies). 'International motivation' is related to use of English in international settings.

Gardner's social psychological, social educational, and ESL/EFL models (e.g., Gardner, 1983, 2006) reveal significant relationships between motivation, language learning, and language outcomes. The relevant literature reveals that integrative motivation has a significant role in achieving native-like English due to the existence of a target ENL nation. Instrumental, developmental, and international motivations play significant roles in misalignment with StE and ENL usages due to the lack of a target (ENL) nation. For instance, Cavalheiro (2015) and MacKenzie (2014) discuss the relationship between motivation and English language learning/usage. They distinguish between motivations for using/learning ESL/EFL and motivations for using/learning ELF. In the former, ESL/EFL learners/users attempt to gain ENL linguistic and cultural knowledge and to align with ENL linguistic usages and communicative styles because their target interlocutors are ENL users. In the latter, ELF learners/users are interested in problem-solving skills that help in achieving ELF contextual functions, rather than mastery of ENL usages, accents, culture-bound expressions (e.g., idioms), and formulaic sequences. The present study investigates whether the lack or existence of a target (ENL) nation plays any role in perception of English, (in)tolerance towards ELF variants, and English reported use.

Although the above-discussed studies give useful insights into motivation, they treat motivation as a stable and measurable state. Dornyei's (2000) motivation-in-action theorisation conceptualises motivation as a complex process. This process-oriented framework for approaching motivations adds to the traditional framework time dimensions (e.g., temporal drives), and contextual dimensions (e.g., environmental contingencies). Based on this extended theorisation, time and context are interconnected dynamically with the motivation processes, and motivation processes are inseparable from other affective, cognitive, conative, and social parts. This treatment of 'motivation' suits the present study because it is interested in exploring how temporal and contextual motives (e.g., convergence and divergence motives) relate to perceptions, experiences, and reported use of English (see Sections 2.2.2 and 2.3.2).

In ELF communication, ELF users' desires to achieve contextual functions motivate them to converge with other ELF users' linguistic and communicative behaviours.

'The desire to be understood has also come to be seen as an important motivating factor underlying convergence in communication' (Dewey, 2011: 206).

Regarding convergence-related aspects of ELF rhetoric, MacKenzie (2014: 140-155) describes ELF perspectives as having 'noble intentions' towards ELF users, and always looking 'at the bright sides of life'. He discusses how ELF research assumes a fantastic collaborative atmosphere, guarantees cultural sympathy, and ignores human cruelty. His criticism is right sometimes, as some ELF studies have done this. Other ELF studies have referred to the attitudinal dimensions of ELF interactions and the possibility of misunderstanding, unwillingness to converge, and lack of awareness or tolerance (see Jenkins, 2006a, 2007, 2009a, 2009b; Wang and Jenkins, 2016). It is necessary to acknowledge that convergence is not always the case in ELF interactions (see Section 2.2.2). Adjustment of speech and communicative behaviours in a way that enhances differences (i.e., divergence strategy) is an indicator of distance and non-accommodation. Maintaining speech and communicative behaviours without any adjustment is an indicator of neutral positioning.

From a sceptical standpoint, MacKenzie (2014: 150) questions ELF data on pragmatic and interactional competences which are collected from lectures, conferences, meetings, seminars, presentations, classrooms, friendly or business discussions, and family gatherings, because in these settings 'people are more likely to converse like this than to punch you in the face'. As inspiration to propose new practical ways, most applied linguistics data come from the setting described by MacKenzie. In an ELF online chatroom, Jenks (2012) has investigated convergence and divergence strategies. ELF chatters' behaviours highlighted boundaries and troubles in communication through laughter, joking, ridicule, and making fun of each other's linguistic and cultural differences. The researcher concluded that contextual and situational factors play a significant role in ELF interactions. On one hand, ELF users may seek to build consensus in business negotiations and academic talks, reflecting their membership of the group. On the other hand, ELF users may highlight distances in the absence of predefined roles, goals, and memberships. Having said that, the next section discusses how language behaviours and perceptions relate to the sense of belonging, group memberships, and identity management.

3.3.5 Multiple memberships and interactive identity management

In the modern world, a single belonging concept is problematic because no one belongs to a single group. From a social cognitive-affective perspective, as suggested by Van Dijk (1998), I view identity as both personal (i.e., perception of the self as a unique human being) and social (i.e., perception of the self as a collection of group memberships). Through a complexity theory lens, Baker (2015a) suggests approaching social identity through ELF in relation to group memberships. Viewing 'identity' as a process of identification, Stets and Burke (2000: 225,226) define one's identities, in plural, as 'self-views that emerge from the reflexive activity of self-categorisation or identification in terms of membership in particular groups or roles'. Some scholars suggest that ELF use is identity-free, but the majority of ELF scholars stresses that ELF use is identity-loaded (see Section 2.3.5). The concept of 'identity-free ELF' may seem true if identity is limited to nationality membership, but ELF is identity-loaded when identity is associated with one's multiplicity of social memberships to many groups including religious, ideological, professional, and official groups (Baker, 2015a). Such a relationship between language and identity are manifested in (local) accents, use of personal pronouns, and use of local idioms because they suggest socially loaded positions (Baird, 2013; Wang, 2012).

A growing body of ELF research suggests that ELF users demonstrate their joint membership to local/cultural habitat and other groups which also make use of ELF (Baker, 2011, 2015a, 2015b; Cavalheiro, 2015; Jenkins, 2007, 2011, 2013, 2015a, 2015b; Mauranen, 2012, 2013; Seidlhofer, 2010; Wang, 2012, 2015a; Wang and Jenkins, 2016). The sense of multiple belongings stimulates identification processes to be (re)established, (re)adjusted, (de)activated, (de)personalised, and (de)motivated simultaneously depending on socially situated contexts. Joseph (2004) differentiates between 'identity-as-sameness' and 'identity-as-difference'.

In the former, we converge with whom we identify as 'our' group, but we diverge with whom we identify as 'their' group. This account suggests that people negotiate their identities and language behaviours depending on the context. Many ELF studies (e.g., Pitzl, 2009, 2012; Wang, 2012) have discussed language usages and communicative styles which represent L1 linguacultural identity such as translation of L1 metaphors, code-switching, modification of ENL ready-made expressions, and making use of L1 communicative styles (see Section 2.3.5). 'Saudi English' studies have discussed variants that represent Saudi identity (see Section 2.4.2). These studies did not take into account that people may change their language behaviours when they want to represent their other identities (e.g., professional and transcultural identities). To investigate this issue, the present study delves into Saudis' experiences with English in relation to identity management and negotiation.

Marotta (2014) discusses notions of the 'complex identities' of 'complex multicultural' people in terms of 'in-between', 'third', and 'hybrid' identifications. He draws attention to three types of identities that emerge for the sake of accommodation across-cultures: multicultural, intercultural, and transcultural. Multicultural identification acknowledges similarities and differences between cultures while maintaining a space between the self and the others. It does not necessitate mutual exchange of cultural norms. Intercultural identification produces multiple identities that show deep understanding and appreciation of the self and the other. It involves a mode of multiple belongings that resists 'universalising' practices. Today, the idea of 'universal' itself is problematic anyway, whether it is about identities, nations, cultures, languages, or ELF practices. Transcultural identity removes the boundaries between cultures and creates a new hybrid culture that has something from both cultures, but is different from each one of them. Through describing the world as one 'English-speaking global village', Archibald, Cogo, and Jenkins (2011) suggest that ELF users have a sense of a global citizenship with a global identity-membership using variant Englishes.

As transcultural and translingual social beings, ELF users may demonstrate these notions of identifications through their uses and perceptions of ELF.

Baker (2015a: 111) discusses Rampton's (1995) notions of 'liminality', 'crossings', and 'code-alteration', which acknowledge hybrid and in-between identities as symbolised by adopting and adapting others' languages for one's own purposes and needs. Viewed through a complexity theory lens, Baker (2015a) argues that one does not have to be 'in-between' or 'hybrid' because one can have several identities, jumping in and out of them to shuttle across group memberships. If ELF interlocutors want to cope with one another, they negotiate their linguistic, communicative, and interactional practices, which, in turn, symbolise identity negotiation in transcultural communications through ELF (Baker, 2015a). In other words, users of English may modify their language behaviours for the sake of identity management.

With respect to identity negotiation and management, Baker (2015a) discusses Pavlenko and Blackedge's (2004) three types of identities: 'imposed identity', which is compulsory and not negotiable; 'assumed identity', which is accepted and not negotiable by one's free choice; and 'negotiable identity', which is negotiable and can be contested. He suggests that ELF use symbolises 'negotiable identity' when users choose it by their own free will. He also suggests that non-negotiable identities (e.g., imposed identities by authorities, assumed identities by dominant ideologies, and assumed identities of belonging to one's own linguacultural habitat) can put limitations on the degree of choice and negotiation that people have. Interactions between negotiable and non-negotiable identities bring their markers to uses and perceptions of ELF.

In the KSA, Elyas's (2011) findings reveal struggles in the identity of ELT Saudi teachers because they are expected to reconcile two highly contrasting outlooks: Islamic vs. Western/ English values (Elyas, 2011; Elyas and Picard, 2012a, 2012b).

Other resources that may bring tensions to the identity of non-native teachers of English are learners' expectations. As a traditional role model for learners, ELT teachers are typically expected to teach ENL usages to which non-native teachers themselves may not conform intentionally or unintentionally (Cavalheiro, 2015; Kirpatrick, 2007a, 2007b). The dynamic account of the present study opens up spaces for exploring how Saudis fashion and negotiate interactive identities beyond a mono-national-lingual identity.

3.4   Summary

In the light of complexity theory approaches, this chapter starts with conceptualising 'perception' as a dynamic contextual(ised) process with cognitive (e.g., beliefs, common sense, and attitudes), affective (e.g., motivations), conative (e.g., behaviours), and social (e.g., experiences, memberships, and socially-biased representations) dimensions in flux and overlaps. The chapter then discusses the interactions among these dimensions and highlights their non-linear interrelationships in ELF phenomena. This discussion problematises the narrow and straightforward treatments of some concepts in transcultural communications (e.g., attitude, motivation, identity, ideology, nativespeakersim, and memberships). This complexity theory-informed framework requires complexity theory-inspired methodological approaches, as discussed in the next chapter.

Chapter 4:   Complexity theory-inspired methodology

4.1   Introduction

This mixed-method sequential exploratory study has a qualitative phase (i.e., follow-up interviews) building on and explaining the initial mixed-method survey phase. Data from 'Saudi English' studies are used in the survey and interviews. This study aims to come up with a holistic description of the relationships between experiences and perceptions of English in the Global Englishes era through the eyes of Saudis. To achieve this aim, the study investigates a complex web of interconnected parts: beliefs; attitudes; common sense; motivations; ideologies; identifications; and reported contextual(ised) uses of English. This investigation aims at offering answers for the following nested research questions:

RQ1. How, and to what extent, do Saudis report (in)tolerance towards misalignment with StE models?

RQ2. How, and to what extent, do Saudis' judgements of (in)tolerance relate to their:

   a. beliefs and attitudes towards their own English, the global spread of English, and English associations with natives and non-natives;
   b. motives for using/learning English;
   c. identifications and feelings of belongings;
   d. contextual factors?

This chapter begins by discussing the philosophical considerations of the present study. This discussion is supported by clarifying the relevance of the complexity theory paradigm to the current study's methodologies. The chapter then justifies the appropriateness of mixed-method approaches to the present study. This chapter then goes on to discuss this project's design, participants, and instruments. It also discusses how I compensated for the limitations of my research methodology. At the end, a discussion is presented about my fieldwork in relation to ethical considerations, pilot study, and main study.

4.2 Relevance of complexity theory paradigm to the methodology of the present study

In social science research, the categorisation most frequently referred to in relation to methodology includes positivism, constructivism, participatory, and pragmatism (Cohen et al., 2013; Grix, 2010). Positivism does not suit the present study's theoretical framework. Complexity theory frameworks reject pre-hypotheses, partialist approaches, solo-reliance on deductive thinking, simple linear cause-effect relationships, determination, and universal generalisations. Constructivism relies on qualitative approaches and inductive thinking. The present study needs mixed-method approaches and uses a back-and-forth process of induction and deduction. Participatory does not suit the present study's questions, purposes, and position because the present study does not have an agenda to reform or situation to change. Pragmatism and this study have some mutual interests such as applied research, real-world practice orientations, problem-centred focus, inductive-deductive orientations, mixed-method approaches, challenging of traditional paradigms, flexibility, pluralistic views, and seeking of both convergence and divergence in data analysis. Unlike pragmatism, the present study does not have any intended consequences to achieve or influence to make.

Cohen et al. (2013) discuss the properties of the complexity theory research paradigm in social science. In alignment with complexity theory paradigm, the present study's methodology transcends the conventional philosophies; it hosts multi-perspectives; it employs a combined deductive-inductive approach by welcoming emergent data-driven themes aside from its pre-established themes; it employs instruments that enable micro- and macro-level analyses to detect interrelationships; it addresses the phenomena through the eyes of as many participants as possible using a range of diverse methods; and it values variability as a positive resource for data collection and analysis procedures. However, the present study belongs to complexity theory-inspired research (not complexity theory research) as it does not use computerised/algorithmic modelling for interrelationships and it does not aim at offering predictions.

4.3 Appropriateness of mixed-method approaches to the present study and reliability issues

The complexity theory research tends to fall into the quantitative inquiry of statistical interrelationships. Cohen et al. (2013) suggest integration of qualitative and quantitative methods in complexity theory-informed social sciences research. In language studies, Wesely (2012) underscores the need for mixed-method approaches when employing complex frameworks. In ELF studies, Baker (2015a) suggests that employing complexity theory perspectives does not mean replacing qualitative inquiries with quantitative inquiries. As an overall, decisions on methodological approaches depends on the research purposes (Bryman, 2006; Greene, Caracelli, and Graham, 1989; Moran-Ellis, Alexander, Cronin, Dickinson, Fielding, Sleney, and Thomas, 2006). The present study employs a mixed-method approach for four purposes, namely complementarity, initiation, development, and expansion. The survey consists of closed and open items to explain one another. It aims to explore a wide range of ELF-relevant issues and collect large scale data from different provinces of the KSA. The present study requires a relatively large number of participants to investigate patterns of responses, examine degrees of regularities, and enable complexity theory-inspired statistical interrelationships tests. The follow-up interviews aim to elaborate on the survey questions, obtain personal explanations, and welcome data-driven relevant issues. Providing accurate knowledge and well justified conclusions can answer questions of reliability of the present study.

4.4 Sequential exploratory research design

The present study used two instruments across two sequential phases. The two phases addressed RQ1 and RQ2 differently. Firstly, the large-scale survey addressed quantitatively and qualitatively the research questions. Secondly, the qualitative follow-up interviews expanded the survey inquires. As a complementary tool, data from 'Saudi English' studies were integrated within the survey and interviews. In addition, I observed and commented on the differences and similarities between what participants had said/written and how they had actually used the language in the survey and the interviews.

4.4.1 Participants variability as a resource for complexity-informed research

This study targeted Saudi users of English who have at least graduated from high school because they represent the Saudi individuals involve with this project's complex research problem (see Section 1.2). These Saudis should be able to use English after several years of formal education. Viewing variability as a positive resource for complexity theory paradigm (Larsen-Freeman and Cameron, 2008, 2012), the present study has welcomed variability in the participants' background characteristics because people experience English in their lives with different identities (as parents, learners, workers, teachers, etc.), which may influence how they use and perceive the language. Through participant's variability, the present study could explore a range of experiences of English communication in relation to other languages, contexts, identities, and motives across wider domains. I have not tried to reduce participants' diversity in order not to lose the information that may shed light on emergence. However, the survey addresses respondents' backgrounds to divide respondents into groups if the data reveals something significant within the interest of the present study. Regional factors are considered in the interviews as enrichment for the qualitative analysis.

4.4.2 Multiphase sampling: 'convenience', 'snowball', and 'confirming and disconfirming' techniques

Data collection of this study adapted the 'multiphase sampling' strategy to move from the wide inquiry of the survey to the focused inquiry of the interviews. In the survey phase, this study employed 'convenience' and 'snowball' techniques, which left participation to participants' willingness. A 'snowball' technique refers to using the researcher's contacts to reach contacts of contacts, contacts of contacts of contacts, etc. (Cohen et al., 2013). The present study employed the 'snowball' technique in order to reach a wide range of participants from different regions. Without a relatively large number of participants, some complexity theory-inspired statistical interrelationships cannot be examined. To minimise the limitations of the 'snowball' technique, extra precautions were taken (see Section 4.5). I employed a 'bottom up/reverse approach' (see Cohen et al., 2013; Dornyei, 2014) to estimate the minimum number that would enable the statistical procedures that suit this investigation. Based on this approach, the quantitative inquires of this study need at least 100 respondents in each potential subgroup. As the survey provides three options for occupation (students, ELT professionals, and professionals in majors other than English), I aimed for at least 100 respondents in each occupation group. In the second phase, the interview sample was recruited from the survey sample based on 'confirming and disconfirming' and 'convenience' techniques. In 'confirming and disconfirming' technique, typical and deviant cases of participants are selected to investigate the reasons for their conformity or disconformity (Teddlie and Tashkkori, 2009 as cited in Cohen et al., 2013). In this project, I selected interview participants from among survey respondents who had written significant comments or represented either typical or deviant cases of the statistical tests. Viewing openness of investigation as a positive orientation in complexity theory-informed approaches (Cohen et al., 2013), the sample size of the interviews was left open to bring data saturation.

4.4.3   First phase: Mixed-method survey

4.4.3.1   Preliminary considerations

A survey is a type of questionnaire. Brown (2001: 6 as cited in Dornyei, 2014: 102) defines questionnaires as 'any written instruments that present respondents with a series of questions or statements to which they are to react either by writing out their answers or selecting from among existing answers'. Surveys differ from questionnaires in terms of their scope. Cohen et al. (2013) suggest using surveys in exploratory studies that aim to examine a wide range of issues by collecting large-scale data from a wide target population or from as representative a sample population as possible. The present study used surveys to investigate ELF wide issues and explore relationships, patterns of responses, and degrees of regularities on a relatively large scale. Surveys are quantitative in nature, but the present study's survey contains open-ended questions that require qualitative analysis to consider any data-driven themes. To construct the survey, I consulted a wealth of relevant literature (e.g., Azuaga and Cavalheiro, 2012; Cavalheiro, 2015; Inal and Ozdemir, 2015; Kitazawa, 2013; Matsuda, 2009; Wang, 2012). I designed the present study's survey with a variety of question types, namely multiple choices, fill in the blanks, optional comment fields, five-point Likert scales (in terms of 'strongly disagree, agree, neutral, agree, and strongly agree' or 'very false, false, neutral, true, and very true'), attitudinal scales (in terms of 'completely unacceptable, unacceptable, neutral, acceptable, and completely acceptable' or 'very unimportant, unimportant, neutral, important, and very important'), and ranking schemes from 0 to 6 (0 represents unimportant/unnecessary/non-priority, where 1 represents the least important/necessary/priority, and 6 represents the most important/necessary/top-priority). The rational of numerical representatives and weights follows standard marking practices in the Arabic context, according to which, '0' represents 'none', '1' represents a negative meaning or the least weight, '3' represents a neutral position, and '5' represents a positive meaning or the most weight. The five-point Likert and attitudinal scales were chosen to allow neutral positions and to shorten the time required for responses. However, I ensured that I asked for clarifications and justifications during the interviews. Instead of including an 'I do not know' category, I included an 'other' category and optional comment fields to stimulate respondents' critical thinking and encourage them to say anything that may be useful to the investigation.

For ease of reading, I used some terms that sound problematic in complexity theory frameworks such as 'native', 'non-native', 'culture', and 'community'. Using these terms does not imply my full compliance with their notions (see Sections 1.1.3, 2.2.3, and 3.3.2). In addition, I ensured that I explored participants' perceptions of these notions during the interviews. When a question requires choosing a 'native' category or a 'non-native' category, the 'native' category is positioned at the first choice because, as suggested by Wang (2012), this positioning may help in exploring if respondents have presuppositions that block careful thinking and reconsiderations. In order to not draw conclusions on such assumptions, I ensured that I investigated participants' perceptions of the 'nativespeakerism' discourse during the interviews. Because the investigation of language ideologies is within the interest of this study, I included 'standard', 'American', and 'British' categories in some of the questions. The reason for this specific categorisation is to investigate Saudis' perceptions in relation to the three prevalent representations of English in the Saudi context (see

Section 1.2). I formulated the last question in the survey to function as a 'trap question' to exclude any participation that would offer haphazard responses. The survey was conducted in three modes (hardcopy, software, online) to compensate for each of the methods' limitations (see Section 4.5). The main survey was formulated in English. As suggested by the pilot study's participants, an Arabic version (hardcopy, software, online) was produced in consultation with two English-Arabic translators (see Section 4.6.2).

4.4.3.2 Survey construction in relation to research questions, objectives, and interviews

It is within the interest of the present study to investigate Saudis' awareness of 'ELF' as a term, field of study, and function. As to not influence the views of respondents in any way, the title of the survey 'Saudis' perceptions of English in relation to globalisation', and the consent/information forms do not provide specific details about the study or definitions of terms, including the term 'ELF'. The survey (See Appendix 1) consists of 22 questions divided into four sections, namely background information, use of English, teaching/learning English, and optional comments. The survey addresses RQ1 and RQ2 quantitatively and qualitatively. RQ1 is addressed in the survey by Q13, Q14.1, Q14.2, Q14.3, Q18.5, Q20, Q21.1, Q21.2, and Q21.4. RQ2.a is addressed in the survey by Q10, Q12, Q14.3, Q14.6, Q15, Q16, Q18.6, Q19, Q20, Q21.2, Q21.3, and Q21.4. RQ2.b is addressed in the survey by Q8, Q9, Q18.1, Q18.2, Q18.3, and Q18.4. RQ2.c is addressed in the survey by Q11, Q13, and Q14.7. RQ2.d is addressed in the survey by Q14, Q17, Q19, Q21, and Q22. It is important to note that the association of a particular survey question with a particular RQ aims to clarify the relevance of the survey questions to the research questions. This association does not mean singling one part out of the whole. Therefore, responses to each survey question do not provide directly answers to each RQ. Statistical interrelationships between items in conjunction with qualitative analysis are what bring comprehensive answers to nested questions. Therefore, I turn to discuss the relevance of the survey questions to the present study's objectives and interviews.

Part (A), the background information, consists of six questions (from Q1 to Q6) that deal with gender, age, occupation, educational qualifications, work experience, and an open question investigating perceived knowledge of 'ELF'. The purpose of this question is to examine how respondents' awareness of ELF relates to their perceptions. To make respondents feel comfortable, the survey does not requires details about living and working locations. However, this issue was considered in the interview to enrich the qualitative analysis. The purpose of part (A) is to divide respondents into groups based on the covered factors if the data reveals something significant within the interests of the present study. Part (B), use of English, consists of eight questions (from Q7 to 14) that facilitate respondents' reflections on their experiences of using English. Q7, Q8, and Q9 examine the perceived extent of English use. Q7 relates to the perceived frequency of English use. Q8 relates to the perceived domains/ purposes/motives of using English. This question provides choices and a free space for writing additional or different perspectives. Q9 asks about one's current interlocutor group in terms of native English users, non-native English users, and Saudi users. The purpose of specifying a 'Saudi' category is to explore whether respondents use English with whom they share an L1. Q10 provides options for labelling one's own English. It also provides a free space to describe one's own English. This question explores whether/how respondents see their own influence on English. With a complexity theory lens, I believe that non-awareness of one's own influence on English does not necessarily represent ideological positions. Therefore, Q11 investigates perceptions of identity projection and perceptions of agency over English use. Inspired by Wang's (2012) suggestion, the 'native English' category in this question is positioned after the 'my English' category to stimulate careful though. However, the interviews investigated participants' descriptions and judgements of their own English and the English associated with native and non-native English users. Q12 is a five-point Likert scale (from strongly disagree =1, agree=2, neutral=3, agree=4, to strongly agree=5). This question explores whether respondents perceive the spread of English as an imposed threat or positive resource. The interviews' investigation elaborated on this issues.

Q13 is an attitudinal scale in terms of acceptability along a five-point continua running from 'completely unacceptable=1' to 'completely acceptable=5'. In the instructions of this question, I underlined the phrase 'linguistic structures' to draw attention to linguistic usages rather than content. The purpose of this question is to examine the extent of (in)tolerance towards ELF variants that are adapted from 'Saudi English' studies (see Section 2.4.2). In this question, I have included Saudis' shared usages that can be classified as variants based on Kachru's (1992) distinction between errors and variants (see Section 2.3.2). The question consists of 17 sentences. The sentences contain the following variants: routinely code-mixed and Islamic expressions (13.1); borrowings from Arabic when words do not have equivalents in English (13.2); expanding the function of the article 'the' from a definite marker to a purposeful list of functions (13.3); the free mobility of adverbial phrases around the sentence to give semantic operations more emphasis, as Arabic works, than syntactic operations, as English works (13.4); using the Arabic style of emphasis on emotional expressions (13.5); using the dummy object as a desirable communicative method to clarify meaning or exhibit emphasis (13.6); preference for gerund forms in purposive meanings (13.7); using the Arabic style in intonations and exclamations (13.8); adding the article 'a/an' before uncountable nouns when used in localised expressions (13.8); using localised lexical items (13.9 and 13.10); expanding the meanings and functions of some words such as 'open' and 'supermarket' (13.9 and 13.10); preference for masculine forms when the gender is not specified in a way that mirrors male-dominant cultures (13.11); mixing British and American usages (13.12); omission of the article 'a/n' from noun phrases to activate the Arabic zero article function of indefiniteness (13.3); providing additional clarifications as desirable in Arabic (13.14); direct translations of Islamic prayers (13.15); adding the plural morpheme '-s' to some uncountable nouns when used in localised expressions (13.16); and using of locally-invented lexical items to expand English usage (13.17). In the interview, I investigated participants' reactions to, contextual reflections on, and adjustments of these specific variants and other Saudis' shared usages of English.

Q14 starts with the phrase 'Based on your experiences' to prompt critical thinking in terms of real-life usages and stimulate responses based on experiences rather than normative way of thinking. The question then asks respondents to rank the necessity of given skills in the success of international communications in English. The given skills include: conformity to StE models; conformity to ENL usages; familiarity with native English cultures; language adjustments depending on situations; fulfilling contextual functions; and accommodating responses to cultural diversities. The purpose of providing these options is to investigate how far respondents report (in)tolerance to misalignment with StE and ENL usages in international settings, and how they perceive the role of a transcultural negotiator in ELF settings. The interviews' investigation elaborated on these issues. After this question, Part (C), starts to investigate perceptions in relation to pedagogical settings. This part consists of eight questions (from Q15 to Q22) that facilitate reflections on motives, objectives, needs, preferences, and experiences in relation to learning/teaching English. This survey design facilitates comparing between (in)tolerance in non-pedagogical settings (Part B) and (in)tolerance in pedagogical settings (Part C). In the interviews, I encouraged participants to talk about their experiences with English in different contexts. I also investigated experiences with ALF, ELF, and ELT to understand how they relate to one another. Q15 examines the image of the 'ideal' ELT teachers in the eyes of respondents. The question provides options of three groups. The first group is 'native English users', the second group is 'non-native English users who have good command of English and are specialised in teaching English', and the third group is 'Saudis who have good command of English and are specialised in teaching English'. Formulation of these options aims to explore whether respondents still prefer ENL teachers without being aware of their qualifications. The 'Saudi teachers' option is specified in order to investigate whether respondents prefer ELT teachers who have a similar background to the student background. To explore the reasons for chosen responses, Q16 asks respondents to justify their choices and stimulates them to express any differing views. This question allows the investigation to obtain unexpected or significant insights. In the interviews, these issues were expanded to explore how participants perceive themselves in relation to other Saudi users of English, non-native users of English, and native English users.

Q17, Q19, and Q20 investigate needs in relation to ELT linguistic, communicative, and cultural dimensions. They also examine whether ELF-oriented ELT suits the Saudi context. Q17 asks about the importance of given activities for development of English using skills. The question used the expressions 'your opinion' and 'English using skills' to encourage respondents to respond based on their own needs (not on what they have experienced).The given options of activities include American usages, British usages, all/any native English usages, non-native English usages, and English usages in international domains. I formulated this question as an attitudinal scale with a five-point continua ranging from 'very unimportant = 1' to 'very important = 5'. The purpose of this question is to explore whether respondents associate ELT with global practices of English or with ENL linguistic usages. Q18 is a five-point scale running from 'very false = 1' to 'very true = 5'. This question consists of six items investigating motives and goals for learning/using English. The question examines the existence/lack of target ENL users/nations, interest in native-like English, and orientations towards language standardisation and English linguistic diversities. Q19 is a multiple-choice task that investigate whether respondents associate ELT with ENL cultures, local cultures, or transcultural practices. The expression 'do you suggest' encourages respondents to choose what suits their needs (not what they have experienced). Q20 is a multiple-choice task with a space for writing relevant ideas about the communicative dimensions of ELT. This question investigate whether respondents associate ELT with linguistic conformity to StE models, ENL communicative competence, local communicative styles, or contextual performativity in international communications. In the interviews, inquires of Q17, Q18, Q19, and Q20 were expanded to identify participants' needs in relation to ELT linguistic, communicative, and cultural dimensions.

Q14, Q21, and Q22 investigate how far (in)tolerance to misalignment with StE and ENL usages relate to context (international settings, teaching/learning settings, and evaluative/assessment settings). In the interview, these issues were discussed with participants to explore what makes 'good' English across a range of different contexts. Q14 and Q21 are ranking schemes, and Q22 is a multiple-choice task with a free space for writing any response that I did not anticipate. The question provides negative and positive opinions about StE-based tests. Instructions inform respondents that more than one option can be chosen. To minimise haphazard responses, I designed Q22 to function as a 'trap question', where contradictory options are expressed in positive and negative voices. Using this method, I could exclude any participation that revealed haphazard responses from the sample. Part (D), additional participation, gives respondents the chance to add comments on relevant issues, and their contact details if they would like to participate in the interviews.

4.4.4 Second phase: follow-up qualitative interviews

4.4.4.1 Values of qualitative research methods

The quantitative approach is useful in identifying statistically significant interrelationships between perceptions and reported practices, though it cannot elicit reflective and contextual insights from language users. Through a complexity theory lens, this study views meaning as inseparable from thick contextual descriptions and reflection. This position justifies the mixed-method survey of this project followed by the qualitative stage. The concept 'qualitative research' is 'an umbrella phrase that refers to the collection, analysis, and interpretation of interview, participant observation, and document data in order to understand and describe meanings, relationships, and patterns' (Tracy, 2013: 36). The scope of this definition recommends encompassing approaches such as ethnography and narrative inquiry.

As stated by Tracy (2013), qualitative methods are useful in approaching the object of study as 'gestalt' (a German word meaning a whole perceived as more than the sum of its parts) and acknowledge and celebrate the role of the researcher as a 'bricoleur' (a creative who (re)constructs something significant from the ingredients that show up in the data). Tracy (2013) suggests that ethnography and observation are useful methods in understanding 'gestalt' meanings. Perceiving a problem with obscuring the voices of those being researched, Baird (2013) questions methods that tend to underemphasise interviews or do not appreciate languaging, cultural alignments, and contextualisation in terms of integrated knowledge and complex social systems.

'The effects of such studies, and their resulting accounts, is a tendency to reify both language and the meaning making behaviours of those observed, without recognising the performative, integrated and complex nature of human culture, knowledge and semiotics... An alternative, but still problematic, tendency in the field is for ethnographic- or social semiotic- oriented accounts to emphasise meaning making being in relation to power relations and asymmetrical symbolic exchange, which, by association, often places the site of meaning making outside the minds and direct experiences of people themselves... It does not, however, situate the performance entirely beyond the speaker, instead with minds and semiotic systems being completely intertwined' (Baird, 2013: 130, 131).

Baird's (2013) position suggests engaging with language users' conscious perceptions and positions to complement and/ or start qualitative forms of research. This study requires qualitative research methods because it is in its interest to reflect critically on 'what is said' and 'how it is said' to make 'second-order interpretations' (explanations of participants' explanations) and illustrations of multi-layers of perceptions and reported practices (ranging from conscious to unconscious and from explicit to implicit meanings). This project manages issues that cannot be observed directly such as experiences and ways of thinking that inform current positions, how people interpret questions, the actions that they describe in relation to the questions that they answer, people's critical insights into language constructs, people's perspectives to understand 'what is said', and the researcher's reflections on 'how it is said'. Interviews provide the opportunity to present observations, provide a forum of probing, and test hunches (Tracy, 2013). The following section discusses these issues with qualitative interviews in relation to the present study.

4.4.4.2 Appropriateness of qualitative interviews to the present project

Section 4.4.3.2 discusses the relevance of the qualitative interviews in the formulation of the present project's research questions and survey. This section discusses qualitative interviews in terms of relevance to the present project's objectives and frameworks. Qualitative interviews are necessary to provide thick descriptions for meanings of research themes from subjects' perspectives in terms of lived experiences in their contexts (Tracy, 2013). This project aims to investigate this area. Therefore, qualitative interviews are appropriate for the project. Considering the objectives of this study, ethnography and observation are not rejected but are not the only approaches that guide the investigation, particularly when a number of issues of the present study require direct questioning in particular contexts in relation to specific questions. It is possible to observe and/or interview a few people, but I seek wide-scale research through a complexity lens to provide a competing narrative to other works that have conducted the same investigation with a simple focus. This contribution adds not only on complexity theory and ELF research, but also on language perception, attitude, and teaching research because it performs similar data collection with a different focus and scale.

Dornyei (2013:134) describes the 'interview genre' as 'turn-taking conversations', and Kvale (1996: 11 as sited in Cohen et al., 2013: 409) describes the 'inter-view' as 'an interchange of views between two or more people on a topic of mutual interest'. In qualitative interviews, participants answer open-ended questions to explain their views. As the present project not only requires 'yes, no, or because' answers, it employs a flexible style of in-depth interviewing with questions that encourage interviewees to produce self-reflectivity, contextual experiences, and thick descriptions. As discussed by Dornyei (2013), the format of qualitative interviews can be structured (i.e., with a fixed list of questions), unstructured (i.e., following participants' directions), or semi-structured (i.e., with a pre-prepared guiding questions to prompt free elaboration on interesting issues). I conducted semi-structured follow-up interviews to obtain personal explanations for orientations, elicit reflective insights from participants, prompt elaboration on the survey questions, and permit comparing different responses in an exploratory manner. The follow-up interview questions depended on the interviewees' choices of items in the survey (see Section 4.4.3.2).

I chose to conduct individual face-to-face interviews to approach individual voices in relation to contextually lived experiences and positions. This kind of interviewing enables using verbal (e.g., questions) and non-verbal (e.g., gestures) techniques that encourage interviewees to produce personally elaborated accounts, information on past events, buried emotions, rationales, explanations, and/or justifications for practices and opinions. These narratives provide a window to explore how others understand and interpret a certain issue or situation and 'create a reality that they, in turn, act upon' (Tracy, 2013: 29). From this point of view, narratives do not necessarily mirror the 'truth' of interviewees' perceptions and practices. Instead, these narratives serve as a mirror of how participants make sense of the world and interpret their positions, motives, identities, and experiences. Baird (2013: 131) asserts that interview responses indicators of 'how people felt inclined to answer particular questions, on a particular topic, with a particular interviewer and in a particular context'. The analysis and interpretation of these responses may inform future research. Through this project, I hope to contribute to the literature by listening to the voices of those in discussion while observing the language that they actually use for expressing their views and telling stories.

4.5 Compensation of limitations

One of the techniques I used for sampling was the 'snowball' technique to support the widespread sharing of the survey across the different provinces of the KSA. The present study required a relatively large number of respondents to enable the examination of complexity theory-inspired statistical interrelationships. Snowballing may enfeeble the data because initial contacts may influence later contacts. Therefore, I did not rely solely on snowballing, and I distributed the survey in my official channels. When any potential respondents contacted me for enquiries, I asked them to invite their contacts. In addition, I ensured that most of the initial contacts invited people through their public social media accounts (e.g., Facebook, Twitter, and Snapchat) to further spread the survey. I also made sure that the initial contacts were scattered across the main five provinces of the KSA (Western, Eastern, Central, Northern, and Southern). It is more effective to use this kind of sampling rather than obtaining an incomplete picture. After the data collection period, the screening of respondents' backgrounds indicated that the spread of the survey went far beyond its initial contacts (see Sections 4.6.3.1 and 5.3). The significant value brought to this study by snowballing was respondents' trust, which encouraged them to talk comfortably about their private experiences (e.g., cultural chocks) and sensitive orientations (e.g., religious positions) in terms of English use.

In terms of survey length, completion of the presents study's survey requires from 30 to 40 minutes. Dornyei (2013) suggests not to exceed the 30-minute completion limit. However, the survey study found a salience from respondents' perspectives and I received 825 participations. Furthermore, I understand that a pre-established set of statements in surveys prevents participants from using their own terms and articulating their own views. To minimise this limitation, the present study's survey includes open-ended questions and optional comment fields. However, there is also a possibility that even if two respondents have chosen the same response, they might have different understanding of the question (Kitazawa, 2013). To take this possibility into consideration, I have made my contact information available for inquires, and all paper-based surveys were completed in my presence to answer inquires. In addition, I conducted interviews, which could reveal differences in interpretations and allowed participants to respond in their own words based on their own ideas and understanding. Another limitation in the methodology of the present study is the use of a web-based survey. This mode may make it possible to obtain multiple participations from the same individual.

Unfortunately, I was unable to offer only one access to each computer because some of my official channels had shortages in computers. After screening the data, I excluded the ones that had identical responses to all items (see Section 5.2.1). To minimise the possibility of haphazardness of responses, the last question in the survey functions as a 'trap question' test for this issue (see Sections 4.4.3.2 and 5.2.1).

4.6 Field Work

4.6.1 Ethical considerations

Ethical approval was obtained (ID 24317) from the ERGO (Ethics and Research Governance Online) at the University of Southampton. Information and consent forms for each phase were formulated (see Appendix 2) and signed by the participants. Data confidentiality, participants' anonymity, permission for audio-recording, and withdrawal rights were declared in the forms. I received official approval from four organisations to host my data collection procedures. Upon their requests, their names are kept anonymous. Due to sex-segregation regulations in the KSA, I administered cautiously the mixed-sex procedures without violating Saudi traditions and Islamic values (see Sections 4.6.3 and 6.4.6). Due to Muslim females' veil-related issues, I avoided video-recording.

4.6.2 Pilot study and modifications

My research leave for data collection (pilot and main study) was permitted for four months (from 14 February to 15 June 2016). Due to time limits, I piloted the survey with 13 participants, who were acquired through personal communications. I knew this sample was not enough to test the feasibility, length, and clarity of the survey. However, these participants' feedback was useful. In response to participants' suggestions, more clarifications were added in the information form; the wording of the survey was edited; and an Arabic version of the English survey was prepared. All Q13 items remained in English in both versions because this question investigates participants' reflections on particular English usages. The Arabic version was revised by two English-Arabic translators to ensure that it mirrored the English version. The Arabic version of the survey was produced to encourage people who may not feel confident or comfortable enough to complete an English version. Although three participants suggested adding an 'I do not know' category, the others argued that the lack of this easy option inspired them to reread, rethink, and reconsider issues to make a decision. Completion of the survey required from 25 to 35 minutes, and some participants expressed their discomfort due to its length. Therefore, I added to the information form that it may take from 30 to 40 minutes to complete the survey. I did not shorten the survey length to maintain the quality of the survey and its data. 6 out of the 13 participants volunteered to join the pilot study's interviews. Each interview lasted from 15 to 30 minutes. Interview participants' feedback was useful in refining my interviewing skills.

4.6.3 Main Study

4.6.3.1 Survey phase: hardcopy, software, and online

I prepared the survey in three modes (hardcopy, software, online) to suit participants' preferences. I created a web-based survey using Google forms. Google itself is widely popular in the KSA, and Saudis tend to trust its associated links. People may not open the link if it seems unfamiliar to them. I distributed the paper-based, email-based, and online surveys across my official channels and 'snowballing' initial contacts to reach contacts of contacts, contacts of contacts of contacts, etc. Initial contacts employed their social media accounts to support the spreading of the survey to a wider audience. Paper-based surveys with women were administered at my official channels or other locations upon requests (e.g., offices, restaurants, coffee shops, libraries, and houses). Due to sex-segregation regulations in the KSA, paper-based surveys with men were administered only at my official channels for this procedure. At the end of the data collection period, I was able to collect 825 questionnaires, but I included 765 questionnaires in the present study (see Section 5.2.1). Through screening respondents' background information, I found high school students, people who left school, graduates still looking for jobs, non-Saudis, employers at airlines, and police officers. This variability indicates that the spread of the survey went beyond its initial contacts of distribution (e.g., engineers, physicians, businessmen, ELT professionals, and university students).

4.6.3.2   Interviews in the light of flexibility

My initial plan was to finish the survey phase before starting interviews. I modified the plan when I learned how to use the advanced functions of Google forms such as tracking changes in descriptive results and tracking typical and deviant cases. In this process, I was able to recruit interviewees who were behind any change in the results, who had written significant comments in the open areas of the survey, or represented either typical or deviant cases of the descriptive analysis. I continued interviewing until the data could satisfy the requirements of my investigation. With these processes, I explored what was left unsaid and unnoticed in the questionnaire, elicited reflective insights from my participants, and obtained personal explanations of orientations.

I started each interview by greetings, introducing myself and the research project, giving the interviewers the chance to introduce themselves, re-explaining confidentiality and anonymity issues, and re-asking interviewees' permission to record. I used survey questions as guidelines to maintain the rhythm of the interview. However, I did not delimit the talk to my predetermined list of questions. I asked unplanned questions depending on the interviewees' given accounts. I attempted to obtain a balance between being open to new horizons and being sensitive to verbal and non-verbal reactions related to the research focus. When unexpected relevant ideas emerged from the interviewees' accounts, I intended to elaborate on them in in-depth levels gradually within the flow of the interviewee's conversation to make the process look like a 'natural' conversation. I attempted to facilitate without directing the interviewees' conversations. As a Saudi user of English who grew up and received English education in the KSA, I had something in common with my participants. We had a common understanding of the Saudis' context, education, and use of English. This advantage was useful in building a rapport with participants and understanding what they said and how they said it. However, I encouraged interviewees to verbalise and clarify what they meant to ensure that I have comprehensive understandings.

All face-to-face interviews with female participants were conducted at my official channels or other locations upon requests (e.g., offices, restaurants, coffee shops, libraries, and houses). Due to sex-segregation regulations in the KSA, all face-to-face interviews with male participants were conducted only at the official channels. I conducted phone interviews only with cases whose voices in the survey seemed significant for the study (e.g., deviant cases of statistical tests), but they restricted their availability to phone methods, such as those located in different cities and religious men who did not want to be in a face-to-face meeting with a woman. When I noticed the emergence of sensitivity signs in some participants' body language, I started to take notes after each interview about this issue. Although body language is not within the interest of the present study, it may be useful in understanding and interpreting participants' accounts (see Section 4.6.5).

At the end of the data collection period, I was able to interview 72 participants, but I included 30 interviews in the present study (see Section 6.2.1). The longest interview lasted 71 minutes and 42 seconds, and the shortest interview lasted 12 minutes and 39 seconds, with the average interview at almost 30 minutes. Language and duration of each interview depended on what suited the interviewee. The flexibility during the interviews encouraged participants to feel comfortable for the duration of the interview. It encouraged some participants to extend the discussions. With this flexibility, I was able to conduct in-depth interviews with those who had dedicate more than30 minutes for the interview. Most ELT professionals used only English, and a few of them used code-switched phrases and words. Some university students and non-ELT professionals used English almost exclusively with code switching. The rest of the participants used both languages to varying degrees. None of the participants used just Arabic. All interviews were audio-recorded.

4.6.4 Consultations on interpretations of interview utterances

I conducted six focus groups at my official channels. Each focus group consisted of four-six members, and all members signed consent forms for this phase. For each group, I prepared a different list of written utterances, which were adopted from the present study's interviews. I emailed each list with an instructional guide to members two days before their meeting. The longest focus group lasted 90 minutes and 56 seconds, and the shortest group meeting lasted 30 minutes and 53 seconds, with the average interview at almost 54 minutes. All focus groups were recorder. This procedure aimed to check participants' interpretations of the interview utterances. The focus group data were not included in this project as they highlighted construction and negotiation of meaning while the present study targets individuals' ideas.

4.6.5 Emergence of sensitivity signs

The pilot study was managed successfully without any difficulty. However, what seems 'innocent to the researcher may be highly sensitive to the researched or to other parties' (Cohen et al., 2013: 166). There are some factors that may seem insensitive to the research, but they cause participants' sensitivity such as having professional informants, social deviance from accepted standards, fear of judgment, intrusion into deeper personal experiences, threat of stigmatisation, risk of exposure, religious practices, and fear of scrutiny, guilty knowledge (i.e., having knowledge that a wrongful action has occurred, but is ignored), oppression, taboo, cross-cultural conflicts, and hidden curriculums. During the present study's interviews and paper-based survey administrations, I noticed some physical reactions of sensitivity from some participants during the interviews and paper-based survey administrations, such as blushing, shaking legs/pens/papers, scratching heads, pressing forehead, sweating, sudden laughing, hesitation, changing answers many times (e.g. see Appendix 7), groaning, and asking for a break, coffee, food, or cigarette. These reactions occurred while answering Q13, Q8.6, Q11.1, Q14.7, and/or Q19, which investigate identity management and negotiation in relation to English use. As I became aware of when these reactions appeared, I continued interviewing with caution.

Chapter 5: Mixed-method survey results and findings (interrelationships among perceptions of English, language judgments, and context)

5.1 Introduction

This chapter presents and discusses the survey results and findings. At a preliminary level, the collected data provided patterns of responses, extent of tolerance towards misalignment with StE models, and perceptions of English in terms of beliefs, attitudes, common sense, motivations, ideological outlooks, identifications, and contextual(ised) positions. The chapter begins with a brief explanation of the procedure through which the data were prepared for analysis, the criteria which were considered for data inclusion and exclusion, the considerations which were taken for descriptive analysis, and the justifications for processing cross-tabulations and Chi square tests in pairs for all the survey items. After presenting respondents' background characteristics, the chapter presents the results and findings of the descriptive analysis, qualitative inquiries of the survey, and (highly) significant interrelationships. The discussion and conclusion are summarised at the end of this chapter. The summary justifies the need for the interviews.

5.2 Statistical considerations

5.2.1 Preparing data for analysis

In total, 825 questionnaires were collected. To increase reliability, I excluded 60 participations because they did not fulfil the criteria I took into consideration. Firstly, I excluded 34 respondents because they did not complete all the questions. Missing responses may decrease the reliability of the Chi square tests and statistical interrelationships. Secondly, I excluded 15 respondents because their background characteristics, such as being school students, indicated that they were not involved in the present study's complex research problem (see Sections 1.2 and 4.4.1). Thirdly, I excluded nine respondents because they did not pass the 'trap question', which tests haphazardness of responding (see Sections 4.4.3.1 and 4.4.3.2). In addition, I found three online identical participations, so I excluded two of them. At the end, 765 questionnaires were included in the present study's data. Each question, item, and questionnaire was numbered. Regarding the open-ended items, I extracted and grouped answers for each relevant question. The data were transferred into Excel 2013 and then to IBM SPSS 22 Software.

5.2.2 Justifications for statistical tests and reliability issues

For Likert measurements in Q12, Q13, Q17, and Q18, the overall responses were calculated in means according to table 1.

Table 1. Mean values of overall responses

Mean	Overall Response			
From 1.00 to less than 1.80	Strongly Disagree	Completely Unacceptable	Very False	Very Unimportant
From 1.80 to less than 2.60	Disagree	Unacceptable	False	Unimportant
From 2.60 to less than 3.40	Neutral	Neutral	Neutral	Neutral
From 3.40 to less than 4.20	Agree	Acceptable	True	Important
From 4.20 to less than 5.00	Strongly Agree	Completely Acceptable	Very True	Very Important

As means hide some elements of the data, the overall responses cannot provide answers for my research questions. Thus, the interview participants were recruited from among the survey respondents based on 'confirming and disconfirming' technique to obtain explanations for the typical and deviant responses/cases (see Sections 4.4.2, 5.5, and 5.6). In addition, I cross-checked whether a particular choice in one question correlated with a particular choice in another question (cross-tabulation). As the purpose of the statistical procedures in the present study was to examine the relationships between the items on the questionnaire, Chi square tests for independence were processed after cross-tabulation processes. The values of Chi square tests (χ^2) and p-values of significance were calculated. The following criteria were considered to judge the significance of the relation:

- If the p-value is £ 0.05, there is a significant relation between the two variables.
- If the p-value is > 0.05, there is no significant relation between the two variables.

The survey validity was not considered because it does not suit mixed-method surveys. Instead, the reliability of the survey was calculated (Total Cronbach's Alpha = 0.759), and the Cronbach's Alpha value for each closed item is less than 0.759. After consultation with statisticians at King Abdulaziz University, the reliability of this survey is good because its total Cronbach's Alpha value is higher than 0.65, and the Cronbach's Alpha value for each closed item is less than the total Cronbach's Alpha value.

As cross-tabulation and Chi square tests were processed in pairs for all the survey items, I found many (highly) significant relationships. Some of those relationships are outside the scope of the present study. For instance, I found some relationships between gender and patterns of responses, between age and patterns of responses, and between educational/professional background and patterns of responses. To save space and sharpen focus, I presented only the (highly) significant relationships that are relevant to my research questions. To investigate the role of ELT professional identity, I have divided the respondents into four groups based on occupation (see table 2) to discuss briefly, in some sections, the considerable differences in perceptions of English among these groups. I divided ELT professionals into two groups (schoolteachers and university instructors) to present some significant differences between them in some areas.

Table 2. Respondent groups based on occupation

Q3. Occupation	Frequency	%
Students	227	29.7
ELT schoolteachers (teachers, teacher supervisors, and teacher educators	118	15.4
ELT university instructors (lecturers, assistant professors, associate professors, professors)	108	14.1
Non-ELT professionals (e.g. businessmen, engineers, physicians, non-ELT teachers, instructors, etc.)	312	40.8
Total	765	100.0

5.3 Respondents' background

Tables 3, 4, 5, 6, and 7 show that there is quit a range of respondents from different demographic backgrounds.

Table 3. Gender

Gender	Frequency	%
Male	300	39.2
Female	465	60.8
Total	765	100.0

Table 4. Age

Age	Frequency	%
(18–23)	145	19.0
(24–29)	121	15.8
(30–35)	176	23.0
(36–40)	126	16.4
(40+)	197	25.8
Total	765	100.0

Table 5. Occupation

Occupation	Frequency	%
Student (undergraduates and postgraduates)	227	29.7
ELT professionals (e.g. schoolteachers, teacher supervisors, teacher educators, and university instructors including teacher assistants, lecturers, assistant professors, associate professors, and professors)	226	29.5
Professionals in majors other than ELT (e.g. businessmen, engineers, physicians, academics in fields other than ELT, employers in different organisations, etc.)	312	40.8
Total	765	100.0

Table 6. Last academic degree

Educational Qualifications	Frequency	%
Still an undergraduate	169	22.1
Bachelor Degree	317	41.4
Master Degree	153	20.0
PhD Degree	126	16.5
Total	765	100.0

Table 7. Working experience

Working Experience	Frequency	%
From 0 to less than 5 years	335	43.8
From 5 years to 10 years	128	16.7
More than 10 years but less than 16 years	115	15.0
16 years or more	187	24.4
Total	765	100.0

5.4   Results and findings

5.4.1   Perceived functions of English

Q6 examined respondents' awareness of the field of ELF. As shown in table 8, 20.1% (154) of the respondents answered 'yes' to Q6. Those respondents were then asked to write briefly what they know about the ELF field. The resulting descriptions of the 154 respondents displayed awareness of the functions of ELF (e.g., 'communication', 'real speaking', 'nonstandard', 'international', 'small mistakes', 'non major grammatical mistakes', and 'understanding before correct grammar'). However, only 15 out of the 154 respondents displayed evidence of some understanding of the field of ELF (e.g., 'new Englishes', 'Kachrue', 'ELF varieties', 'nativisation of English', 'standard ideology', and disassociation of English from ENL usages and cultures). Descriptions of 139 respondents showed evidence of mistaking the field of ELF for ESL/EFL/ELT courses that focus on conversation skills (e.g., 'IELTS conversation', 'speaking and listening in TOEFL', 'Fluency in English courses', 'talking skills in English for Academic purposes', and 'communication section in English courses', and 'English for specific purposes'). These responses were explored in more depth in the interviews to investigate the role of this awareness in perceptions and reported uses of English.

Table 8. Perceived knowledge of ELF field

Q6. Have you ever received formally a course or training on the field of English as a Lingua Franca? If yes, please write about it.	Frequency	%
Yes	154	20.1
No	611	79.9
Total	765	100.0

Responses to Q7, as shown in table 9, displayed respondents' acknowledgment of their extensive use of English. 77.3% of the respondents indicated that they (almost) always use English. From an ELF standpoint, a language that is perceived as a foreign language is not used on a daily basis.

Table 9. Frequency of using English

Q7. How often do you use English?	Frequency	%
Never	2	0.3
Rarely	40	5.2
Sometimes	132	17.3
Often	215	28.1
Always	376	49.2
Total	765	100.0

Q9 asked about the current interlocutor group. As displayed in table 10, 77.6% of the respondents reported that most of their current interlocutors are non-native English users, including Saudis. From an ELF standpoint, a language that is perceived as a foreign language is used with its native users, while a language that is perceived as a LF is used with anyone who can use it, including interlocutors who share an L1. Regarding Saudis' use of English with other Saudis, table 10 shows that 26.1% of the respondents reported that most of their current interlocutors are other Saudis. The interviews explored in more depth participants' experiences in relation to these practices.

Table 10. Current Interlocutors

Q9. You may use English with different interlocutors for different purposes. In most cases, you use English to communicate with...	Frequency	%
Native English users	171	22.4
Non-native English users	394	51.5
Saudi users of English	200	26.1
Total	765	100.0

Table 11 compared responses to Q9 based on occupation. As displayed in table 11, 33% of the students and 41.35% of ELT professionals reported that most of their communications in English occur with other Saudis. Only 9% of non-ELT professionals reported this practice. Considering the contact in English between students and ELT professionals in teaching/learning contexts, this is not surprising. However, the interviews explored this practice in more depth.

Table 11. Current interlocutors based on occupation

Q3. Occupation	Q9. In most cases, you use English to communicate with...	Frequency	%
Students	Native English users	50	22.0
	Non-native English users	102	44.9
	Saudi users of English	75	33.0
	Total	227	100.0
ELT professionals	Native English users	26	11.65
	Non-native English users	105	47
	Saudi users of English	95	41.35
	Total	118	100.0

Non-ELT professionals	Native English users	95	30.4
	Non-native English users	187	59.9
	Saudi users of English	30	9.6
	Total	312	100.0

Q8 explored domains/purposes of English use. Table 12 shows that respondents reported their use of English in wide domains starting with tourism, education, and social networks and ending with communications with friends, family, and ENL users. From an ELF standpoint, a language that is perceived as a foreign language is not used in wide domains for both international and intranational settings. The results of this question and the previous questions show that English, for respondents, functions as a common LF to communicate with anyone who can use it in both international and intranational settings. Section 5.4.4.1 discusses the results of table 12 (Q8) and its open-ended item in relation to motives and purposes.

Table 12. Domains of English use

Q8. What are your purposes for using English? (more than one option can be chosen)	Frequency	%	Rank
Education	566	74.0	2
Work	481	62.9	4
Tourism	568	74.2	1
Friends and family	415	54.2	5
Social networks (e.g. WhatsApp, Facebook, Twitter, LinkedIn, professional forums, etc.)	516	67.5	3
Integration with native English users	107	14.0	7
Other (please specify)	210	27.5	6

5.4.2 Extent of tolerance towards misalignment with StE models

As displayed in table 13, each item in Q13 examined (in) tolerance towards a particular variant. Routinely Islamic code-mixed expressions, as in item 13.1, are considered completely acceptable (mean = 4.23, Std. Deviation = 1.07). Borrowing from Arabic when words do not have equivalents in English, as in item 13.2, is also considered completely acceptable (mean = 4.25, Std. Deviation = 1.04). Giving the article 'the' additional functions, as in item 13.3, is considered acceptable (mean = 4.01, Std. Deviation = 1.22). Regarding the free mobility of adverbial clauses, as in item 13.4, respondents' position is considered neutral (mean = 3.32, Std. Deviation = 1.28). Using the Arabic style of emphatic expressions, as in item 13.5, is considered acceptable (mean = 3.47, Std. Deviation = 1.25). Regarding using a dummy object to clarify meanings, as in item 13.6, respondents' position is considered neutral (mean = 2.89, Std. Deviation = 1.41). Using gerund forms instead of infinitive forms for purposive meanings, as in item 13.7, is considered acceptable (mean = 3.85, Std. Deviation = 1.26).

Using the Arabic style in intonation, missing exclamation marks, and/or changing noun countability when the noun is used in a localised English expression, as in item 13.8, is considered acceptable (mean = 3.54, Std. Deviation = 1.33). Using localised lexical items and/or expanding meanings of some words, as in item 13.9, is considered acceptable (mean = 3.94, Std. Deviation = 1.15); regarding such usage and expansion, but as shown in item 13.10, respondents' position is considered neutral (mean = 3.23, Std. Deviation = 1.41). Preference for masculine forms when the gender is not specified, as in item 13.11, is considered acceptable (mean = 4.08, Std. Deviation = 1.17). Mixing British and American usages, as in item 13.12, is considered completely acceptable (mean = 4.45, Std. Deviation = 0.88). Omission of the article 'a/n' in noun phrases for the purpose of indefiniteness, as in item 13.13, is considered acceptable (mean = 3.98, Std.

Deviation = 1.22). Providing unnecessary clarifications, as in item 13.14, is considered acceptable (mean = 3.86, Std. Deviation = 1.20). Direct translation of Islamic prayers, as in item 13.15, is considered acceptable (mean = 3.72, Std. Deviation = 1.31). Changing noun countability when the noun is used in a localised English expression, as in item 13.16, is considered acceptable (mean = 3.88, Std. Deviation = 1.31). Using locally invented vocabulary, as in 13.17, is considered acceptable (mean = 4.02, Std. Deviation = 1.25).

The overall response to 'Saudi English' variants, which have sociolinguistic/sociocultural explanations, is acceptable (mean = 3.81, Std. Deviation = 0.80). I selected the interview participants from among the survey respondents who had represented the 'acceptable', 'neutral', or 'unacceptable' positions to obtain personal explanations. Respondents' additional comments in part (D) displayed awareness of these variants among Saudis. In contrast to variationist perspectives, respondents' additional comments suggested a tendency to negotiate on the usage and judgment of English (see Section 5.4.8). Some comments displayed intentional and purposeful misalignment with StE and ENL usages in favour of Islamic usages (see Section 5.4.8). I selected the interview participants from among the survey respondents who had written interesting comments about these issues to search for the data that may shed light on emergence and complexity.

Table 13. Extent of tolerance towards misalignment with StE models

'Saudi English' variants (Q13)	Completely unacceptable		Unacceptable		Neutral		Acceptable		Completely acceptable		Weighted Mean	Std. Deviation	Overall Response (in Mean)
	f	%	f	%	f	%	f	%	f	%			
13.1. Mashallah, she is successful.	38	5.0	13	1.7	103	13.5	189	24.7	422	55.2	4.23	1.07	Completely acceptable
13.2. She is wearing her Abaya and Niqaab.	28	3.7	22	2.9	110	14.4	175	22.9	430	56.2	4.25	1.04	Completely acceptable
13.3. We love the talented children.	43	5.6	55	7.2	142	18.6	138	18.0	387	50.6	4.01	1.22	Acceptable
13.4. I ran to you as a friend more than as a mother.	89	11.6	100	13.1	227	29.7	172	22.5	177	23.1	3.32	1.28	Neutral
13.5. It is a very very interesting story.	76	9.9	85	11.1	198	25.9	213	27.8	193	25.2	3.47	1.25	Acceptable
13.6. Riyadh is the city which she lives in it all her life.	182	23.8	122	15.9	195	25.5	127	16.6	139	18.2	2.89	1.41	Neutral
13.7. I sometimes go to Jeddah for shopping with my family.	60	7.8	56	7.3	140	18.3	190	24.8	319	41.7	3.85	1.26	Acceptable
13.8. What a good luck.	89	11.6	69	9.0	187	24.4	180	23.5	240	31.4	3.54	1.33	Acceptable
13.9. Let's go to one of the hypermarkets.	44	5.8	42	5.5	142	18.6	222	29.0	315	41.2	3.94	1.15	Acceptable
13.10. Don't open the computer.	124	16.2	120	15.7	174	22.7	148	19.3	199	26.0	3.23	1.41	Neutral

'Saudi English' variants (Q13)	Completely unacceptable		Unacceptable		Neutral		Acceptable		Completely acceptable		Weighted Mean	Std. Deviation	Overall Response (in Mean)
	f	%	f	%	f	%	f	%	f	%			
13.11. A good teacher is flexible with his students.	38	5.0	47	6.1	123	16.1	163	21.3	394	51.5	4.08	1.17	Acceptable
13.12. This is my favorite colour.	16	2.1	10	1.3	78	10.2	173	22.6	488	63.8	4.45	0.88	Completely acceptable
13.13. He is facing difficulty solving the problem.	40	5.2	62	8.1	149	19.5	140	18.3	374	48.9	3.98	1.22	Acceptable
13.14. They should set up natural settings with authentic data.	39	5.1	58	7.6	200	26.1	142	18.6	326	42.6	3.86	1.20	Acceptable
13.15. May God give you a long life.	70	9.2	72	9.4	161	21.0	163	21.3	299	39.1	3.72	1.31	Acceptable
13.16. My mother always gives me advices.	64	8.4	64	8.4	130	17.0	152	19.9	355	46.4	3.88	1.31	Acceptable
13.17. The Saudi government supports Saudization.	57	7.5	36	4.7	136	17.8	139	18.2	397	51.9	4.02	1.25	Acceptable
Total	1097	8.44	1033	7.94	2595	19.95	2826	21.73	5454	41.94	3.81	0.80	Acceptable

5.4.3 Beliefs and attitudes in relation to perceived language use

5.4.3.1 Beliefs and attitudes towards the spread of English

Table 14 shows that the overall responses to the items of Q12 did not display negative positions towards the spread of English. The overall response to [English is today's worldwide lingua franca] is strongly agree (mean = 4.58, Std. Deviation = 0.79). The overall response to [English is a threat to my culture and first language] is disagree (mean = 2.28, Std. Deviation = 1.36). The overall response to [English enriches our linguistic skills] is strongly agree (mean = 4.36, Std. Deviation = 0.86). The overall response to [English is a trend which we are forced to follow] is neutral (mean = 2.84, Std. Deviation = 1.47). The findings of this section and previous sections revealed that respondents' positive attitudes towards English chime with how they perceive the function of English as a useful LF in intranational and international interactions. From an ELF standpoint, viewing the language as a resource, not a threat, encourages users to exploit it intensively in both international and intranational settings. However, the additional comments in part (D) displayed respondents' emphasis on the Arabic language and its LF function (see Section 5.4.8). I selected the interview participants from among the survey respondents who has represented positive, neutral, or negative positions to explore how attitudes and beliefs relate to the reported practices of English. Through a complexity theory lens, the following sections continue this investigation in relation to (in)tolerance towards ELF variants, perception of one's own English, common sense, StE ideology, identity projection, motivations, and contextual functions.

Table 14. Opinions about the spread of English

Q12. Opinions	Strongly Disagree		Disagree		Neutral		Agree		Strongly Agree		Weighted Mean	Std. Deviation	Overall Response (in Mean)
	f	%	f	%	f	%	f	%	f	%			
12.1. English is today's worldwide lingua franca.	11	1.4	11	1.4	46	6.0	154	20.1	543	71.0	4.58	0.79	Strongly Agree
12.2. English is a threat to my cultural values and Arabic language.	325	42.5	133	17.4	143	18.7	95	12.4	69	9.0	2.28	1.36	Disagree
12.3. English enriches our linguistic skills.	12	1.6	11	1.4	91	11.9	224	29.3	427	55.8	4.36	0.86	Strongly Agree
12.4. English is a trend which we are forced to follow.	219	28.6	99	12.9	169	22.1	138	18.0	140	18.3	2.84	1.47	Neutral

5.4.3.2 Relationship between self-description of one's own English and one's (in)tolerance towards ELF variants

Q10 examined respondents' descriptions of their own English. It provided options with a free space to stimulate respondents to write their own views. As displayed in table 15, 52.2% of the respondents chose to label their own English as English with Saudi/Arabic imprints. 4.4% (34) of the respondents chose to write their own descriptions.

Table 15. Labelling of one's own English

Q10. Description of one's own English	Frequency	%
American English	155	20.3
British English	48	6.3
Mixture of American English and British English	129	16.9
English with Saudi/Arabic imprints	399	52.2
Others (please specify)	34	4.4
Total	765	100.0

Descriptions of the 34 respondents were categorised into ten themes: ownership of English, intelligibility, simplicity, acceptability, non-standardisation, normality, similarity with the English used by other Saudis, projection of Islamic identity, and awareness of translingualism impact. Table 16 shows examples of respondents' descriptions according to these themes. All the themes displayed interactions of perceptual dimensions and contextual dimensions with one's views on English. Through a complexity theory lens, the following sections explore interrelationships between self-descriptions of one's own English and these dimensions.

Table 16. Qualitative descriptions of one's own English

Theme	Frequency	Examples
Ownership of English	2	'my own way', 'my additional language'
Intelligibility	3	'clear', 'easy to be understood', 'understandable'
Simplicity	1	'simple but good'
Acceptability	2	'not as bad as English of some Arabs and some Saudis, but not perfect', 'at least English of Gulf people is better than English of some unnative speakers from other countries'
Non-standardisation	2	'not standard', 'informal'
Normality	2	'normal English', 'ordinary English of Saudis'
Similarity with the English used by other Saudis	9	'Saudi English', 'Saudi version of English', 'Informal with a Saudi touch', 'slang English of Saudis', 'like all other Saudis' English'
Projection of Islamic identity	2	'It mirrors the Islamic identity', 'It is influenced by Arabic language and Islamic religion'
Awareness of translingualism impact	11	'more British with something else. I don't know', 'It seems like a translation from Arabic to English', 'It's influenced by Arabic and French', 'It has traces from Arabic and Japanese', 'It is influenced by Arabic, Italian, and Germany... they all influence each other'

As displayed in table 17, Chi square testing showed that there is a highly significant relation (χ^2 = 139.496, p-values = 0.000) between self-description of one's own English and the extent of one's (in)tolerance towards misalignment with the StE model. In 54.5% of the cases, non-rejection of ELF variants is accompanied with acknowledgment of Saudi/Arabic traces on English.

Table 17. Relationship between self-description of one's own English and one's (in)tolerance towards ELF variants

One's overall (in)tolerance towards 'Saudi English' variants (Q13)	Q10. Description of one's own English						Conclusion		
	American English	British English	Mixture of American English and British English	English with Saudi/Arabic imprints	Other	Total	χ^2_{16}	Sig. (p-value)	Sig.
	f. (%)	f. (%)	f. (%)	f. (%)	f. (%)	f. (%)			
Completely unacceptable	3 (0.4)	2 (0.3)	1 (0.1)	5 (0.7)	0 (0.0)	11 (1.4)			
Unacceptable	13 (1.7)	2 (0.3)	11 (1.4)	10 (1.3)	1 (0.1)	37 (4.8)			
Neutral	59 (7.7)	19 (2.5)	39 (5.1)	72 (9.4)	4 (0.5)	193 (25.2)	139.496	0.000	Sig.
Acceptable	63 (8.2)	19 (2.5)	54 (7.1)	110 (14.4)	4 (0.5)	250 (32.7)			
Completely acceptable	17 (2.2)	6 (0.8)	24 (3.1)	202 (26.4)	25 (3.3)	274 (35.8)			
Total	155 (20.3)	48 (6.3)	129 (16.9)	399 (52.2)	34 (4.4)	765 (100.0)			

5.4.3.3 Relationship between perceptions of English standardisation and (in)tolerance towards ELF variants

Q18.5 investigated respondents' perception of English standardisation. As displayed in table 18, 81.9% of the respondents did not show an explicit bias towards StE models, and 18.1% of the respondents showed an explicit bias towards language standardisation. Q18.6 investigated respondents' perceptions of English linguistic diversities. As displayed in table 18, 51.1% of the respondents value the necessity of familiarity with English linguistic diversities, 27.2% of the respondents showed a neutral position, and 21.7% of the respondents denied the necessity of familiarity with English linguistic diversities. The overall response to the necessity of sticking to one standard model is false (mean = 2.31, Std. Deviation = 1.32), and the overall response to the necessity of familiarity with non-standard and non-native English usages is true (mean = 3.45, Std. Deviation = 1.29). I recruited the interview participants from among the survey respondents who has represented false, neutral, or true positions to explore personal justifications for positions.

Table 18. Perceptions of English standardisation vs. perceptions of English linguistic diversities

Statements	Very false		False		Neutral		True		Very true		Weighted Mean	Std. Deviation	Overall Response (in Mean)
	f	%	f	%	f	%	f	%	f	%			
Q18.5. It is necessary to stick to a single standard model (e.g. only British model).	293	38.3	157	20.5	177	23.1	63	8.3	75	9.8	2.31	1.32	False
Q18.6. Today, it becomes necessary to be familiar with non-standard and non-native English usages.	85	11.1	81	10.6	208	27.2	188	24.6	203	26.5	3.45	1.29	True

Table 19 shows that there is a highly significant relation ($\chi^2 = 113.904$, p-values = 0.000) between explicit rejection of language standardisation (Q18.5) and implicit tolerance towards using a mixture of different Englishes (Q13.8). In 79.9% of the cases, implicit tolerance towards using a mixture of American and British usages is accompanied by either explicit rejection of or a neutral position towards language standardisation. However, perceptions of this practice (using a mixture of different Englishes) was explored in more depth in the interviews.

Table 19. Relationship between explicit rejection of language standardisation and implicit tolerance towards using a mixture of different Englishes

Q18.5. It is important to stick to a single standard model (e.g. only standard British model).	Q13.8. This is my favorite colour.					Total f. (%)	Conclusion	
	Completely unacceptable f. (%)	Unacceptable f. (%)	Neutral f. (%)	Acceptable f. (%)	Completely acceptable f. (%)		χ^2_{16}	Sig. (p-value)
Very false	7 (0.9)	1 (0.1)	9 (1.2)	32 (4.2)	244 (31.9)	293 (38.3)		
False	1 (0.1)	2 (0.3)	22 (2.9)	40 (5.2)	92 (12.0)	157 (20.5)	113.904	0.000
Neutral	2 (0.3)	3 (0.4)	29 (3.8)	59 (7.7)	84 (11.0)	177 (23.1)		
True	1 (0.1)	4 (0.5)	8 (1.0)	23 (3.0)	27 (3.5)	63 (8.2)		Sig.
Very true	5 (0.7)	0 (0.0)	10 (1.3)	19 (2.5)	41 (5.4)	75 (9.8)		
Total	16 (2.1)	10 (1.3)	78 (10.2)	173 (22.6)	488 (63.8)	765 (100.0)		

5.4.4 Motives in relation to language perceptions and judgments

5.4.4.1 Interrelationships among language perceptions, language judgments, and the lack of a target nation

In Q18, respondents were allowed to choose more than one purpose. In addition, they were given a free space to write their own purposes. The qualitative responses written by 210 respondents were extracted and grouped into three categories: entertainment (e.g., movies, songs, and online gaming); social mobility (e.g., requirements of education, jobs, and publishing); and intranational communication with non-Arabs who live/work in the KSA. The three themes displayed instrumental and developmental motives. As displayed in tables 12 and 20, 14% of the respondents expressed interest both in integration with ENL users and in use of English with anyone who uses English for developmental/instrumental purposes. The rest of the respondents (86%) showed orientations towards instrumental motivations (e.g., tourism, education, work, communication, and social mobility) and developmental motivations (e.g. personal hobbies) for using English with anyone who uses English. 54.2% of the respondents showed orientation towards intranational use of English with family and friends. Through a complexity theory lens, I realise that (categories of) motivations are not necessarily divisible, separate, or fixed/permanent. Therefore, the interviews explored in more depth how changes in motives influence, and are influenced by, participants' outlooks on 'good' English practices.

Table 20. Purposes of using English

Q8. What are your purposes for using English? (more than one option can be chosen)	Frequency	%	Rank
Education	566	74.0	2
Work	481	62.9	4
Tourism	568	74.2	1
Friends and family	415	54.2	5
Social networks (e.g. WhatsApp, Facebook, Twitter, LinkedIn, professional forums, etc.)	516	67.5	3
Integration with native English users	107	14.0	7
Other (please specify)	210	27.5	6

As displayed in table 21, there is a significant relation (χ^2 =11.647, p-value= 0.020) between the lack of a target nation and lacking/neutral interest in producing native-like English. In 49% of the cases, lacking/neutral interest in producing native-like English is accompanied by the lack of a target nation.

Q18.3. One of my ultimate goals for learning/ using English is to produce native or native-like English.	Q8. Integration with native English users		Total	χ^2	Sig. (p-value)	Conclusion
	0	1				
	f (%)	f (%)	f. (%)			
Very false	160 (20.9)	15 (2.0)	175 (22.9)			
False	68 (8.9)	10 (1.3)	78 (10.2)			
Neutral	147 (19.2)	29 (3.8)	176 (23.0)	11.647	0.020	Sig.
True	129 (16.9)	33 (4.3)	162 (21.2)			
Very true	154 (20.1)	20 (2.6)	174 (22.7)			
Total	658 (86.0)	107 (14.0)	765 (100.0)			

Table 21. Relationship between the lack of a target nation and lacking/neutral interest in producing native-like English

MacKenzie (2014) discusses data indicating that ELF users/ learners lack a target ENL nation, which he argues, in turn, results in the lack of interest in acquiring ENL cultural-bound expressions (e.g., idioms) and ENL accents. In contrast, EFL/ ESL users/learners underscore ENL formulaic sequences, pitches, intonations, and accents because they have target ENL interlocutors (see Section 5.5). Statistical tests of the present study displayed reference to the existence of a target ENL nation relates to placing importance on ENL usages. As displayed in table 22, there is a highly significant relation (χ^2 = 56.279, p-values = 0.000) between (in)tolerance towards missing the exclamation/intonation mark (in Q13.8) and perception of ENL accents (in Q14.2). In 51.6% of the cases, tolerance towards missing the exclamation mark is accompanied by devaluing the necessity of acquiring ENL accents.

Table 22. Relationship between (in)tolerance towards missing the exclamation mark and perceptions of ENL accents

Q14.2. Sounding like native English accents	Q13.8. What a good luck.						Conclusion		
	Completely unacceptable	Unacceptable	Neutral	Acceptable	Completely acceptable	Total	χ^2_{24}	Sig. (p-value)	Sig.
	f. (%)	f. (%)	f. (%)	f. (%)	f. (%)	f. (%)			
Unnecessary	8 (1.0)	7 (0.9)	22 (2.9)	11 (1.4)	29 (3.8)	77 (10.1)			
Least necessary	6 (0.8)	6 (0.8)	31 (4.1)	29 (3.8)	40 (5.2)	112 (14.6)			
Little necessary	6 (0.8)	6 (0.8)	14 (1.8)	29 (3.8)	40 (5.2)	95 (12.4)			
Necessary, but not critical	18 (2.4)	15 (2.0)	48 (6.3)	37 (4.8)	65 (8.5)	183 (23.9)	56.279	0.000	Sig.
Necessary and critical	21 (2.7)	16 (2.1)	26 (3.4)	25 (3.3)	28 (3.7)	116 (15.2)			
Very necessary	10 (1.3)	12 (1.6)	23 (3.0)	29 (3.8)	15 (2.0)	89 (11.6)			
Most necessary	20 (2.6)	7 (0.9)	23 (3.0)	20 (2.6)	23 (3.0)	93 (12.2)			
Total	89 (11.6)	69 (9.0)	187(24.4)	180(23.5)	240 (31.4)	765 (100.0)			

Table 23 shows that there is a highly significant relation (x^2 =41.938, p-values = 0.000) between perceptions of ENL accents (Q21.2) and perceptions of ENL cultural-bound expressions (Q14.3). In 46.8% of the cases, lacking/neutral interest in producing ENL accents is accompanied by lacking/ neutral interest in ENL idioms. When responses to motives (Q18) were compared based on occupation, 33.3% of ELT university instructors referred to the existence of a target ENL nation. As displayed in table 24, this percentage is higher than the percentages of students (12.3%), non-ELT professionals (9.6%), and ELT schoolteachers who referred to the existence of a target ENL nation. The interviews explored the reasons behind this position and its role on perceptions and reported practices. In addition, respondents' additional comments in part (D) suggested a possibility for a change in perceptions, motives, goals, and target proficiency (see Section 5.4.8). The interviews explored in more depth this issue.

Table 23. Relationship between perceptions of ENL accents and perceptions of ENL cultural-bound expressions

Q14.3. Use of native English idioms	Q21.2. Sounding like native English accents								χ^2_{36}	Sig. (p-value)	Conclusion
	Non-priority f. (%)	Last priority f. (%)	Fifth priority f. (%)	Fourth priority f. (%)	Third priority f. (%)	Second priority f. (%)	First top-priority f. (%)	Total f. (%)			
Unnecessary	35 (4.6)	35 (4.6)	27 (3.5)	23 (3.0)	3 (0.4)	2 (0.3)	2 (0.3)	127 (16.6)			
Least necessary	11 (1.4)	22 (2.9)	26 (3.4)	31 (4.1)	2 (0.3)	3 (0.40)	2 (0.3)	97 (12.7)			
Little necessary	3 (0.4)	9 (1.2)	26 (3.4)	19 (2.5)	7 (0.9)	8 (1.0)	5 (0.7)	77 (10.1)			
Necessary, but not critical	6 (0.8)	13 (1.7)	23 (3.0)	49 (6.4)	22 (2.9)	10 (1.3)	17 (2.2)	140 (18.3)			
Necessary and critical	7 (0.9)	8 (1.0)	13 (1.7)	16 (2.1)	27 (3.5)	26 (3.4)	16 (2.1)	113 (14.8)	41.938	0.000	Sig.
Very necessary	2 (0.3)	4 (0.5)	6 (0.8)	15 (2.0)	30 (3.9)	33 (4.3)	23 (3.0)	113 (14.8)			
Most necessary	4 (0.5)	1 (0.1)	3 (0.4)	6 (0.8)	16 (2.1)	20 (2.6)	48 (6.3)	98 (12.8)			
Total	68 (8.9)	92 (12.0)	124 (16.2)	159 (20.8)	107 (14.0)	102 (13.3)	113 (14.8)	765 (100.0)			

Table 24. Purposes of using English based on occupation

Occupation	Purposes for using English	Frequency	%
Student	Education	207	91.2
	Work	66	29.1
	Tourism	149	65.6
	Friends and family	123	54.2
	Social network (e.g. WhatsApp, Facebook, Snapchat, etc.)	155	68.3
	Integration with native English users	28	12.3
	Other	73	32.2
ELT schoolteachers	Education	71	60.2
	Work	100	84.7
	Tourism	76	64.4
	Friends and family	76	64.4
	Social networks (e.g. WhatsApp, Facebook, Twitter, LinkedIn, professional forums, etc.)	95	80.5
	Integration with native English users	13	11.0
	Other	32	27.1
ELT university instructors	Education	104	96.3
	Work	102	94.4
	Tourism	85	78.7
	Friends and family	71	65.7
	Social networks (e.g. WhatsApp, Facebook, Twitter, LinkedIn, professional forums, etc.)	87	80.6
	Integration with native English users	36	33.3
	Other	25	23.1

Non-ELT professionals	Education	184	59.0
	Work	213	68.3
	Tourism	258	82.7
	Friends and family	145	46.5
	Social networks (e.g. WhatsApp, Facebook, Twitter, LinkedIn, Professionals Forums, etc.)	179	57.4
	Integration with native English users	30	9.6
	Other	80	25.6

5.4.4.2 Interrelationships between goals of learning/ using English, language perceptions, and language judgments

Table 25 shows responses to Q18.1, Q18.2, Q18.3, and Q18.4, which investigated respondents' primary goals of learning/ using English. The overall response to [One of my primary motives for learning/using English is to interact with native English users] is neutral (mean = 2.90, Std. Deviation = 1.51). 301 (39.3%) respondents chose (very) true in response to this goal, and 337 (44.1%) respondents chose (very) false in response to this goal. The overall response to [One of my primary motives for learning/using English is to communicate with anyone who can use it (native and non-native English users)] is very true (mean = 4.65, Std. Deviation = 0.71). 709 (92.7%) respondents chose (very) true in response to this goal, and 16 (2.1%) chose (very) false in response to this goal. The overall response to [One of my ultimate goals for learning/using English is to acquire native or native-like English] is neutral (mean = 3.11, Std. Deviation = 1.46). 336 (43%) respondents chose (very) true in response to this goal, and 253 (33.1%) respondents chose (very) false in response to this goal. The overall response to [One of my ultimate goals for learning/using English is to produce understandable English, and I do not mind if it seems different from standard and native English usages] is very true (mean = 4.29, Std. Deviation = 0.99). 618 (80%) respondents chose (very) true in response to this goal, and 50 (6.5%) respondents chose (very) false in response to this goal.

As very few respondents had negative responses to Q18.2 and Q18.4, I selected the interview participants from among the survey respondents who represented positive, neutral, or negative positions to explore what was left unsaid in mean values and statistical tests. In addition, I cross-checked if any particular goals correlate with any particular choices in other questions. The previous section showed that the lack of a target nation relates (χ^2=11.647, p-values = 0.020) to lacking/neutral interest in acquiring/producing native-like English and tolerance to ELF variants, which, in turn, relates (χ^2= 56.279, p-values = 0.000) to devaluing the necessity of producing ENL accents, which, in turn, relates (χ^2=41.938, p-values = 0.000) to the lack of interest in ENL cultural-bound expressions. The coming section presents the (highly) significant interrelations between these positions, identity, and language judgments.

Table 25. Primary goals of learning/using English

Q18. Primary goals	Very false		False		Neutral		True		Very true		Weighted Mean	Std. Deviation	Overall Response (in Mean)
	f	%	f	%	f	%	f	%	f	%			
18.1. One of my primary motives for learning/using English is to interact with native English users.	208	27.2	129	16.9	127	16.6	135	17.6	166	21.7	2.90	1.51	Neutral
18.2. One of my primary motives for learning/using English is to communicate with anyone who can use it (native and non-native English users).	5	0.7	11	1.4	40	5.2	136	17.8	573	74.9	4.65	0.71	Very true
18.3. One of my ultimate goals for learning/using English is to produce native or native-like English.	175	22.9	78	10.2	176	23.0	162	21.2	174	22.7	3.11	1.46	Neutral
18.4. One of my ultimate goals for learning/using English is to produce understandable English, and I do not mind if it seems different from standard and native English usages.	16	2.1	34	4.4	97	12.7	186	24.3	432	56.5	4.29	0.99	Very true

5.4.5 Identity in relation to language perceptions and judgments

5.4.5.1 Interrelationships between identity projection, language perceptions, and (in)tolerance towards ELF variants

Q11 investigated whether respondents tend to promote L1 linguacultural identity projection. Table 26 shows that 75.4% of the respondents chose the statement which displays orientations towards projection of L1 linguacultural identity.

Table 26. English as an identity marker

Q11. Circle the statement that best describes you.	Frequency	%
Most of the time, I want my own English to represent my Saudi identity when I use it (e.g. using my accent, local expressions, and communicative styles in English)	577	75.4
Most of the time, I want the English I use to be recognised as native English (e.g. American, British, Canadian, Australian, and New Zealand English)	188	24.6
Total	765	100.0

Furthermore, respondents' additional comments in part (D) displayed emphasis on Islamic and Arabic identities (see Section 5.4.8). Although respondents did not reject variations in communications (as found in the previous sections), this section reveals that respondents still position themselves symbolically with others; they are still influenced by, and influence, social ideologies and practices. Respondents might have arrived at these orientations for different reasons, and they can put these orientations into practice in different ways. Therefore, the interviews explored how participants perceive identity management in ELF settings, how they perceive the role of a transcultural mediator in ELF settings, and to what extent they are ready to adjust their practices and converge with other interlocutors in ELF settings. In addition, the interviews explored why some participants wanted their use of English to be recognised as 'native English'.

As displayed in tables 27 and 28, one's identity projection on English relates significantly to both self-description of one's own English (χ^2 = 106.717, p-values = 0.000) and one's (in)tolerance to ELF variants (χ^2 = 51.476, p-values = 0.000). As displayed in Section 5.4.3.2, both self-description of one's own English and one's (in)tolerance to ELF variants relate significantly to each other (χ^2 = 139.496, p-values = 0.000). Table 27 shows that the orientation towards projection of the Saudi identity is accompanied by acknowledging the impact of Saudi/Arabic traces on English in 50.6% of the cases. Table 28 shows that non-rejection of 'Saudi English' variants is accompanied by willingness to project Saudi identity in 71.1% of the cases. These statistical results suggest respondents' acceptance of sociolinguistically/socioculturally justified misalignment with StE and ENL usages. The interviews investigated participants' understanding of 'justified misalignment' in ELF settings in relation to their experiences with ELF and ALF.

Table 27. Relationship between self-description of one's own English and one's identity projection on English

Q10. Self-description of one's own English	Q11. English as an identity marker		Total f. (%)	Conclusion	
	I want my own English to represent my Saudi identity.	I want the English I use to be recognised as native English.		χ_4^2	Sig. (p-value)
	f. (%)	f. (%)			
American English	85 (11.1)	70 (9.2)	155 (20.3)		
British English	31 (4.1)	17 (2.2)	48 (6.3)		
Mixture of American English and British English	74 (9.7)	55 (7.2)	129 (16.9)		
English with Saudi/Arabic imprints	356 (46.5)	43 (5.6)	399 (52.2)		
Other	31 (4.1)	3 (0.4)	34 (4.4)		
Total	577 (75.4)	188 (24.6)	765 (100.0)		

Table 28. Relationship between one's identity projection on English and one's (in)tolerance towards ELF variants

Q13. One's overall (in)tolerance towards ELF variants	Q11. English as an identity marker		Total f. (%)	Conclusion		
	I want my own English to represent my Saudi identity.	I want the English I use to be recognised as native.		χ^2_4	Sig. (p-value)	Sig.
	f. (%)	f. (%)				
Completely unacceptable	10 (1.3)	1 (0.1)	11 (1.4)	51.476	0.000	Sig.
Unacceptable	24 (3.1)	13 (1.7)	37 (4.8)			
Neutral	126 (16.5)	67 (8.8)	193 (25.2)			
Acceptable	171 (22.4)	79 (10.3)	250 (32.7)			
Completely acceptable	246 (32.2)	28 (3.7)	274 (35.8)			
Total	577 (75.4)	188 (24.6)	765 (100.0)			

5.4.5.2 Interrelationships among L1 linguacultural identity, lack of a target nation, and perception of proficiency in English

The findings of the previous sections indicated the interests of respondents in integration/interaction/communication with the whole world, rather than with particular nations. As displayed in table 29, there is a highly significant relation ($x^2 =$ 74.729, p-values = 0.000) between the lack of a target nation and L1 linguacultural identity projection. In 69.5% of the cases, the lack of a target nation is accompanied by a willingness to represent L1 linguacultural identity. As displayed in table 30, there is a highly significant relation ($x^2 =$ 88.553, p-values = 0.000) between one's identity projection and one's perception/target of proficiency in English. In 48.9% of the cases, intention of projecting L1 linguacultural identity is accompanied by lacking/neutral interest in producing native-like English. As displayed in table 31, there is a highly significant relation ($x^2 =$ 60.667, p-values = 0.000) between willingness to project linguacultural identity and lacking/neutral interest in producing native-like English. In 73.1% of the cases, the willingness to project L1 linguacultural identity is accompanied by targeting/accepting proficiency in terms of intelligibility, not conformity with StE and ENL usages. To conclude, identity projection relates to the motives, goals, and perceptions of language proficiency. Through a complexity theory lens, the interviews explored in more depth how these perceptual dimensions relate to temporal and contextual experiences.

Table 29. Relationship between the lack of a target nation and linguacultural identity projection

| Q8. Integration with native English users | Q11. English as an identity marker | | Total f. (%) | χ_1^2 | Sig. (p-value) | Conclusion |
	I want my own English to represent my Saudi identity. f. (%)	I want the English I use to be recognised as native English. f. (%)				Sig.
No	532 (69.5)	126 (16.5)	658 (86.0)			
Yes	45 (5.9)	62 (8.1)	107 (14.0)	74.729	0.000	
Total	577 (75.4)	188 (24.6)	765 (100.0)			

Table 30. Relationship between one's identity projection and one's target of proficiency in English

| Q18.3. One of my ultimate goals for learning/using English is to produce native or native-like English. | Q11. English as an identity marker | | Total f. (%) | χ^2_4 | Sig. (p-value) | Conclusion |
	I want my own English to represent my Saudi identity. f. (%)	I want the English I use to be recognised as native English. f. (%)				
Very false	168 (22.0)	7 (0.9)	175 (22.9)	88.553	0.000	Sig.
False	68 (8.9)	10 (1.3)	78 (10.2)			
Neutral	138 (18.0)	38 (5.0)	176 (23.0)			
True	102 (13.2)	60 (7.8)	162 (21.2)			
Very true	101 (13.2)	73 (9.5)	174 (22.7)			
Total	577 (75.4)	188 (24.6)	765 (100.0)			

Table 31. Relationship between willingness to project linguacultural identity and lacking/neutral interest in producing native-like English

Q18.4. One of my ultimate goals for learning/using English is to produce understandable English, and I do not mind if it seems different from standard and native English usages.	Q11. English as an identity marker		Total f. (%)	χ^2_4	Sig. (p-value)	Conclusion
	I want my own English to represent my Saudi identity. f. (%)	I want the English I use to be recognised as native English. f. (%)				Sig.
Very false	8 (1.0)	8 (1.0)	16 (2.1)	60.667	0.000	
False	10 (1.3)	24 (3.1)	34 (4.4)			
Neutral	71 (9.3)	26 (3.4)	97 (12.7)			
True	130 (17.0)	56 (7.3)	186 (24.3)			
Very true	358 (46.8)	74 (9.7)	432 (56.5)			
Total	577 (75.4)	188 (25.6)	765(100.0)			

5.4.5.3 Interrelationships between perceptions of ELT professional identity and EFL/ESL-oriented perceptions

The findings of Section 5.4.4.1 revealed that 14% (107 respondents) from the whole sample (765 respondents) displayed interest in integration with ENL nations. This group of the 107 respondents consists of 28 students, 30 non-ELT professionals, and 49 ELT professionals. The previous sections also found that reference to the existence of a target ENL nation relates to one's ESL-oriented outlook, and the lack of a target nation relates to one's ELF-oriented outlook. For instance, the ELT professional group tended to associate ELT linguistic components with British/American linguistic usages before international settings, while the other groups tended to associate ELT linguistic components with international settings before British/American usages (see Appendix 6). In addition, a high percentage (44.9%) of schoolteachers associated students' needs in ELT with 'correct' grammar and conformity to StE models, while all the other groups tended to associate students' needs in ELT with international communication skills (see Appendix 6). Ironically, responses to Q15 and Q16 (see tables 32 and 33) suggested a contextual(ised) switch in perceptions, as the ELT professional groups displayed a preference for qualified Saudi ELT teachers, while the non-ELT professionals displayed a preference for native English ELT teachers who have some familiarity with Saudi/Islamic values (whether they are qualified or not). The interviewed explored reasons behind these contextualised switches in perceptions. As an overall, 50.1% of the respondents chose native English ELT teachers even though this option does not provide any information about qualifications. 47.1% of the respondents chose qualified Saudi teachers. From a complexity theory perspective, we cannot know what respondents were imagining or assuming about this hypothetical teacher, this issue needed to be further explored qualitatively in Q16.

Table 32. Preferable ELT teacher group based on occupation

Q3. Occupation	Q15. Which of the following teacher groups do you prefer for teaching English in Saudi Arabia?	Frequency	%
Students	Native English users	124	54.6
	Non-native English users with good command of English and specialised in teaching English	9	4.0
	Saudis with good command of English and specialised in teaching English	94	41.4
	Total	227	100.0
ELT schoolteachers	Native English users	43	36.4
	Non-native English users with good command of English and specialised in teaching English	2	1.7
	Saudis with good command of English and specialised in teaching English	73	61.9
	Total	118	100.0
ELT University instructors	Native English users	24	22.2
	Non-native English users with good command of English and specialised in teaching English	8	7.4
	Saudis with good command of English and specialised in teaching English	76	70.4
	Total	108	100.0
Non-ELT professionals	Native English users	192	61.5
	Non-native English users with good command of English and specialised in teaching English.	3	1.0
	Saudis with good command of English and specialised in teaching English	117	37.5
	Total	312	100.0

In Q16, respondents were asked to write their justifications for their own preferences. Explanations for preferring native English ELT teachers were categorised into four themes: common sense (53 respondents), desires to grasp ENL accents (74 respondents), interest in ELT latest teaching methods (87 respondents), and conditional preference (196 respondents). Conditions were categorised into four subthemes: qualifications (50 respondents), teaching in any city except Makkah and Madinah cities (11 respondents), teaching adult learners (51 respondents), and introducing teachers to Islamic/Saudi values (57 respondents). Examples of respondents' answers are shown in table 33 according to these themes and subthemes.

As displayed in table 33, 169 out of 383 respondents (who chose native English teachers) displayed conditional preference in favour of qualification and/or protection of Islamic values. This position means that the absence of the condition cancels out the preference. Justifications for preferring qualified Saudi teachers were categorised into five themes: explicit bias towards Saudis (66 respondents), sharing L1 (34 respondents), sharing of Islamic/Saudi values (87 respondents), clarity of accent (52 respondents), and capability of teaching English as a Saudi tool for communications (121 respondents). Examples of respondents' answers are shown in table 34 according to these themes.

Table 33. Desires and (conditional) preferences for native English ELT teachers

Theme	Frequency 383	Examples
Common sense and unquestioned assumptions	53	'Justify? It's their language', 'By logic, it's their mother language', 'Simply because it's their mother tongue', 'There is no need to say it. They are English NATIVES', 'Of course, it's their native tongue', 'Everybody knows why. It's their first language. No one can teach it better than them', 'No wonder. It is their mother tongue', 'It goes without saying', 'Who else can teach it better?', 'To learn it from its original source', 'They are the only ones who use it correctly'
Desire to grasp ENL accents	74	'natural beauty of their accent', 'grasp the right accent from the right source', 'acquire correct accent', 'imitate pure accent', 'magnetic accent', 'alluring accent', 'attractive accent', 'produce pleasant accent'
Interest in ELT latest teaching methods	87	'They are updated with latest methods', 'They work on improving our communicative skills', 'not like Saudi teachers, they don't talk about grammar all the time', 'They provide interactive environment', 'Interesting practical techniques', 'They let us practice not just do grammar questions', 'They talk about slang and everyday use, not only English of the book'

Conditional preference upon:		
- Qualifications	50	'with qualifications in teaching', 'If all of them are equally qualified, native speakers have an extra advantage of their mother tongue', 'only experienced ones'
- Teaching in any city except Makkah and Madinah	11	'except Mecca and Medina', 'not in Holy cities', 'away from the two holy Harameen'
- Teaching adult learners	51	'not for children', 'only for colleges', 'at universities', 'not for school levels', 'not for elementary', 'just for adults'
- Introducing teachers to Islamic/Saudi values before they start teaching Saudis	57	'but they should be introduced to Islamic concepts before they come', 'It's necessary to give them an idea about what works for our Saudi culture', 'someone should tell them, before they start teaching, about our red lines', 'but they should know how to react to Islamic values which don't match western styles'

Table 34. Reasons for preferring qualified Saudi teachers

Theme	Frequency 360	Examples
Bias towards Saudis	66	'I just feel comfortable with my people', 'I have a bias in jobs towards educated and skilled Saudis', 'They are Saudi citizens, and the job in their country', 'Citizenship right', 'For saudization purposes', 'Jobs should given to locals', 'Why giving high salaries to non Saudis?', 'I am just biased in favour of Saudis', 'It's just human nature to have some bias towards your race', 'Citizens must be prioritised for home country careers', 'The priority for jobs should be given to Saudis in all majors', 'Declination of economy in Saudi can't afford native teachers of English'.
Sharing L1	34	'They have the capability to switch', 'They understand what language difficulties we encounter because they have been there once', 'They can use code-switching wisely as a teaching strategy'

Sharing of Islamic/Saudi values	87	'They know how to consider the religious sensitivity of our Saudi community', 'Sharing the same religion, first language, and nationality can facilitate learning and teaching', 'They have the same Islamic identity which we have', 'Saudi context is sensitive to some Taboo issues which only Saudi teacher can handle', 'Saudi teachers can teach the English language with an Islamic flavour', 'Saudi teachers are more capable of dealing with our complicated context of learning English', 'Natives may not understand our complicacy', 'To guarantee that English is taught with respect to Saudi traditions and Islamic rules'
Clarity of accent and articulation of sounds	52	'Most of un-native teachers use unclear or annoying accents, but Saudis' accent is clear and good', 'Some non-natives have irritating accent. Saudi and Gulf people have moderately good accent of English', 'I prefer Saudi and Gulf teachers with good command of English', 'Other not native speakers may have distorted accent. Saudis' accent is tolerable', 'Our articulation of sounds is more capable than others'
Capability of teaching English as a Saudi tool for communications	121	'They can add a Saudi touch to the English', 'to bring a link between the English and locals' needs', 'Saudis know how to teach English as a neutral tool for communication as recommended by the ministry policies', 'We teach it just as a medium of communication. There is no necessity to have native teachers', 'As a tool for communication, English should be taught by teachers who can connect this tool with its learners' local culture', 'As long English is taught to be a medium of communication, not a second language, local teachers are preferable', 'As long as English is taught and used in Saudi Arabia as a foreign language, teachers' nativeness is not a must', 'In Saudi Arabia, we teach and use English as a tool for communication. The best persons who can teach it in this way and for this purpose are Saudi teachers', 'They also use English as an additional language without its cultural ingredients', 'I would prefer Saudi teachers to teach Saudi students because they can deliver language learning as a medium of communication without its cultural aspects'

In light of these qualitative and quantitative results, the native English ELT teachers' group is ranked as a top-preference if qualifications and/or familiarity with Saudi/Islamic values exist. The Saudi qualified ELT teacher group is ranked as a top-preference if qualifications and good command of English exist. If the condition(s) do(es) not exist, the preference is cancelled out. This result suggests that non-qualified native English ELT teachers who have some familiarity with Saudi/Islamic values rank alongside qualified Saudi ELT teachers. This finding is interesting compared with findings of previous sections, where respondents did not reject variations in ELF communications and did not have strong orientations to StE and ENL usages. Education seems to throw up an area of ideological, common-sense, or positional conflicts of interests. Respondents who value ENL accents and/or have unquestioned assumptions displayed a preference for native English teachers, whether these teachers are qualified/experienced or not. Respondents who value similarity of linguacultural identity or who are worried about the loss of Islamic/Saudi values displayed a preference for qualified Saudi teachers. Respondents who outweigh pedagogical needs displayed a preference for teachers who, regardless of their L1, can satisfy learners' needs. The interviews explored in more depth how perceptions of English relate to pedagogical experiences and needs.

5.4.6 Relationship between context and language judgment

This section presents how perception/judgment of English relates to context. Q14 dealt with international non-pedagogical ELF settings, Q21 dealt with ELT teaching/learning settings, and Q22 dealt with ELT evaluative/assessment settings. In the interviews, these context-related issues were explored in comparison with ELF intranational settings and experiences of ELF and ALF.

5.4.6.1   International non-pedagogical ELF settings

Q14 investigated how respondents rank the necessity of given skills for the success of international communications in English. The instruction of the question emphasised the expression 'based on your experience' to stimulate responses based on real-life usages, rather than habitual ways of thinking.

As shown in table 35, the overall ranking of 'communication skills' is 6 (most necessary, mean = 5.30). Then, 'fulfilling contextual functions' is ranked as 5 (very necessary, mean = 5.13), and 'accommodating responses to cultural diversities' is ranked as 4 (necessary and critical, mean = 4.75). 'Accuracy of grammar based on StE models' is ranked as 3 (necessary but not critical, mean = 4.19), 'familiarity with ENL cultures/societies' is ranked as 2 (little necessary, mean = 3.98), 'sounding like ENL accents' is ranked as 1 (least necessary, mean = 3.03), and 'use of ENL idioms' is ranked as 0 (unnecessary, mean = 2.98). In this context, there was not a considerable difference between the way in which the ELT professional group ranked these skills and the way in which the students and non-ELT professional groups ranked them. The interviews explored how participants perceive 'good' English in both international and intranational ELF settings and how they negotiate their linguacultural and transcultural identities in ELF international settings.

Table 35. Criteria of language judgment in international non-pedagogical settings

Q14. Criteria	Ranks							Mean	Overall Ranks
	0 Unnecessary	1 Least necessary	2 Little necessary	3 Necessary, but not critical	4 Necessary and critical	5 Very necessary	6 Most necessary		
14.1. Accuracy of grammar and conformity to standard English	24	23	64	178	108	120	248	4.19	3 Necessary, but not critical
14.2. Sounding like native English accents	77	112	95	183	116	89	93	3.03	1 Least necessary
14.3. Use of native English idioms	127	97	77	140	113	113	98	2.98	0 Unnecessary
14.4. Fulfilling contextual functions (e.g. achieving mutual understanding or building relations)	5	4	26	63	84	157	426	5.13	5 Very necessary

14.5. Communication skills (e.g. clarity, resolution conflict, adjustment depending on audiences and situations)	2	7	18	37	73	159	469	5.30	6 Most necessary
14.6. Familiarity with native English cultures/societies	39	70	114	190	101	116	135	3.98	2 Little necessary
14.7. Accommodating responses to cultural diversities	23	17	30	85	112	134	364	4.75	4 Necessary and critical

5.4.6.2 Teaching/learning settings

Q21 investigated how respondents rank the priority of development of given skills in teaching/learning contexts. As shown in table 36, the overall ranking of 'international communication skill's is 6 (first top-priority, mean = 5.24). Then, 'appropriateness to discourse' is ranked as 5 (second priority, mean = 5.17). 'Writing in ENL styles' is ranked as 4 (third priority, mean = 4.42), 'accuracy of grammar based on StE models' is ranked as 3 (fourth priority, mean = 4.37), 'sounding like ENL accents' is ranked as 2 (fifth priority, mean = 3.18), 'use of ENL idioms' is ranked as 1 (last priority, mean = 3.09), and 'familiarity with ENL cultures/societies' is ranked as 0 (non-priority, mean = 3.03). In both contexts (international non-pedagogical settings and teaching/learning settings), the respondents prioritised international communication skills and appropriateness to situations/discourse over conformity to StE models and ENL usages. In these settings, there was not a considerable difference between the way in which the ELT professional groups ranked these skills and the way in which the students and non-ELT professional groups ranked them.

Table 36. Priorities of skills in teaching/learning settings

Q21. Skills	Ranks							Mean rank	Overall Rank
	0 Non-priority	1 Last priority	2 Fifth priority	3 Fourth priority	4 Third priority	5 Second priority	6 First top-priority		
21.1. Accuracy of grammar and conformity to standard English.	16	16	49	153	139	140	252	4.37	3 Fourth priority
21.2. Sounding like native English accents	68	92	124	159	107	102	113	3.18	2 Fifth priority
21.3. Writing in native English styles	14	25	50	140	110	162	264	4.42	4 Third priority
21.4. Use of native English idioms	123	97	78	129	108	125	105	3.09	1 Last priority
21.5. Appropriateness to discourse (e.g. formal or informal, written or spoken, friendly or business)	8	7	11	45	93	184	417	5.17	5 Second priority
21.7. Familiarity with native English cultures/societies	56	68	116	183	128	117	97	3.03	0 Non-priority
21.8. International communication skills (e.g. clarity, resolution conflict, adjustment depending on audiences and situations)	4	6	13	54	80	150	458	5.24	6 First top-priority

5.4.6.3 Evaluative/assessment settings

Q22, as displayed in table 37, investigated respondents' opinions about StE-based tests and allowed respondents to choose more than one option. It also provided a free space to write additional/different opinions. 23.1% (177) of the respondents had wriiten their own opinions in the free space. Their opinions were extracted and categorised into two main themes. The first theme consisted of unquestioned assumptions as displayed by 16 respondents (e.g., 'I didn't try TOEFL nor IELTS, but I think they are the best and they know what they are doing', 'I don't know...I think they are well established organisations... they know their job', 'I don't know...I assume that they are accurate, updated, and academic', and 'I haven't registered in them before but most probably they are sufficient and updated'). The second theme questioned the soundness or rigidity of StE-based test as displayed by 161 respondents. Table 38 categorises these doubts into six sub-themes: profit tasks, mismatch of test results with actual skills, criticism of multiple-choice tests, bias towards American and British usages/cultures, unfair comparison with StE and ENL usages, and non-attention towards real-life practices in international settings.

As displayed in tables 37 and 38, respondents showed orientations towards questioning the rigidity and/or soundness of StE-based tests because such tests do not consider English using/communicative skills and/or the global use of English. However, these doubts are accompanied, in 303 cases, by approval of the idea of focusing on the basic skills and breaking those skills into sections (e.g., listening, speaking, vocabulary, grammar, reading, and writing) and/or the idea of non-integration of communication skills within ELT assessment methods. In non-pedagogical settings, respondents did not display interest in the basic skills (see Section 5.4.6.1). In non-pedagogical settings, 701 respondents displayed interest in communication skills. In teaching/learning settings, 688 respondents displayed interest in communication skills.

In evaluative/assessment settings, only 166 respondents displayed interest in integration of communication skills within assessment techniques. These findings indicated contextual(ised) changes in preferences. The interviews explored this issue in more depth.

Table 37. Opinions about standard-based English tests

Q22. Circle the choice(s) which reflect(s) your opinion(s) about internationally standard-based English courses and tests (e.g. TOEFL and IELTS) and courses.	Frequency	%
They use accurate measurements of English language proficiency.	167	21.8
They are based on outdated methods.	119	15.6
They use the right benchmark.	90	11.8
They should display some sort of flexibility with non-standard and non-native English usages.	282	36.9
I agree with the idea of focusing on the basic skills and breaking them into sections (e.g. listening, speaking, vocabulary, grammar, reading, and writing).	303	39.6
They should integrate some assessment techniques that consider international communication skills.	166	21.7
Other opinions (please specify)	177	23.1

Table 38. Doubts on standard-based English tests

Doubts	Frequency 161	Examples
Profit/ commercial tasks	16	'The real goal of these tests is profit', 'they have a commercial task'
Mismatch of results with actual skills	28	'They don't reflect your mastery', 'results don't match actual competence', 'results are below expectations', 'I got a higher score than what I really deserve because I chose some answers from my mind', 'My score doesn't reflect my real proficiency. It's unfair. I got a low score because I couldn't manage time', 'I don't know what's wrong but my mark is lower than what I really deserve'
Critics on multiple-choice techniques	41	'it measures speed, not achievement', 'It depends on speed and luck', 'Rigid technique is not accurate for assessing English proficiency', 'It measure your knowledge of their techniques, not your real skills in English', 'If you study their templets, you can get high score'
Bias towards American and British usages/ cultures	34	'it measures knowledge of native issues which we don't know and are not interested to know', 'their bias towards American or British accent is prejudiced', 'I think their measurements have bias towards accents, communicative style, and cultural issues of particular nations', 'racist', 'The content should include general topics from all around the world, not only UK and USA', 'Topics of reading and listening sections should be international', 'Choices of topics should not be derived mainly from American and British nations', 'English as a medium of communication should be taught and assessed without any cultural dimensions'

	24	'not fair requirements', 'it suits those who use English as a second language, not those who use it as a foreign language like Saudis', 'I think it is not fair to request natives' achievements from non natives', 'It evaluates us as if English is our native language, this isn't fair', 'English tests should not deduct marks for minor errors because they assess proficiency of an additional language, not L1', 'They should put in their minds that we are not native English speakers and English is not our first language', 'I am a linguist in Arabic language. I am one of those who prepare tests for measuring none Arabs' proficiency in Arabic. We do not compare their achievement with Arabs, We understand that they use Arabic as a lingua franca. I imagine that there should be an English test for this purpose without comparing non English speakers with English speakers'
Unfair comparison with StE and ENL usages		
Non-attention towards real-life practices in international settings	17	'It neglects interactive skills', 'they miss formative techniques', 'Intercultural communication should be included in English exams', 'English exams should take throughcultural communication into consideration', 'They should find a way to measure communicative skills required for international interactions'

5.4.7 Respondents' needs in ELT linguistic, communicative, and cultural dimensions

Q17, Q19, and Q20 examined whether ELF-oriented ELT approaches suit respondents' needs (see section 1.4). The instructions for the three questions used several expressions (e.g., 'in your opinion' and 'do you suggest') that would stimulate responses based on personal needs/ideas, rather than on what has been experienced.

5.4.7.1 Needs for inclusion of English linguistic diversities into ELT linguistic components

Q17 investigated whether respondents prefer association of ELT linguistic components with British English, American English, all/any ENL usages, non-native English usages, or English usages in international domains. Table 39 shows that inclusion of non-native English usages into ELT settings is viewed overall as unimportant (mean =2.55, Std. Deviation = 1.28). Ironically, familiarity with non-native English usages is viewed overall as necessary for the success of English real-life interactions (see Section 5.4.3.3). As displayed in table 40, inclusion of American English usages (mean = 3.59, Std. Deviation = 1.14) and British English usages (mean = 3.58, Std. Deviation = 1.14) into ELT is viewed overall as important. Ironically, conformity to StE and ENL usages is viewed overall as least/unnecessary for the success of English real-life interactions (see Section 5.4.6.1). Inclusion of English international settings (mean = 3.74, Std. Deviation = 1.37) into ELT settings is viewed overall as important. According to the weighted means of these overall responses, inclusion of English for international settings into ELT dimensions is viewed as more important than solo reliance on American English and British English usages. This position aligns with respondents' reluctance to stick to one StE model (see Section 5.4.3.3). In addition, American English linguistic usages seem more preferable than British English linguistic usages based on these weighted means. Comparisons of responses based on occupation revealed that the ELT professional group tended to associate ELT linguistic components with British/American English usages before international settings, while non-ELT professionals tended to associate ELT linguistic components with international settings before American/British English usages (see Appendix 6). The interviews explored the reasons behind these tendencies.

Table 39. Needs in ELT linguistic components

Q17. Activities on …	Very unimportant		Unimportant		Neutral		Important		Very important		Mean	Std. Deviation	Overall Response (in Mean)	Rank of overall responses
	f	%	f	%	f	%	f	%	f	%				
17.1. American English usages	43	5.6	72	9.4	241	31.5	209	27.3	200	26.1	3.59	1.14	Important	Second Importance
17.2. British English usages	40	5.2	76	9.9	254	33.2	191	25.0	204	26.7	3.58	1.14	Important	Third Importance
17.3. All/any native English usages	165	21.6	95	12.4	298	39.0	132	17.3	75	9.8	2.81	1.23	Neutral	Neutral
17.4. Non-native English usages	230	30.1	125	16.3	237	31.0	108	14.1	65	8.5	2.55	1.28	Unimportant	Unimportant
17.5. English usages in international domains	84	11.0	48	6.3	191	25.0	100	13.1	342	44.7	3.74	1.37	Important	First Importance

The findings of Q17 indicated respondents' need for integration of ELF-oriented ELT approaches, but a lack of awareness regarding how to implement this idea within ELT practices. I selected the interview participants from among the different survey respondent groups (students, Non-ELT professionals, ELT schoolteachers, and ELT university instructors) to explore in more depth these needs in relation to practices.

5.4.7.2 Needs for inclusion of international communication skills into ELT communicative components

Q20 investigated whether respondents prefer mastering/developing of StE-based linguistic competence, ENL communicative competence, local communicative competence in English, or contextual performativity in international communication in English. Table 40 shows that 45.3% of the respondents selected communicative skills required for global use of English. 34.5% of the respondents selected StE models, and 8.8% of the respondents selected ENL communicative styles.

Table 40. Needs in ELT communicative dimensions

Q20. Which of the following options should be obtained/mastered in order to build/develop English communication expertise?	Frequency	%
Correct grammar and accurate usages based on standard English models	264	34.5
Communicative styles of native English users	67	8.8
Communicative styles of students' own locale	19	2.5
Communicative skills required for global use of English	347	45.3
Other (please specify)...	68	8.9
Total	765	100.0

As shown in table 40, the question provided a free space for respondents to write their own preferences and needs. 68 respondents wrote their own ideas. Nine out of the 68 respondents displayed needs for vocabulary expansion (e.g., 'synonyms and antonyms'). Three out of the 68 respondents displayed needs for developing skills required for academic settings (e.g., 'formal purposes', 'critical thinking and writing', and 'academic writing'). 56 out of the 68 respondents displayed needs for developing transcultural awareness and the ability to achieve ELF contextual functions, such as 'good grammar, but not necessarily like the native', 'clear accent without forcing the tongue to be twisted like native speakers', 'proper use of English which delivers clear messages', 'appropriate English depending on situations', 'conversation skills', 'discussion skills', 'negotiation and argument skills', 'interactive skills of international settings', 'practical techniques', 'actual usages as they take place in real life', 'real practices', 'international communication', 'awareness of other nations', 'tolerance to differences', 'etiquettes of interaction with non-Saudis', 'what to do and what not to do when communicating with non-Arabs', 'how to deal with racism and extremism', 'communication in countries of scholarships', 'how to avoid misunderstanding', 'how to avoid literal translation', 'the difference between English in books and English in real use', 'understandable English', and 'skills for making understandable language'. Comparisons of responses based on occupation showed that all respondent groups tended to associate students' developmental needs with international communication skills except the ELT schoolteacher group (see Appendix 6). 44.9% of the ELT schoolteachers associated students' developmental needs with StE-based linguistic competence, and 44.9% of ELT schoolteachers associated students' needs with contextual performativity. These findings suggested respondents' needs for integration of ELF-oriented ELT approaches, but also that respondents do not know how to implement this idea within ELT practices. The interviews explored the reasons behind these positions. Interestingly, respondents' additional comments in part (D) suggested purposeful misalignment with ENL communicative competence in favour of local/Islamic values (see Section 5.4.8). I selected the interview participants form among the survey respondents who had written some suggestions for pedagogical implementations.

5.4.7.3 Needs for transcultural awareness

Q19 investigated whether respondents prefer enriching ELT cultural dimensions with American, British, all/any ENL, their own local, or different worldwide cultural sources. Table 41 shows that 74.4% of the respondents chose different worldwide cultural sources including the learners' locally cultural sources. Noticeably, small percentages of respondents displayed interests in association of ELT with all ENL cultural sources (12.8%), British cultural sources (6.5%), American cultural sources (4.7%), or learners' local cultural sources (1.6%). Comparisons of responses based on occupation revealed that all groups tended to show a preference for inclusion of different worldwide cultural sources, in addition to learners' locally cultural sources. These findings indicated respondents' need for integration of ELF-oriented ELT approaches, but also that respondents do not know how to put this idea into practice. Respondents' additional comments in part (D) displayed both the need for transcultural awareness and worries about the sensitivity of the Saudi/Islamic context (see Section 5.4.8). I selected the interview participants from among the survey respondents who had written useful comments about this issue.

Table 41. Needs in ELT cultural dimensions

Q19. If we plan to enrich English language subjects/courses with cultural/social topics, which of the following sources do you suggest for this supplementation? (Choose only one)	Frequency	%
American sources	36	4.7
British sources	50	6.5
All/any native English sources	98	12.8
Learners' local sources	12	1.6
Different worldwide sources including the learners' local sources	569	74.4
Total	765	100.0

5.4.8 Respondents' additional comments

Part (D) gave respondents the option to write any relevant comments. The comments were categorised into themes as shown in table 42.

Table 42. Additional comments of respondents

Theme	Frequency	Examples
Emphasis on ALF and Islamic identification	4	'Arabic is one of the international lingua francas before English' 'It's better to say Islamic identity' 'Arabic identity' 'It's a good idea to include different worldwide cultures and communicative skills required for global use of English because English becomes language of science, but this change should not be at the expense of the Arabic language of the religion of Islam, nor at the expense of the Islamic values'
Intentional misalignment with StE and ENL communicative competence in favour of Islamic usages	5	'I would like to invite you to be one of our members. We administer groups on social media to raise awareness among Muslims about usages which contradict with Islamic values and how we can modify them to match our beliefs' 'Your topic seems related to concepts of globalisation, and I don't think our community is ready to embrace these concepts in English subjects' 'It is a good idea to introduce the students to others' cultural traditions, and national festivals, but not religious occasions. Topics which can be covered should be general like currency, food except pork and alcohol, weather, parks, museums, educational systems, etc. Only topics which have Islamic morality can be covered like visiting families, helping others, and charity, but not dating and friendship with the opposite gender' 'Although we encourage broadening the cultural elements in the curriculum, this expansion should be done with exclusion of the forbidden issues in Islam' 'The curriculum of English courses should expose the students to different worldwide cultures including native English native cultures and the Saudi culture. This exposure should exclude Taboo topics and all un-Islamic occasions and life styles'

Awareness of 'Saudi English' variants and tendency towards negotiation of both usages and judgments	11	'Unusual self-negotiation came up by marking the number which represents one's opinion about English sentences which give the impression of being too Saudi. I recommend exploring this issue deeper' 'Question 13 is misleading. It is not clear what you are trying to figure out' 'Question 13 is indirect, as if you are looking for something in the subconscious, and I would like to know what this thing is before I participate in the interview' 'I don't think that Q13 is about linguistic usages. I recommend clarifying that it includes Saudi-cultural/ religious meanings' 'Question 13 seems like a vague test. I think you should provide clearer explanations for the aim of this question' 'Question 13 is interesting. It derives my internal contradictions about Saudi English' 'Items of question 13 are very tricky. They raise doubts over the real purpose of this study' 'The 13th question is strange. I don't know if it is an indirect test or an attempt to collect opinions on hidden messages behind the structure. However, it piqued my curiosity' 'I found it written in a Saudi way similar to this one used in question 13. You can understand it, you know it is different from standard English, but you hesitate to judge its correctness' 'No.13 can represent a typical model for Saudis' distinctive phraseology' 'From your survey in general and question 13 in particular, I can sense a new field in applied linguistics is about to appear on the horizon of the Saudi context. It seems interesting'
Changes in perceptions and usages	1	'My big dream used to be a native like acquisition, and I tried hard to achieve this goal. After years of trials, I have realised that I have reached the maximum limit which a non native user can. To compensate this pain, I enrolled my children in international schools. When I have noticed that their Arabic is negatively influenced, I registered them in Saudi schools. The ability to read Qura'n perfectly is more than important than the ability to speak English perfectly. As a Muslim researcher, you are expected to think about this carefully while dealing with globalisation'

Request for raising transcultural awareness at a global level as a necessity for global peace and civilisation	4	'Contrary to what some extremists think, Islam encourages learning languages and it also encourages knowing traditions of other nations. Allah says in Quran: O mankind! We have created you male and female, and made you into nations and tribes, that you may know one another. This from Al-Hujraat Verse No:13. Exposing students to different cultures goes in line with this core value of Islam. I hope we can deliver this message appropriately'
		'Exposure of students to worldwide cultures is recommended for all native and nonnative English communities. To make the world a better place living in global peace, we should expose our Saudi students to others' cultures, and others should expose their students to our Gulf culture as well'
		'I suggest gradual exposure of school students to general crosscultural issues which are compatible with Islam. University students should be exposed gradually to all kinds of crosscultural issues including TABOO TOPICS and popular religious celebrations. The purpose of this gradual exposure is to develop students' civilized responses with the globe's differences'
		'I am an open-minded person, and I believe we should discuss with adult students others' life styles like dating and drinking alcohol, communication ways of other communities like mixed-sex meetings, and others' religious beliefs to raise their knowledge of the others. When I advocate for this idea, most of Saudis attack viciously my views. They are not ready enough for globalisation of education. Saudi parents whose children are enrolled in international schools still make sure that these issues are avoided in books and classes. Ministry supervisors still put regulations for international schools to modify the curriculum and avoid such topics in order to suit the local mindset'

As displayed in table 42, comments of 11 respondents showed awareness of 'Saudi English' variants and the tendency towards negotiating usages of and judgments on these variants. Therefore, interviews explored in more depth contextual(ised) reflections and reported adjustments on Saudis' shared usages of English. Four respondents showed interest in ELF functions for the sake of global interactions, but the four respondents expressed explicitly unwillingness to negotiate Arabic and Islamic identifications. Therefore, the interviews explored in more depth how perception of Arabic language and Islam relate to perception of English.

More in line with the findings of the previous sections, five respondents displayed orientation towards misalignment with StE usages and ENL communicative competence in favour of Islamic usages and local cultural practices. The interviews explored in more depth how identity management (e.g., Islamic, linguacultural, transcultural, and professional identities) relate to the perceived use of English. Interestingly, one respondent reported temporal changes in her perceptions and practices of English in favour of Saudi/Islamic identification. More in line with the findings of the previous sections, four respondents emphasised the necessity of raising transcultural awareness at a global level, and they justified their opinions by citing the need for 'global peace' and 'civilisation'. The interviews explored these issues in more depth.

5.5   Discussion

This section discusses to what extent the survey provided initial answers for my research questions and justifies the need for the interviews. The findings displayed that the overall tolerance towards 'Saudi English' variants, which have sociolinguistic/sociocultural justifications, is acceptable (mean = 3.81, Std. Deviation = 0.80). In cross-tabulations and Chi square processes, tolerance towards ELF variants is accompanied by explicit rejection of StE ideology in 79.9% of the cases, willingness to project Saudi identity in 71.1% of the cases, lacking/neutral interests in acquiring/producing ENL linguistic usages in 51.6% of the cases, and lacking/neutral interests in acquiring/using ENL cultural-bounded usages in 46.8% of the cases. The deviant cases, distributions of responses to the items, scratches on responses to some items in paper-based surveys (e.g. see Appendix 7), sensitivity signs on body language while responding to Q13 (see Section 4.6.5), and the qualitative comments (see Section 5.4.8) suggested a need for further qualitative inquiry to explore what was left unsaid. The interview participants were selected from among the survey respondents who had written useful comments or represented either typical or deviant cases.

Regarding respondents' perceptions of their own sociolinguistic realties, the majority (77.3%) of the respondents reported that they (almost) always use English for both international and intranational practices. This is not surprising, considering what previous studies have reported about the facts of today's sociolinguistic realities of the KSA and Saudis' extensive use of English in intranational communications (see Sections 1.2 and 2.4.2). The majority (77.6%) of the respondents reported that most of their current interlocutors are non-native English users, including Saudis. Given what previous studies have reported about interlocutors with whom Saudis interact in English, this finding is not surprising either. Previous studies have reported Saudis' use of ALF and ELF in the KSA to interact with non-Arabic expatriates and visitors, and the majority of them are non-native English users of English (see Sections 1.2 and 2.4.2). 56.6% of the respondents displayed awareness of Saudi markers in their use of English.

Respondents' descriptions of their English use included 'our/ my English', 'non-standard', 'informal', 'slang', 'English with a Saudi touch', 'Saudi version' of English, 'Saudi phraseology' of English, 'understandable', 'acceptable', 'clear English', 'normal English', and 'ordinary English of Saudis'. Apparently, respondents employ Firth's (1996) 'make it normal' principle in a positive way through acceptance of differences as normal/ natural cases. In cross-tabulation and Chi square processes, acknowledgment of the impact of Saudi/Arabic traces on English is accompanied by tolerance towards 'Saudi English' variants in 45. 5% of the cases and by one's willingness to project Saudi identity in 50.6% of the cases. From an ELF standpoint, a foreign language is not exploited extensively and intranationally as a linguacultural/translingual marker by members who share an L1, while a lingua franca can be chosen on purpose to be used in local and international settings by users who share an L1.

Respondents' non-negative opinions on their use of English chime with their overall positive positions towards today's functions of English. Respondents' descriptions of the spread of English includes 'lingua franca', 'additional language', 'world language', 'international language', and 'communication language' with 'minor grammatical errors'. Similarly, findings of recent previous studies have reported Saudis' positive attitude towards English as an international means for communication with the world (e.g., Al Khateeb, 2015; Elyas, 2011, 2014; Elyas and Badawwod, 2017; Kronick, 2014; Nouraldeen and Elyas, 2014). In the present study, 86% of the respondents did not refer to a target nation, as they referred to English as an additional means for communication with the world for instrumental, developmental, and international motives. From an ELF standpoint, a second language is used/learned to integrate or interact with its native users, and a foreign language is used/learned to interact or communicate with its native users; a lingua franca, in contrast, is used/learned to integrate/interact/communicate with anyone who uses English, not with members of a particular nation. The typical cases of statistical tests showed that the lack of a target nation relates to ELF-oriented perceptions, and the reference to the existence of a target ENL nation relates to ESL/EFL-oriented perceptions (χ^2=11.647, p-values = 0.020).

75.4% of the respondents displayed their willingness to project their Saudi identity on their use of English. Findings of Elyas (2011, 2014) displayed Saudis' willingness to promote their global, Saudi, and Islamic identities in English interactions. These orientations towards projection of the Saudi/Islamic identification and use of English as a tool for international communications are shared by the KSA government and its educational and language policies (Al Khateeb, 2015; Elyas, 2011, 2014; Elyas and Badawood, 2017; Faruk, 2014). In cross-tabulation and Chi square processes, willingness to project Saudi identity is accompanied by the lack of a target nation in 69.5% of the cases, by perception/target of proficiency in terms of contextual performativity in 73.1% of the cases, and by lacking/neutral interest in acquiring native-like English in 48.9% of the cases. In alignment with the present study's findings, MacKenzie (2014) refers to data that found that learners/users who are highly motivated to integrate with ENL users tend to acquire/use ENL culture-bound expressions (e.g., idioms) and formulaic sequences, although these expressions are difficult to acquire. ENL ready-made expressions are resistant to acquisition because 'they are highly pronunciation-sensitive requiring a particular stress, pitch, intonation, and tone of voice' (MacKenzie, 2014: 104). Still, ESL/EFL users/learners underscore these expressions for many reasons such as: achieving comprehensibility, which is more advanced than intelligibility, with ENL users; maintaining relations with ENL users; and/or representing ENL memberships. MacKenzie (2014) also refers to data that found that ELF users/learners who use English for international purposes and/or who expect to use English mostly with other non-native English users tend to avoid using/learning ENL usages and ready-made expressions because they view them as obstacles in ELF interactions. To gain a holistic understanding, the interviews explored participants' contextual(ised) reflections on and experiences of ELF and ALF interactions.

To examine how perception relates to context, the survey investigated how respondents perceive English in different settings (e.g., international non-pedagogical settings, teaching/learning settings, and evaluative/assessment settings). In international non-pedagogical settings, respondents tended to prioritise communication skills, fulfilment of contextual functions, and appropriateness to situations/discourse over conformity to StE and ENL usages. Respondents' ranking in the present study resembles the opinions of Nouraldeen and

Elyas's (2014) Saudi participants, who showed a reasonable liking for ENL accents, but emphasised the priority of clarity and mutual understanding before the 'beauty of ENL accents'. Alharbi's (2016) data evidenced that the actual English practices of both Saudis and non-Saudis in a multinational workplace prioritise communicative skills (e.g., negotiation of meaning, code-switching, paraphrasing, hedging, and backchannels) in smoothing conversations and achieving contextual functions. The interviews explored how participants perceive the role of a transcultural mediator in ELF settings.

Osman's (2015) findings showed mismatch between Saudi ELT teachers' opinions and practices. Although Saudi teachers' opinions tended to prioritise being a transcultural mediator in English interactions before producing StE or ENL usages, the teachers have not put this idea into practices. Al Asmari's (2014) findings suggested that the majority of university instructors in the KSA are familiar with the field of ELF, and that they acknowledge the significance of its perspectives on pedagogy, but they still display a preference for sticking to StE and ENL usages in their teaching practices. In non-pedagogical settings, the present study's findings have not found a considerable difference in perception between the ELT professional group and non-ELT groups. However, considerable differences in perceptions emerged among these respondent groups in pedagogical settings. ELT schoolteacher and university instructor groups tended to associate ELT linguistic dimensions with British/American usages before international diversities of usages. In contrast, the students and non-ELT professional groups tended to associate ELT linguistic dimensions with international diversities of usages before British/American usages. Student, non-ELT professional, and ELT university instructor groups tended to associate competence with both contextual performativity and transcultural awareness. Differently, the ELT schoolteacher group tended to associate competence with both StE-based linguistic competence and contextual performativity. The interviews explored the reasons behind these contextual(ised) positions. All groups tended to associate ELT cultural dimensions with worldwide cultures besides the students' local culture. Latest studies on ELT cultural components have reported that the majority of Saudi students and teachers have interest in moving across languages and cultures in transcultural contexts without emphasis on a particular nation (Ahmed and Ahmed, 2015; Ahmad and Shah, 2014; Al-Asmari and Khan, 2014; Elyas, 2011, 2014; Mekheimer and Aldosari, 2011; Osman, 2015). However, respondents' additional comments in the present study emphasised the necessity of balance between protection of the Arabic language and the Islamic identification on the one hand, and transcultural awareness on the other. The interviews explored in more depth perceptions of this sensitive balance and pedagogical needs.

Due to the sensitivity of the Gulf context and the worries about the loss of traditional 'Bedouin' values, the majority of expatriate teachers of English are from other Middle East countries (Raven, 2011). In the present study, the ELT professional groups displayed a preference for qualified Saudi ELT teachers over non-qualified native English teachers in favour of qualifications and familiarity with learners' local settings. Stimulated by the desire to satisfy expectations/needs, the students and non-ELT professional groups displayed a preference for (qualified and non-qualified) native English ELT teachers who have familiarity with Saudi/Islamic values. These conditional preferences manifested the sensitivity of Saudis' expectations regarding the role of ELT teachers. Findings of Alseweed (2012), Kronick (2014), and Nouraldeen and Elyas (2014) have demonstrated that Saudis feel more comfortable with ELT teachers who have a similar linguacultural background, use an intelligible accent, tolerate 'minor errors' and code switching without blaming, and prioritise communicative/interactive/practical approaches before alignment with StE and ENL usages. Moreover, the findings of the present study showed respondents' orientations towards questioning the rigidity and/or soundness of StE-based tests because these tests do not consider contextual performativity. Similarly, previous studies showed that Saudis complained about the unrealistic and/or inaccuracy of StE-based measurements, and that norm-based tests contributed to constructing a sense of inferiority and reducing confidence (Al-Asmari and Khan, 2014; Alzayid, 2012; Elyas, 2014; Kronick, 2014; Nouraldeen and Elyas, 2014). In the present study, the ELT professional groups seemed interested in inclusion of international communication skills and interactive techniques within ELT assessment/evaluative methods. Despite the doubts, the students and non-ELT professional groups seemed reluctant towards this integration. The interviews explored in more depth these contextual(ised) positions.

5.6   Overall findings of the survey study

This section summarises the initial answers for my research questions and highlights the need for the interviews. The extent of tolerance towards 'Saudi English' variants, which have sociolinguistic/sociocultural justifications, is acceptable (mean = 3.81, Std. Deviation = 0.80). Responses to these variants indicated that perceptions of 'acceptable' English cover a range of dimensions (e.g., linguistic, domain-driven, and identity related). However, acceptance of such variants is not a stable outcome as the statistical tests displayed (highly) significant interrelationships between (in)tolerance and the other dimensions of perceptions: beliefs, attitudes, (habitual) ways of thinking, motivations, ideological outlooks, identifications, and perceived context. In conclusion, self-description of one's own English relates to both one's identity projection on English (χ^2 = 106.717, p-values = 0.000) and one's (in)tolerance towards ELF variants (χ^2 = 139.496, p-values = 0.000). One's implicit (in)tolerance to ELF variants relates to both one's explicit position towards language standardisation (χ^2 = 113.904, p-values = 0.000) and one's identity projection on English (χ^2 = 51.476, p-values = 0.000). The extent of one's (in)tolerance towards ELF variants relates to one's motives (χ^2 =11.647, p-values = 0.020). One's identity projection on English relates to one's motives for using English (χ^2 = 74.729, p-values = 0.000), one's perception of native-like English (χ^2 = 88.553, p-values = 0.000), and one's perception/target of proficiency in English (x^2= 60.667, p-values = 0.000). In the typical cases of the present study's statistical analysis, the lack of a target nation relates to ELF-oriented perceptions (x^2= 11.647, p-values = 0.020) and tolerance to misalignment with StE and ENL linguistic usages (x^2= 56.279, p-values = 0.000), which, in turn, relates to devaluing ENL cultural-bound usages (x^2 =41.938, p-values = 0.000). These statistical interrelationships suggest that the outcome of the typical cases is not fixed as it depends on co-adaptations and self-organisations in response to any perceptual, temporal, or contextual change (see Section 5.5). To gain a holistic understanding, the interview participants were recruited from among the survey respondents who presented either typical or deviant cases.

Respondent's additional comments (see Section 5.4.8) displayed emphasis on protection of Arabic language, ALF functions, and Islamic identifications. Some comments displayed awareness of the tendency of both usages and judgments to change. Other comments displayed the need for aligning ELT practices with real-life usages in a way that suits the Saudi context. To explore these issues in more depth, the interview participants were recruited from among the survey respondents who had written useful comments. Interestingly, I have noticed that respondents' use of English in their written comments has some characteristics of so-called 'Saudi English', such as code-switching as in 'two holy Harameen' (see Table 33), using Islamic expressions as in 'O mankind!' (see Table 42), using localised lexical expressions as in 'put in their mind' and 'from my mind' (see Table 38), and free mobility of adverbial clauses as in 'my views viciously' (see Table 42).The interviews examined the 'Saudi English' variants and their sensitivity to change in participants' reported use of English. Studies that see an 'English variety' break down the pragmatic, form-based, and various other parts that travel in the variability of language and the complexity of communication. Through a complexity theory lens, the interviews investigated participants' contextual(ised) reflections on and experiences of ELF and ALF communications. The survey findings in conjunction with the interview findings can provide holistic answers for the nested research questions of the present study.

Chapter 6: Interview Results and Findings (Patterns and interrelationships among reported usages, perceptions, and context)

6.1 Introduction

The survey study helped to answer my research questions at a preliminary level. The findings provided insights into the extent of tolerance towards ELF variants, and the statistical interrelationships displayed how language perceptions/judgments relate to beliefs, attitudes, (habitual) ways of thinking, motivations, ideological outlooks, identifications, and contexts. Based on complexity perspectives, the same choices may not necessarily have the same meanings to different people in different cases. To investigate the survey respondents' voices in more depth, I selected the interview participants from among the survey respondents who had written useful comments and/or represented either typical or deviant cases of the statistical tests (see Sections 5.5 and 5.6). The interviews aimed to apply a lens of complexity to approach individual experiences with English communication through open questions and free dialogues.

Unlike previous studies on how Saudis use English, which focused on linguistic features, the interviews in the present study investigated multiple dimensions of communication, such as: how Saudis perceive LF functions (ELF and ALF); how they perform religious practices in English; and how they relate English practices to national and transcultural identities. To achieve the aims of this project, the interviews explored how participants reflected on their survey responses, what makes English a transcultural mediator in their version of the world, why they reported changes/adjustments in their outlooks and reported uses, and what factors were behind any change/ adjustment. With the 30 participants who joined the two phases (survey and interview), the analysis could apply a complexity lens to understand accounts at deep levels as I could compare and contrast responses in the two phases and explore the roles of time and context on their perceptions. I also could observe and analyse how participants used English in their written comments (in the survey) and in their oral discussions (during the interviews). This chapter begins with a brief description of the participants. This description is followed by an explanation of the procedure through which the data were prepared for analysis. This explanation discusses data inclusion, exclusion, translation, transcription and coding. Next, the chapter presents the thematic framework and discusses the results and findings in terms of the themes. Finally, the chapter summarises the main insights gained through analyses of interview data in relation to the research questions.

6.2 Preparing data for analysis

6.2.1 Participants

I interviewed 72 participants (25 were ELT professionals, 25 were students, and 22 were professionals in fields other than ELT). However, some participants were more cooperative and disclosed more information than others. Therefore, I excluded the interviews which were not conducted in depth and included 30 interviews in the present study. The background characteristics of the participants are presented in Appendix 3. To maintain participant anonymity, codes have been used. I refer to students as S with a number (e.g., S1, S2, etc.), to ELT university instructors as ELT-U with a number (e.g., ELT-U1, ELT-U2, etc.), to ELT schoolteachers as ELT-S with a number (e.g., ELT-S1, ELT-S2, etc.), and to non-ELT professionals as NON-ELT-P with a number (e.g., NON-ELT-P1, NON-ELT-P2, etc.).

6.2.2   Data transcription and translation

I transcribed each interview in a Microsoft Word file and named it with a code (e.g., S1, ELT-U1, etc.). I did not systematically include silent moments, conventions, and prosodic features of speech (e.g., laughter, overlapping, interruption, pauses, emphasis, and intonations), as they were not the focus of the enquiry and my interpretations of identifiable aspects of speech tended to be grounded in more objective treatments of language and meaning making than the classical approaches suggest. However, I noted them when they contributed and were relevant to the areas of interest (see Appendix 4). In most utterances, participants used both English and Arabic. When English was used, I transcribed accounts in the participants' own words. When Arabic was used, I translated the utterances into English, and I then consulted a translator to assure that the English utterances mirrored the content of the Arabic utterances (see Appendix 5).

6.2.3   Data analysis methods and procedures

Section 6.2.1 discusses how I assigned a code of a letter and a number to each participant. For instance, S1 refers to the first student that I interviewed, ELT-S1 refers to the first schoolteacher I interviewed, ELT-U-1 refers to the first university instructor that I interviewed, and Non-ELT-P1 refers to the first non-ELT professional that I interviewed. The reason for this specific categorisation is that the results of some survey questions revealed differences in perceptions among these four groups, namely students, ELT schoolteachers, ELT university instructors, and non-ELT professionals. Section 6.2.2 discusses how I transcribed the interview data and saved it in a Microsoft word document with a naming code. For instance, S1 document refers to the interview data of the student that I interviewed. This section explains and justifies what was performed in order to produce qualitative findings and discussions of the present study.

After data transcription, I submerged myself in breadth of the data by re-reading the data, re-listening to the interviews' audio recordings, and re-visiting notes taken during and after interviews in order to absorb the data without jumping to judgments or conclusions. Because I had a large number of interviews producing a large amount of data to organise and report, I began with highlighting utterances linked to my research questions, which may be useful in exploring the survey study more comprehensively and providing content that answers questions undiscovered by the survey study. I used a grounded concept-driven approach integrated with emergent themes by looking for utterances related to areas the survey study could not explore (see Sections 5.5 and 5.6). The acts of highlighting was achieved carefully with cautious as a process of considering relevant meanings and weaving them into a coherent whole rather than reduction. I attempted to avoid biased selections and reflect what the data represented. I used the 'cycle' method of qualitative data analysis. This method refers to the circular reflexive processes of highlighting, coding, code refinement, categorisation, theme development, reflections, and salient narratives that occur more than once (Saldana, 2013; Tracy, 2013). These procedures are taken in order to facilitate working in a flexible way with manageable and organised data.

As I wanted to stay close to the data and treat them within their own contexts, I decoded, encoded, and categorised them using Microsoft Word and its tools (e.g., documents, files, copy, paste, colours, and highlighters) in order to mark codes and collect utterances of each theme in a file. In this way, I could compare and contrast what a participant said with who s/he was, what s/he said before or afterwards, and what s/he said in different phases (surveys and interviews). I decided not to use qualitative analysis programmes (e.g., NVIVO) because they could not help me treat what participants said in relation to their identities, what they did, and their narratives. The way these programmes treat extracts as pieces of data isolated from their whole context cannot give complex meanings; in addition, their reliance on codes which are taken directly from what the participants themselves say did not suit the present study's complexity theory framework. As Saldana (2013) noted, these programs may offer false justifications because they quantify qualitative data and may remove the interpreter's judgments by 'chopping things up'.

I began with 'first-level' descriptive coding by assigning names that capture the data essence and/or summarises the primary topic of highlighted utterances (see Saldana, 2013). In this phase, I assigned and typed interpretively names of codes in the 'comment' function of Microsoft Word documents (e.g., attitudes and motives). I used 'copy' and 'past' Microsoft Word functions to group relevant utterances into separate Microsoft Word documents based on the themes of this paper's research questions: reported use, beliefs, attitudes, common sense, ways of thinking, ideologies, identification, motivation, and context. Under each descriptive theme in each document, I used 'emergent coding' in the form of inclusion of data-driven subthemes (e.g., ALF, Islam, and ELT taboo topics). The most important aspect of moving from the main descriptive coding to the emergent descriptive coding was that the former, main descriptive coding, had to represent what was being said in relation to this paper's research questions, whereas the latter, emergent descriptive coding, was open to all possibilities of thematisation to represent what was being said in relation to ELF phenomena.

When the descriptive coding was complete, I re-arranged and re-categorised utterances into themes based on the outcomes of the interactions of the interconnected themes. In this stage, I used 'second-level' analytic coding that interprets complexity in the data, relationships, and/or case-effect progressions (Saldana, 2013; Tracy, 2013). For instance, explanations for language patterns, how perceptions of ALF, and Islam play significant roles in perceptions of English and identity management, and how perceptions of English relate to perceptions of time and contextual factors. As the procedures progressed, I continued adding notes constantly using the 'comment' function. These notes included notes taken during and after interviews (e.g., interviewees' non-verbal reactions) and considerations of literature. These notes were invaluable in interpreting what was said and how it was said. To approach the data with a more open mind and make the account more coherent, I allowed themes to emerge, codes to change, multiple codes to belong to a single utterance, and notes to reflect on patterns, groupings, and organisation. This cycle was repeated several times until the organisation was complete, level alignment, and representativeness of themes to which they were assigned. I then organised the data according to level of their descriptive and analytic coding (See Appendix 4). Section 6.3 discusses the results and findings based on the final analytic and interpretive frameworks of these processes.

6.3   Results and findings

6.3.1   Patterns in complex adaptive systems

This section describes language and perception patterns that were detected in the qualitative data. It also reveals regional impacts on co-adaptation and self-organisation of these patterns. Further, it examines the sensitivity of these patterns to change in response to contextual dimensions.

6.3.1.1   Language and perception patterns

I asked participants to justify the extent of their acceptance or non-acceptance for each sentence in Q13 in the survey (See Appendix 1). Then, I asked them to adjust each sentence to convey the same meaning in their own way. As discussed in this section, participants' reported paraphrases matched, with varying degrees, the description of 'Saudi English' patterns in a closer way than the way that had already been offered in Q13 (See Appendix 1). I did not expect to find such a strong match and clearly identifiable regularity. However, as presented in this section, the regularity of these patterns is not a product of random usages. It is a by-product of repeated practices with translingual, religious, sociocultural, and sociolinguistic justifications. Looking at this phenomenon through the lens of language patterns alone would mislead researchers. The nature of language patterns in ELF use has been examined in the literature (see Chapter 2). Baird et al. (2014) offered a complexity theory-informed insight:

'Furthermore, emergentism and complexity theory would also suggest that the patterns are learnt as part of communicative repertoires gained through repeated participation in contextualised communication, as opposed to drawing on abstract grammatical rules. Therefore, what is shared in ELF interactions that enables the participants to refer to the language as English is related to social experience rather than abstract rules. In many cases these shared experiences will be learning "English" as a subject at school and then later engaging with wider communities which also make use of English. Thus, ELF users share overlapping repertoires of communicative practices and the associated conventionalised, but adaptable and variable, linguistic forms which form part of these practices' (Baird et al., 2014: 182).

In the present study, participants reported certain categories of repetition, justified their reasons, limited their uses and acceptance to non-pedagogical communications among Saudis, and acknowledged their tendency towards negotiation depending on the context (See Sections 6.3.1.3 and 6.3.2.4.1). The linguistic features of the language patterns which were captured by the survey and interview studies are listed below, followed by the participants' comments and my observations and interpretations.

1. The use of Islamic code-mixed expressions and direct translation of Islamic prayers was acknowledged by all interviewees, but it was perceived and treated differently.

Some participants, such as S2, felt that this usage happens unintentionally as a result of habitual religious practices:

S2: Unintentionally, I use Islamic words in English.

From a different perspective, some participants, such as NON-ELT-P3, noted that this usage is practiced intentionally to reflect Islamic identification. In some cases, this purpose resulted in rejecting item 13.1 (Mashallah, she is successful) in favour of the use of 'Masha Allah', rejecting item 13.15 (May God give you a long life) in favour of the word 'Allah', rejecting item 13.8 (What a good luck) in favour of the word 'fate' or 'destiny', and/or rejecting the use of English itself in favour of the use of Arabic for all Islamic expressions and prayers. This position suggests resistance against matching StE and ENL usages in favour of Islamic identification (see Section 6.3.3.3), as NON-ELT-P3's statement demonstrates below:

NON-ELT-P3: No English with holy words. Being a native speaker of the language of Islam and the Quraan is a blessing... We are able to say them in the perfect way, we shouldn't mix them with other languages.

However, this usage seems under negotiation, which is contextual in nature. Regarding this, some interviewees have shown reluctance towards the use of the Islamic expressions in transcultural and multi-religion interactions (see Sections 6.3.1.3 and 6.3.2.4.1). For instance, NON-ELT-P7 stated that using Islamic expressions with non-Muslims may disrupt the communication as it suggests distance and highlights divergence.

NON-ELT-P7: It depends on the situation. We can use them with other Saudis or Muslims, but it's inappropriate to use religious words with people who have a different religion from the one you have.

This negotiation indicates that people do not have one rigid style with which they communicate with others; they use language to communicate in a constant process of contextualisation, which entails awareness of themselves and others, and which offer choices and creates diversity in people's preferences and practices.

2. The use of Arabic words was common when words do not have equivalents in English. Awareness of the mutual influence of Arabic and English on each other was demonstrated regularly in the data. Participants' accounts provided evidence of wider trends in sociolinguistic research that no longer assume linear divides between languages in people's lives, as discussed in Chapter 2 (e.g., flowing symbolic meanings vs. fixed models, and functions vs. forms).

NON-ELT-P6: Both languages influence each other.

This recognition of the mutual influence results in participants' awareness and, sometimes, acceptance of the insertion of Arabic words in the middle of English sentences.

NON-ELT-P1: Sometimes, we speak Arabic, and then suddenly, we insert one of the widely shared invented English words in the middle of an Arabic sentence like 'kansalt' to Arabitise and summarise the expression 'I have cancelled'.

S9's reaction shows another layer of the complexity of language identification. As shown below, she rejected item 13.2 (She was wearing her Abaya and Niqab) because the words 'Abaya' and 'Niqab' were capitalised. She did not like the sense of 'othering' of these two Arabic words in the written text.

S9: Like any common nouns that describe clothes, the words 'Abaya' and 'Niqab' should not be capitalised. Do we capitalise nouns that describe nuns' clothes? Why do you capitalise nouns that describes Muslim females' clothes?

Such an account demonstrates how a simple signifier (e.g. capitalisation) may have a significantly semiotic meaning. Capitalisation of the clothes 'Abaya' and 'Niqab' sent S9 a message that she is not a part of the group who uses English and that her clothing is not a normal item of clothing. S9 views herself as an agent who has the authority over her own language use. The sense of agency and the acknowledgment of the mutual influence result in participants' awareness and sometimes acceptance of their own accent and justified differences from StE and ENL usages.

ELT-U4: I know it's impossible to sound like native speakers of English, as it's impossible for non-Arabs to sound like native Arabs. Arabic will always influence our English, or at least our English accent... No matter how you try to sound like native English speakers, your Saudi accent, which is not bad, will always exist.

The above accounts provide evidence of a specific status of Arabic and the possibility of others' desire to sound native in Arabic (another LF), but there is also a choice of 'impossibility' rather than 'undesirability', so perhaps this is a reluctant position rather than a desired one. However, participants' positions towards mixing Arabic with English showed flexibility depending on the interlocutors' backgrounds and context (see Sections 6.3.1.3 and 6.3.2.4.1). For instance, NON-ELT-P8 prefers not to use any Arabic word while speaking with non-Arabs and not to use any Islamic expressions that suggest extreme positions while speaking with non-Muslims.

NON-ELT-P8: Non-Saudis may not know the meanings of 'Abaya' and 'Niqab', and non-Muslims may get scared of these words if they know their meanings. It's better to use the word 'Hijab' or provide more explanations when we borrow from Arabic while speaking to non-Arabs.

This way of thinking suggests that participants try to converge, to some extent, with their interlocutors in a constant process of contextualisation, which creates diversity in their practices.

3. Emphasis was given to semantic operations, as is the case in Arabic, more than to syntactic operations at the surface structure.

Although the instructions for Q13 (See Appendix 1) made it clear that opinions were being requested about the linguistic structures (not content) of the given sentences, the interviews showed that some participants rejected items 13.4, 13.8, and 13.16 for their meanings, not 'incorrectness' and mismatch with StE models. Emphasis on meaning stimulates the free mobility of adverbial clauses (e.g., item 13.4: I ran to you as a friend more than as a mother) and changing noun countability to serve the exact content of particular localised English expressions (e.g., item13.8: What a good luck, and item 13.16: My mother always gives me advices). Some participants displayed an awareness of Saudis' tendency towards the free mobility of adverbial clauses, changing the countability of the nouns 'luck' and 'advice', and/or missing the exclamation mark. Participants perceived that these usages are common among Saudis although these usages are not unique to Saudis (see Section 6.3.1.2). For instance, ELT-S1 stated clearly his awareness of Saudis' emphasis on semantic operations at the expense of the syntactic operations:

ELT-S1: I know Saudis do it, but I don't.

Some participants did not notice or say anything about mismatch of these usages with StE models. However, they rejected these items because they did not like their meanings and preferred the use of 'fate' over 'luck' to reflect Islamic values (as shown previously) and/or preferred other options which mirrored their own regional backgrounds, as shown in what follows:

ELT-U2: I don't see anything wrong in this sentence (13.16: My mother always gives me advices), but I rejected it because its case doesn't suit me. My mother doesn't give me always advices. Sometimes, not always.

ELT-U2 did not comment on the mismatch with StE models in this sentence and he used the word 'advices' in the plural form as well.

S10: Saudi may say 'I stand with you as a friend more than as a mother'.

ELT-U1: I can accept it if one says 'I came to you as a friend more than as a mother', but not 'I ran to you as a friend'.

S10 and ELT-U1 replaced the word 'ran' with other words and mobilised the phrase 'as a friend more than as a mother' in a non-standard position. The expected structure in StE models is: I ran as a friend more than as a mother to you. However, participants showed flexibility in the extent of their acceptance and adjustment of the mobility of adverbial clauses and countability of nouns depending on the content and the context (see Sections 6.3.1.3 and 6.3.2.4.1).

ELT-S2: Some people say this is right. Some people say this is wrong. I don't know who is right. Native English speakers themselves don't agree on what is right and what is wrong. I saw them arguing in social networks about this. Anyway, at the end, I choose what I remember, what I like, or what I think it suits the situation.

As an ELT professional, ELT-S2 emphasised the notions of 'right' and 'wrong' and displayed a sense of agency over his own use of English. He also added the dummy object 'it' to the phrase 'what I think it suits the situation'. As discussed later in this section, insertion of the dummy object is one of the 'Saudi English' variants, which is practised to exhibit emphasis. The agency and flexibility of participants' positions indicate that they use English to communicate in a constant process of co-adaptation with the contextual(ised) surroundings.

4. Giving the article 'the' additional functions derived from its equivalent in Arabic was viewed as a normal expansion to linguistic functions. NON-ELT-P1 and ELT-U3 presented examples of this usage with the following comments about item 13.3 (We love the talented children).

NON-ELT-P1: I love the smart children.

ELT-U3: Is this a validation sentence? It seems very correct... If I want to paraphrase it I would say I love the talented toddlers.

NON-ELT-P1 and ELT-U3 inserted the article 'the' before the noun phrases 'talented toddlers' and 'smart children'. Some participants, such as S3, rejected item 13.3 because they did not like the content of the sentence, not the non-standard insertion of the article 'the'.

S3: I didn't like its bias towards the talented kids. I love the children, all the kids, not only the talented ones.

Although the instructions for Q13 (See Appendix 1) made it clear that opinions were being requested about the linguistic structures (not content) of the given sentences, S3 focused on the meaning and repeated the non-standard insertion of the article 'the' before the phrase 'talented kids' to emphasise semantic operations, as is the case in Arabic. However, this expansion seems under negotiation depending on meaning making and context (see Sections 6.3.1.3 and 6.3.2.4.1). ELT-U5 displayed this negotiation in the following comment:

ELT-U5: I know we overuse the word 'the', and we may add it or delete it from time to time depending on the meaning of the sentence... I try to follow standard rules, but I don't deduct marks for such usages because I understand most Saudis use them.

As an ELT professional, ELT-U5 related this usage to her role as a 'corrector' and evaluator. She suggested that some common usages can be treated as local flavours of English rather than as errors.

5. Participants displayed a preference for masculine forms when the gender was not specified, in a way which mirrors the male-dominant cultures of Saudi Arabia and the use of the Quraan's language. When I asked participants if they thought that item 13.11 (A good teacher is flexible with his students) assumes that the teacher is a man, participants regularly perceived this use as somewhat desirable because it seemed common for them or/and it matched the use of the Quraan's language when referring to human beings. This position was clearly expressed by ELT-S3 in the following utterance:

ELT-S3: So, what? We follow the use of the Quraan.

Those who displayed neutrality or rejection towards item 13.11 (A good teacher is flexible with his students) justified their positions by their disapproval of the content of the sentence or their preference of other words that seemed more common to them than the word 'flexible'. Utterances of ELT-U3 and NON-ELT-P8 displayed these positions.

ELT-U3: Any teacher must be strict with his students, not flexible.

NON-ELT-P8: I hear Saudis use lenient. Flexible is right, but not common... The teacher has to be lenient with his pupils.

ELT-U3 and NON-ELT-P8 paraphrased item 13.11, but they used the masculine forms. However, ELT-S4's account suggests that some people are willing to co-adapt when meeting other practices, discourses, and ideologies.

ELT-S4: In international papers, it would seem more convenient to use 'his/her' or the plural form of the noun with 'their'... It's a sign of professionalism to match updated trends.

Such an account displays an awareness that signifiers do not have universal meanings across contexts, even when they relate to strong associations with people's deeply-held beliefs and cultural backgrounds, and that co-adaptation on different scales (e.g., gender, user, and purpose) can elicit variations.

6. Participants displayed a preference for gerund forms more than infinitive forms for purposive meanings. None of the participants rejected the gerund form in item 13.7 (I sometimes go to Jeddah for shopping with my family).

Some participants rejected this item because they did not like the content of the sentence, not the linguistic structure. Examples of this position were shown in the following utterances:

NON-ELT-P4: I go sometimes for shopping with my friends, not family.

S4: I don't like shopping.

ELT-S4: Not in Jeddah. I don't go to Jeddah for shopping.

NON-ELT-P4, S4, and ELT-S4 focused on the meaning and changed the given sentences to suit their cases, but they used the gerund forms. Participants perceived that the preference for gerund forms is common among Saudis although this is not unique to Saudis. However, NON-ELT-P9 suggested that this preference for gerund forms is sensitive to change:

NON-ELT-P9: I don't know. I can't judge. It depends on the meaning or the mood we want to convey in a particular conversation with a particular person.

Such an opinion showed an awareness that preference of language practices are not stable, and that they co-adapt with temporal and contextual dimensions (see Sections 6.3.1.3 and 6.3.2.4.1).

7. Stressing emotional and emphatic expressions was found to be a desirable Arabic style to express the extent of emotions or the importance of the emphasis. For instance, NON-ELT-P7 thought that the double use of 'very' in item 13.5 (It's a very very interesting story) is an 'irresistible way' of communication among Saudis.

NON-ELT-P7: We can't resist this way of saying 'very very'. It just happens naturally. I think it's not an error... It's just how Saudis communicate.

As NON-ELT-P7 knew that this usage did not match the StE model, he tried to justify it and defended it as a Saudi way of communication, not an error. S3 perceived the double use of 'very' as an acceptable 'mistake'.

S3: I know that 'very very' is a mistake, but we all do it. Our teachers got used to see it and accept it.

Although S3 described such a usage as a 'mistake', she thought that it should be accepted because its commonality has meaningful purposes. As an ELT professional, ELT-US judged such a usage as a 'major error' which functions as a 'Saudi habit' in favour of stressing emotions or emphasis.

ELT-U2: It's a major error. Students don't have any excuse. They can stop doubling. It's not that difficult, but they still say 'very very' as if it's a Saudi habit.

The tendency of ELT professionals towards judging 'correctness' shows that ELT professionals relate their perceptions with their professional roles. Another example of this tendency was shown by ELT-S5 who evaluated the correctness of this usage and categorised it as a 'minor error'.

ELT-S5: I don't deduct marks for such a minor error.

Participants perceived the double use of the word 'very' and the free mobility as a common usage among Saudis although this is not unique to Saudis. In addition, participants showed flexibility in the judgments on such usages and the use of emphatic expressions depending on the context (see Sections 6.3.1.3 and 6.3.2.4.1).

8. The dummy object was used sometimes as a communicative way to clarify meanings or exhibit emphasis.

When participants were asked to paraphrase item 13.6 (Riyadh is the city which she lives in it all her life) in their own way, some participants did not notice any variation in this sentence from the StE model (e.g., NON-ELT-PS).

NON-ELT-P6: This is the way I say it... To change this sentence, we can say 'Riyadh is the city where she is still lives in it'.

Other participants showed awareness of Saudis' tendency towards inserting a dummy object, but they hesitated to judge this tendency. As a student, S5 expressed how confused he feels because his teachers criticise this usage, but they themselves do it.

S5: I don't know. Teachers say don't add 'it', but the sentence seems incomplete without 'it', and teachers do the same tempting mistakes we do. This is confusing.

The student S5 referred to the mismatch between what some teachers do and what they say. Sometimes, she is right. For instance, the schoolteacher ELT-S2 has done used the dummy object 'it' in the following utterance:

ELT-S2: Anyway, at the end, I choose what I remember, what I like, or what I think it suits the situation.

As presented previously, the university instructor ELT-U2 changed the countability of the word 'advice' in the following utterance:

ELT-U2: My mother doesn't give me always advices.

While student S5 described the insertion of a dummy object as 'tempting' among Saudis, the schoolteacher ELT-S3 acknowledged its commonality and related its usage to non-correctness.

ELT-S3: It is grammatically incorrect. I can't understand why students repeat it. I tell them. I correct them. Nothing works... I don't do it... As I know it's common, I don't deduct marks for it.

While some schoolteachers such as ELT-S3 could not find explanations for such a usage, some university instructors such as ELT-U5 explained it in terms of L1 negative transfer and preferable practices.

ELT-U5: This is an L1 negative transfer. It's one of the favourable grammatical mistakes of the students.

Describing this variant as a 'tempting' and 'favourable' practices suggests resistance against matching StE models in favour of meaning clarity. However, this usage seems under negotiation with contextual functions (see Sections 6.3.1.3 and 6.3.2.4.1).

9. Expanding the meanings and usages of specific words, such as 'open', was considered to be common among Saudis. Participants showed awareness of how Saudis expand the meanings of the word 'open', as it functions in Arabic. When participants were asked to paraphrase item 13.10 (Don't open the computer) in their own way, some

participants emphasised that the word 'open' can be used in English to mean 'turn on'. This emphasis was expressed explicitly by S10:

S10: It's right to say open the computer. Why not? ... English people don't use it like this, but we do.

Student S10 viewed this expansion as a normal 'right' usage, but ELT professionals noted its difference from StE models. This notice was accompanied by tolerance of some ELT professionals, such as ELT-S4, to this expansion due to its commonality among Saudis:

ELT-S4: I don't use it in this way, but I don't deduct marks for such a common usage.

It seems that ELT professionals relate variations with their professional practices in relation to evaluation as they talk about correction, marks, and errors as shown in the preceding and following examples. In addition, some ELT professionals limited their tolerance towards the expansion of the meanings and functions of some words such as 'open' to specific contexts (e.g., informal communication). For instance, ELT-U4 did not like using such an expansion with non-Saudis:

ELT-U4: It's not right, especially in exams... but it's OK as many Saudis extend the meanings of the word 'open', but I don't prefer doing this with non-Saudis, as they may not understand or may judge it negatively.

Such a position indicates that people may abandon some of their own styles to assimilate the style of their interlocutors in order to satisfy the expected roles and/or meet the contextual purposes (see Sections 6.3.1.3 and 6.3.2.4.1).

10. Mixing British and American usages was viewed by the whole sample as acceptable due to the popularity of British and American usages in the Saudi context. When

participants were asked to rewrite item 13.12 (This is my favorite colour), participants did not reject mixing British and American usages in this sentence, but their preferences were different. Examples of their preferences are shown in the following utterances:

NON-ELT-P6: I write 'favorite' with u like this (favourite), *but both ways are right.*

S9: No need to rewrite it...This is how I write it.

ELT-U5 referred to the influence of the media and education on Saudis' practices and perceptions of English:

ELT-U5: I know it's better to use either British or American, but almost all Saudis use a mixture of this and that as American English and British English are popular in the Saudi context due to the media and the educational curricula.

These accounts suggest the influence of professional identity, media, and education on what constitutes 'good' or 'acceptable' English. Other factors were detected in the data, such as dual nationality (See Section 6.3.2.3), birth place (See Section 6.3.2.3), and place of residence (See Section 6.3.1.2).

11. It was considered common among Saudis to omit the article 'a/n' from some noun phrases to activate the zero article function of indefiniteness in the same way it works in Arabic. When participants were asked to paraphrase item 13.13 (He is facing difficulty solving the problem.), only three participants suggested adding the article 'a' before the word 'difficulty'. However, ELT-U5 thought that this omission may seem acceptable in informal and oral communications.

ELT-U5: It still seems OK in some cases like in informal or oral chats.

Some participants justified their rejection of item 13.13 by disapproving of the choice of words. This position was supported by various participants:

ELT-S5: I rejected this sentence in the survey because I prefer to say 'he has, not is facing, difficulty in making decisions'.

S3: It's better to say 'he is having, not facing, difficulty'.

NON-ELT-P4: I would say 'he faces difficulty in problem-solving'.

As shown in the above comments and other previous examples, many participants gave priority to semantic operations over syntactic operations, as is most often the case in Arabic practices. ELT-S5, S3, and NON-ELT-P4 changed item 13.3 in different ways, but they omitted the article 'a' before the word 'difficulty'. However, participants displayed flexibility in their judgment and adjustment of the omission of the article 'a/n' from noun phrases depending on the meaning and the context (see Sections 6.3.1.3 and 6.3.2.4.1).

12. Locally-invented lexical items were re-produced by some users to enrich their use of English. For instance, participants showed awareness of how Saudis invented the word 'Saudization'. However, participants reacted differently to such a usage in item 13.15 (The Saudi government supports Saudization).

Some participants restricted their tolerance towards locally-produced lexical items to specific contexts (see Sections 6.3.1.3 and 6.3.2.4.1). For instance, S6 rejected using these items with non-Saudis as they may hinder communication and intelligibility:

S6: Not with non-Saudis. How can they understand our Saudi English words?

As English communication is not only about intelligibility, one of the ELT teachers, ELT-S5, displayed her preference for the British way through replacement of 'z' with 's' in the word 'Saudization'. Her position took the side of the British curriculum she teaches at the school level.

ELT-S5: Not with 'z', I would like to use it with 's', Saudisation.

It seems that legitimate resources (e.g., ELT teaching materials and dictionaries) influence the positions of ELT professionals. As an ELT professional, ELT-U4 rejected using such words/ phrases. Despite her rejection, she showed willingness for acceptance in response to changes in surroundings (e.g., changes in meanings of legitimacy).

ELT-U4: I have heard of this word, but I don't use it. I will start using it when it becomes legitimate on a broader level or in an authentic resource.

In contrast, the accounts of non-ELT participants showed how they authorised themselves to modify these locally invented words. They stated their position as follows:

NON-ELT-P3: I think the word 'Sauditisation' with 't' and 's' is better than 'Saudization'.

S6: We should make it 'Saudiation' with 'ation' to mean an action that is happening.

Giving the self this authority to modify and create indicates exploiting multiple competences. Interestingly, NON-ELT5 speaks three language: Arabic, English, and Italian. He acknowledged that his confidence in his English drives him to construct his own sentences in his own way without the need for a legitimate reference.

NON-ELT-P5: When I use English, I don't try to copy native examples because I feel confident enough to compose my own

English sentences... When I speak Italian, I try hard to copy native examples because I know that I'm not capable enough to compose my own Italian sentences.

As NON-ELT-P5 does not trust his proficiency in the Italian language, he memorises and copies native Italian usages.

6.3.1.2 Regional impacts on language and perception patterns

Some participants displayed a preference for usages that are common in their place of residence. For instance, item 13.4 (I ran to you as a friend more than as a mother) was rejected by some participants because it does sound like something that would be stated by a Saudi. S10 expressed this opinion clearly:

S10: I rejected this sentence because I don't think Saudis say I ran to you as a friend more than as a mother. I think Egyptians or people from Al-Sham may say it in this way, not Saudis... Saudi may say 'I stand with you as a friend more than as a mother'.

Also, ELT-U1 considers L1 transfer a positive or normal influence if it reflects characteristics of the Saudi Arabic language.

ELT-U1: I tolerate some L1 transfer, I mean the natural ones, but this one does not seem a natural Saudi Arabic transfer to me. I can accept it if one says 'I came to you as a friend more than as a mother', as we say it in Saudi Arabic, but not 'I ran to you as a friend'. No, this use doesn't sound Saudi.

S10 and ELT-U1 replaced the word 'ran' with other words and mobilised the adverbial phrase 'as a friend more than as a mother' in a non-standard position. The expected structure in StE models is: I ran as a friend more than as a mother to you. However, S10 and ELT-U1 judge L1 transfer as a negative or abnormal influence when it reflects characteristics of non-Saudi Arabic varieties. Furthermore, accounts of some participants exemplified other regional impacts on preferences. For instance, NON-ELT-P9, who is from the Western (Hijaz) area of Saudi Arabia, did not accept the usages which mirror the characteristics of the language used by non-Hijazi Saudis.

NON-ELT-P9: 'What a good luck' sounds Bedouin or Eastern Saudi or from the Gulf. I like to sound Western Hijazi Saudi... Hijazi people may say 'this is a good luck'.

NON-ELT-P9 did not reject changing the countability of the word 'luck' and missing the exclamation mark '!'. She commented on mismatching with the English usages of Hijazi Saudis. In line with this position, ELT-U5, who lives in the Western (Hijaz) area of Saudi Arabia, rejected the expression 'What a good luck' because she thought it is uncommon in the western area of Saudi Arabia.

ELT-U5: 'What a good luck' seems like L1 literal translation... Saudis do that. Sometimes, it doesn't seem bad when it sounds familiar... I rejected this sentence because I have never heard of it here... People here say 'she has a good luck'.

The accounts of NON-ELT-P9 and ELT-U5 represents regional variations, but these variations have something in common, which is the use of the article 'a' before the uncountable noun 'luck'.

S10, who is from the Middle Eastern area of Saudi Arabia, voiced intolerance towards item 13.7 (I sometimes go to Jeddah for shopping with my family) because its action takes place in the Western area where Jeddah is located. In the following utterance, S10, who is from the Middle area of Saudi Arabia, used the gerund forms and clearly stated his bias:

S10: I rejected this sentence because I don't like Jeddah... I sometimes go to Dammam for shopping.

NON-ELT-P7 reflected his awareness of regional language practices and preferences.

NON-ELT-P7: *'May God give you a long life' seems from Najd or other Gulf countries. I don't think people in Makkah area use it or like it... Here, we have other English Islamic or Arabic expressions like 'May Allah helps you'.*

This awareness was also expressed by S5, who lives in the Northern area of Saudi Arabia:

S5: *'Hypermarket' is a common word in Dubai and Bahrain, but not Hijaz. The word 'supermarket' is used in the Western area of Saudi Arabia for both 'supermarket' and 'hypermarket'.*

These accounts demonstrate identity positions and different levels of local associations, as the language indexes 'others' and 'in-groups' from/in physical locations. When people are talking, they are identifying who are with or against particular language constructs.

Such accounts suggest instability and diversity of English practices. S2 supported this idea:

S2: *The person who knows one way of English will not be able to interact successfully with others who don't use his own way. We should use, change, and update our ways depending on the situation.*

The following section examines these issues in relation to the sensitivity of language patterns to changes.

6.3.1.3 Sensitivity of language and perception patterns to the context

The sensitivity of a LF to change is higher and faster than the sensitivity of a 'language variety' to change (see Section 2.4.3). This section examines the sensitivity of the above-reported language patterns to change. Some participants criticised Q13 (See Appendix 1), which investigates the tolerance towards ELF variants, because it asks for judgments on heavily context-based usages without providing information about the context. I intended to not give any information about the context in Q13, but I provide a free space for writing to examine reactions and reflections. In the interviews, some participants reported their struggle to make context-free judgments on the given variants. For instance, S1 asked for information about the context as her language judgments and adjustments rely heavily on the context:

S1: In order to judge or express something in English, you should give me some information about its setting.

The same position was taken by ELT-S2 who refused to give clear-cut judgments about the given sentences and did not like the idea of making context-free judgments on the given variants:

ELT-S2: These usages can be considered acceptable in some contexts, but unacceptable in other contexts.

Such a position indicates that context-free judgments are met with resistance. Some participants avoided the extreme positions of 'completely acceptable' and 'completely unacceptable' towards ELF variants because the extreme positions suggest stability. These findings present that people are likely to know more than researchers about how and why they use the language they do. For instance, NON-ELT-P1 and ELT-S3 explained their understanding this way:

NON-ELT-P1: I chose acceptable, not very acceptable, because my opinion may change.

ELT-S3: I chose the neutral position because I couldn't judge. It depends on the situation.

Such statements show that the neutral position, in some case, suggests negotiation. Some participants negotiated usages and/or perceptions in response to changes in motives, goals, context or time. For instance, NON-ELT-P10 changed her judgments and adjustments on the given sentences on Q13 (See Appendix 1) many times during the interview and came to a conclusion:

NON-ELT-P10: It depends on the situation.

Similarly, NON-ELT-P2 *and* S8 changed their responses, judgments, and adjustments on the given sentences and commented:

NON-ELT-P2: I chose acceptable at the beginning, then I thought twice, what if someone uses this in a contract or official document? It wouldn't be acceptable, so I decided to change my response to neutral.

S8: I changed my choice from 'very acceptable' to 'neutral'... After thinking, I realised that it would acceptable to say 'Insha Alla' and 'Masha Allah' with anyone, but it wouldn't seem acceptable to say 'Allahu Akbar' with non-Muslims because it is related to terrorist actions when they commit their crimes... This may frighten some people.

This desire to smooth interactions through convergence strategies has been voiced by other participants (see Section 6.3.2.4.1). The role of desires on changing practices and perceptions is also represented by NON-ELT-P10 as follows:

NON-ELT-P10: Many years ago, I tried to acquire British English, but I discovered that this was an unreachable goal for me and other Saudis who are my age because schools introduced us to English at age 13... Finally, I stopped dreaming of and doing this.

When NON-ELT-P10 realised, after making significant effort for many years, that late introduction to a language influences its usage, she abandoned her desire of acquiring native-like English and accepted the way she and other Saudis use English. These reflections suggest that participants' practices and perceptions of English are highly sensitive to change and co-adaptation as they are distinctly related to the scope of the regional background of their users, the context of use, and the background of the interlocutors. Empirical evidence from the present study indicates the openness of these patterns to negotiation and that the sensitivity of these language patterns to their surroundings is high and, therefore, change happens quickly in a noticeable way. This means that these language patterns belong to a LF (not a variety). This finding explains the issues which the survey study could not explore. Furthermore, Davis's (2003) rejection of traditional perspectives on language use (see Section 3.3.2) implies that language users have agency in the treatment of their own language use. The empirical evidence of this project supports the contention that Saudis do not want their use of English to be treated as a 'stable variety' and that it is unsuitable to use the label 'Saudi English' for these emergent language patterns.

ELT-U1, who is aware of ELF as a field of study, announced explicitly that she uses ESL, not EFL or ELF. This is why her perception of English is ESL-oriented, as shown in the previous sections. However, she thought that Saudi students use ELF. This is why she believed that native-ness of ELT teachers in the Saudi context is not necessary. She could clearly explain that her perspectives were a result of an ELF course she had taken, and this course had helped her to differentiate between her needs and her students' needs. She explained this as follows:

ELT-U1: Q15, in the survey, specified a context. I responded to the given context. Saudi students are taught EFL or it could be ELF. I don't know. I'm not sure. Anyway, in such contexts, native-ness of ELT teachers is not a must. It's a plus, but not a necessity... EFL and ELF users may not use English in the native English-speaking community itself. Most likely, they will communicate in English with other non-native English speakers. So, they need a qualified teacher who is a member in this non-native speaking community. If learners want to get a high score in TOEFL, a different context, I would advise them to be trained by an American ELT teacher to satisfy the purposes of the exam. If they want to get a high score in IELTS, it's better for them to be taught by a British ELT teacher.

It is worth pointing out how she positioned teachers in this way. In alignment with the survey findings, it seems that there is a hierarchy here, and there are circumstances in which a native English-speaking teacher is not necessary, but never a circumstance when such a teacher is not 'a plus'.

6.3.2 Interactions among language adjustments, perceptions, and contexts

This section presents how perceptions and practices of English relate to perceptions and experiences of ALF, temporal and/ or multiple motives, identity management/negotiation, and contexts.

6.3.2.1 Role of ALF

Some participants could not resist comparing ALF with ELF as a tool for communication before I asked them about ALF. This comparison was evidenced by the following comments:

NON-ELT-P5: Others can tolerate our English and we can tolerate others' Arabic when the language can convey understandable and clear messages and contents. Minor errors and personal accents mean nothing to us in work, tourism and oral conversations.

S7: I think native speakers of English may judge our English in the same way we judge their Arabic. In the end, English natives will get used to our English in the same way we got used to others' Arabic.

S1: It seems weird when non-Arabs try to use standard Arabic with us because we use it only in Arabic and Religion classes... We don't use it elsewhere... It would be weird to use standard English in UK and USA streets.

These opinions suggest awareness and influence of the status of ALF. Some participants seemed proud of their L1 (Arabic Language) as they believed that it enabled them to speak English in an acceptable way. Some of the participants expressed this as follows:

NON-ELT-6: As we can pronounce all the sounds, including the difficult ones, our English sounds clear and good.

S1: I think most educated Saudis can use English in a clear, not perfect, nothing is perfect, but good way... I think 70% of Saudis agree with this view.

NON-ELT-P9: Saudis' accent in English is good.

In line with this position, some participants criticised survey item 12.1 (English is today's worldwide lingua franca), as they thought it exaggerated the status of ELF at the expense of the status of ALF. I intended to use exaggeration in this survey item and to provide a free space for writing to examine their reactions and reflections. Rejection of the exaggerated expression in item 12.1 was explicitly expressed by S9:

S9: I strongly disagreed with this sentence because I didn't like the way it describes English as a worldwide lingua franca. You can say it's one of the lingua francas, as Arabic is one of the lingua francas.

Participants' familiarity with the functions of ALF increased their tolerance for non-conformity with StE and ENL usages and motivated their attempts to accommodate their interlocutors. S8 explained how she, as a native user of Arabic, adjusts her use of Arabic depending on the linguistic background of her interlocutors:

S8: We native speakers of Arabic, use different kinds of Arabic depending on the interlocutors... We use Saudi Arabic with Saudis, we use simple Arabic with non-Arabic speakers who use Arabic as a lingua franca... I think native English speakers do this with us.

She also believed that native users of English adjust their use of English depending on the linguistic background of their interlocutors. This reflection indicates that perceptions and experiences of ALF play a significant role in the perceptions and practices of ELF. This role is manifested by the following comparison:

S10: American English equals Egyptian Arabic because both of them are friendly, easy, and popular in movies and media. British English equals Saudi and Gulf Arabic because both of them are prestigious and their speakers can change from everyday dialects to use the right and perfect standard of their languages. Saudis are the best speakers of the standard Arabic, and British people are the best speakers of the standard English.

Such comparisons in relation to specific nations were made by S10 and other participants, as their accounts showed that their opinions on the English used by some nations related to their opinions on the Arabic used by these nations:

S10: Indian English is good, but I don't like their body language and I feel annoyed when Indian accent changes some sounds or extends some vowels. They do this when they speak Arabic as well... It's understandable, but its sound is annoying.

NON-ELT-P5: Chinese English accent teases my ears. Their accent in Arabic is not pleasing as well... It's their voice tone what I dislike.

ELT-S3: When an Italian person speaks Arabic, it seems different, but alluring...Their English is alluring, too.

Looking on language use through a complexity lens, these perceptions indicate that what constitutes 'appropriate' English does not rely only on intelligibility. Clearly, there is more going on, and intelligibility is just one part of a whole communicative context. Despite the differences in participants' views on different types of English and Arabic, participants appreciated standard models of both Arabic and English in pedagogical settings and formal documents, but they displayed a reluctance to use and accept them in non-pedagogical settings (see Section 6.3.2.4). For instance, S1 voiced her rejection of standard language models in everyday life use:

S1: Who uses standard English? It's only for books and educational purposes. Do we use standard Arabic? Nope. It will seem funny. We use everyday language.

Similarly, NON-ELT-P2 expressed rejection of non-standard models in official written documents:

NON-ELT-P2: The non-standard use, in Arabic or in English, is for oral, informal communications, but in written, formal, especially legal, documents, it isn't acceptable because it may cause misunderstandings or lawsuits.

Such reflections evidence that perceptions of English practices are influenced by the perception of L1 practices.

6.3.2.2 Role of Islamic identification

Participants had positive attitudes towards learning/using English. They justified their positive attitudes by referring to Islamic values. Such a justification was explicitly expressed by two participants:

ELT-S4: We learn and teach languages because Islam encourages multilingualism.

S10: Islam encourages education from any nation... For education today, we need English... It's our duty as Muslims to acquire any language that improves science, education, and knowledge.

Some participants criticised survey item 12.1 (English is a threat to my cultural values and Arabic language) because they disliked the idea of coupling language and culture in one item and they justified their choice of the neutral position to item Q12.1 in the survey for this reason. In this case, I had intentionally coupled language and culture one item to examine their responses, leaving a free space for writing reflections. Separation of language and culture was expressed as follows:

NON-ELT-P10: I chose to take a neutral position towards this statement because English is a threat to our language, but it's not a threat to our culture or religion.

When I divided the question into different parts in the interviews, most participants reported that they believe that English is not a threat to their cultural/Islamic values. Some participants referred to the spread of Islam through the spread of English, but they tended to think that English might be a threat to the Arabic Language and its status as a lingua franca. One participant stated it this way:

NON-ELT-P1: English doesn't threaten Islam, but it influences our Arabic language... It may damage the purity of Arabic or result in abandonment of Arabic in favour of English...We shouldn't allow this to happen.

Such a reflection indicates the willingness to protect Islamic identification, giving priority to Arabic and (unconscious) resistance to English. These desires may result in (un)intentional mismatches with StE and ENL usages. One participant stated this succinctly:

NON-ELT-P7: The spread of English supports the spread of Islam around the world, and the spread of Islam supports the spread of Arabic around the world.

This commentary shows how language ideologies intersect with practices. The participants expressed their belief that it is difficult for English to threaten Islam and/or Arabic in Saudi Arabia because English is not really used in worship places and practices (See Section 6.3.1.1). Arabic is institutionally protected in Saudi Arabia; Saudis themselves insist that people use modern standard Arabic in education (See Section 6.3.2.4.2.1); and most Muslims, even those who are not Arabs, often use Quranic/Islamic Arabic in worship (See Sections 1.2, 6.3.1.1 and 6.3.2.1). These practices and perceptions indicates that ELF and ALF are not just neutral tools for communication. They are fully loaded with many issues, including identity, religion, ideology, and culture. However, many participants described English as an identity-free and culture-free medium of communication:

NON-ELT-P2: English is just a communication language for work, education, and tourism.

S7: It is just an instrument to communicate. It is taught here separately from its native culture... It is just a neutral tool for communication.

Despite their insistence on the idea of neutral English, their reported practices (see Section 6.3.1) and accounts in this section indicate how their use of English is religiously, culturally, socially, and ideologically loaded. NON-ELT-P7, as a specialist in Islamic studies, explicitly expressed how Islamic resources in English sometimes intentionally mismatch StE and ENL usages to purposefully convey a particular message:

NON-ELT-P7: In translation of the Quraan and Hadith, grammar is changed purposefully to serve the meaning which is more important than the linguistic structure.

Such reflections and reported practices evidence that the use of English is influenced by the religious identification of its users.

6.3.2.3   Role of multiple and hybrid identifications

Some participants criticised Q11 in the survey (Do you want your English to project your Saudi identity or to be recognised as native English?). In this case, I had again intentionally limited the choices for the survey item to examine their reactions, leaving a free space for writing critical reflections. As an ELT professional who had taken an ELF course, ELT-U1 criticised this question because its simplicity ignores the fact that a person uses different ways to represent different identities in different situations:

ELT-U1: It doesn't have to be that way. When I say I would like my English to be recognised as native speaking English, I mean I want my L2 to sound professional enough for teaching ESL. I use my L1 to express my L1 identity and I use my L2 to express my L2 professional identity.

This supports the idea that a person can switch identities and some usages on/off depending on the context. In addition, S2, as a Saudi Canadian individual who was born and lived most of his life in Canada, criticised the same question because it did not take into consideration that a person can be a native user of both Saudi Arabic and ENL:

S2: I don't know why this question assumed that one should have either Saudi or un-Saudi identity. I'm both. I use Canadian English, but I have a Saudi Canadian Muslim identity.

Interestingly, pursuing studies in ENL countries plays a significant role in Saudis' sociolinguistic realities and their perceptions and practices of English. For instance, S1 and S2 were born and had lived most of their lives in an ENL country and had an ENL nationality while their parents were studying there. I asked S1, who has an American mother and a Saudi father, why she crossed out and changed her choice in Q11 (I would like the English I use to be recognised as native English); she replied:

S1: I didn't know what to choose... I use my American English with Mom and American people, but I don't use it with Saudis because my Saudi friends may think I'm showing off, or they may not understand... With Saudis or Arabs, I try to slow the speed of speech, give more clarifications, use their popular phrases, and produce clear sounds such as the sound /t/ in words like 'beautiful'.

Such cases show that people practise the language differently with different people for different reasons in different contexts. S9, who lives with her Saudi-American cousins in the same house, noticed that her English was changing to sound more American:

S9: Suddenly, I find myself using the English in their American way.

Accounts of those participants who have dual nationalities or ENL relatives indicated that the motive to integrate with ENL users does not necessarily mean abandonment of membership in one group in favour of membership in another group. In some cases, this motive suggests multiple memberships in different groups. NON-ELT-P6, whose ex-wife is Australian, expressed this position:

NON-ELT-P6: My kids are Saudi Australians... so, yes, Australians are my people too... My English has something Australian, too.

As shown here, one's language practices interact, intentionally or unintentionally, with the practices of his/her interlocutors, especially when there is continuously intensive contact with the same interlocutors.

6.3.2.4   Role of context

6.3.2.4.1   Contextual motives and functions in non-pedagogical settings

As presented in Section 6.3.1, some sentences of Q13 in the survey were viewed as unacceptable because they seemed to some participants as not sufficient for achieving mutual understanding with non-Saudis and/or non-Muslims. For instance, ELT-S5 suggested adding more details to clarify the meanings of 'Abaya' and 'Niqab' or replacing them with other common words to facilitate mutual understanding:

ELT-S5: If they aren't Saudis, it's better to clarify the meanings of the Saudi expressions, like Niqab, or replace them with 'Hijab'.

In line with this position which prioritises contextual convergence in communication, S10 and ELT-S4 preferred avoidance of using any idioms or complex structures in ELF settings. They explained this:

S10: I don't use idioms from any language, and I don't use my cultural expressions or jokes with people whose background is different from mine... These things interrupt interactions. I use these things if others ask to know more about me, but I don't impose my own things on them.

ELT-S4: I don't use native English idioms with non-native English speakers because I'm not sure if they know their meanings.

In communication with ENL users, ELT-U1 preferred replacing Islamic and Saudi expressions with ENL expressions and idioms to facilitate mutual understanding:

ELT-U1: We shouldn't bring L1 metaphors to L2 use. This use is one of the major causes of miscommunication. When I talk with native English speakers, I try to assimilate my English to their English... I use their idioms.

Furthermore, other participants preferred avoidance of using Islamic expressions in communication with non-Muslims because they did not want to scare non-Muslims and did not want to be accused of terrorism or extremism. NON-ELT-P1, S1, and NON-ELT-P9 expressed this concern:

NON-ELT-P1: I don't use Islamic words with non-Muslims... I use some Saudi non-religious proverbs and I like to explain their meanings.

S1: I don't use any Islamic expressions with non-Muslims. I don't want to terrify others. They may think I am a terrorist.

NON-ELT-P9: I don't use Islamic words with non-Muslims, but I like to tell people about our Saudi traditions.

This issue leads us to another area about language that goes beyond language and speech intelligibility. It indicates the complex communication in which language use interacts dynamically with contextual dimensions, including politics and religion. These data evidence that language and practice intersect with who is talking to whom, when, and why. People change their styles according to what the content is, what the domain is, and who the interlocutors are. Bearing this in mind, the idea of modelling a 'Saudi English variety' ignores the ongoing interactions among the interrelated parts of language use which result in variability.

6.3.2.4.2 Needs in ELT

6.3.2.4.2.1 The value of StE models and ELF practices for ELT

For the ELT linguistic dimension, participants displayed a preference for the standard American and/or the standard British models. The data in this section display some factors which play a role in such a preference. For instance, NON-ELT-P1, who had lived in the UK during her husband's university studies, displayed overt preference for what she is familiar with.

NON-ELT-P1: I know American English seems easier for Saudis, but, for me, I am more familiar with British English... Standard British is the one for education.

S1, who is Saudi-American, showed a preference for what she feels a sense of belonging:

S1: I don't suggest the superiority of standard American English, but I chose it because I have the right to love the English of my people.

S2 showed a need for inclusion of both standard British and standard American models within ELT linguistic dimension:

S2: I think we should learn both of them, so we can understand both of them... Saudi youths like American because of gaming and movies. British is seen as prestigious, but not friendly.

These comments indicate an awareness that certain national varieties of English have particular social characteristics or are associated with particular activities (See Section 6.3.2.1).

Chapter 6

Ironically, some participants, such as NON-ELT-P2, who showed in the previous sections high tolerance towards ELF variants in non-pedagogical settings, evidenced extreme intolerance towards ELF variants, code-switching, non-native ELT teachers, and non-StE usages in pedagogical settings. This was expressed in detail:

NON-ELT-P2: Non-natives should not teach English because their English is a mix, like mine, like yours, like any non-native. Can you imagine what will happen to the standard language when every generation learns a mix and adds to it its own mixes? I know accent, correctness of grammar, and standard use aren't important for informal communications, but in English classes, students should hear and learn the right accent and speak the right English, and when I say the right English, I mean professional English, and when I say professional English I mean firstly standard British, then, Standard American... One standard model should be used in a class, no mixed English, no Arabic... In education, only standard languages.

This intolerance towards any non-standard usages in pedagogical settings was voiced by ELT-S4 as well:

ELT-S4: In class, English or Arabic, standard should be used and taught... Using non-standard or different varieties will damage the language.

Here, the concern about language damage/loss plays a role in such a preference. In contrast, other participants displayed interest in code-switching and the inclusion of English linguistic diversities into ELT linguistic components. Such practices are perceived, by these participants, as useful for preparing learners for real-life usages. Various participants noted this:

S4: I like teachers who can use code-switching in a purposeful way to extend their explanations.

S5: It would be more interesting and useful to add non-standard usages to English subjects. Standard is important, but boring, not real.

NON-ELT-P8: Anyway, I think it's good to have an idea about other varieties and communicative ways of English. Why not? I think it would help learners communicate with others.

6.3.2.4.2.2 Needs for inclusion of transcultural awareness into ELT

In line with the survey findings, participants showed interest in broadening the cultural dimensions of ELT. However, they expressed different worries about putting this idea into practice. Some participants expressed the belief that this implementation should exclude taboo topics from ELT materials in order to protect the students and the education system from too much outside influence. This reason for this concern was stated by a number of participants:

NON-ELT-P6: To protect students from Westernisation.

NON-ELT-P9: To keep the students safe from brainwashing.

NON-ELT-P8: I think ELT teachers, even Saudis, are not qualified enough to talk about taboo topics.

S4: Not ELT classes. I think the knowledge of ELT teachers about Islam is weak...They are specialised in English, and we can't trust their opinions... I think their major westernised them.

The above statements display different ideas on the same position (i.e., exclusion of taboo topics from ELT textbooks). NON-ELT-P9 clearly sees in English a wider agenda of a political/ imperialist power 'brainwashing' Saudi Arabians and believes that such an agenda must be actively resisted. NON-ELT-P6 and S4 think that there is a natural process that comes with English 'Westernisation' and that they have to be aware of it.

NON-ELT-P8 focuses on some elements inside the textbooks as taboo topics that might be inappropriate in the Saudi/Islamic context. As they do not trust English itself, NON-ELT-P8 and S4 are not sure whether or not ELT teachers, including Saudi ones, are influenced by non-Islamic values. In contrast, some participants believe that taboo topics should be included in ELT materials in order to raise transcultural awareness among Saudis in order to prepare them to communicate on a global level. One argued this position as follows:

S9: We need to know everything to be ready for scholarships and international careers.

NON-ELT-P2 believes that a blocking strategy is useless because different experiences expose the people, including children, to all different kinds of lifestyles:

NON-ELT-P2: Deleting taboo topics from English materials and forbidding English subject teachers from discussing these issues can't protect your kids from hearing different, Westernised, and un-Islamic views. They will find out everything anyway from anywhere, movies, the Internet, and friends. I think it's better for our kids to know these issues and hear different opinions firstly from schools and Muslim teachers than other wrong sources.

This position was expressed by different participants from their specific perspectives. For instance, NON-ELT-P1 stated that school students should not be exposed to taboo topics:

NON-ELT-P1: With the Internet and globalisation, nothing can be blocked. It's better to expose university students to everything, including taboo topics, but this exposure should be at the university level and should be combined with an emphasis on Islamic values... I am not sure if other Saudis accept this idea.

NON-ELT-P7, who specialises in Islamic studies, aligned his position with Islamic practices of Islamic resources. He also sees that inclusion of taboo topics from different worldwide cultures should be implemented under the supervision of Saudi leaders of Islam:

NON-ELT-P7: This is wrong. Quraan and Sunnah discuss these issues. English books can include them too... new generations need global awareness to survive successfully... They can be discussed in English books, but after getting approval from religious leaders of Islam in Saudi Arabia.

NON-ELT-P7 argues that blocking taboo topics influences negatively the students and does not match the 'right' Islamic practices.

6.3.2.4.2.3   Calls for context-based assessment

Accounts in this section indicate perceiving a difference between competence in language (based in communication) and performance against abstract testing regimes. Some participants raised doubts about StE-based tests. For instance, NON-ELT-P1 and S8 think that a person can end up just randomly answering multiple-choice questions:

NON-ELT-P1: I got a higher score than I deserved, and I made many choices randomly.

S8: The score depends on how fast you can respond... If time is about to run out, you can choose whatever without thinking or even reading.

NON-ELT-P3, who took the TOEFL many times, does not believe that his scores mirrors his real proficiency. He believes that his score only reflects how familiar he is with the TOEFL techniques.

NON-ELT-P3: It has nothing to do with proficiency... Last time I took TOEFL, I practised a lot on the templates and this is how I got the score requested for college admission.

Despite these doubts, ELT-S2, as an ELT professional, still prefers StE-based techniques because they have clear-cut standards for evaluation:

ELT-S2: I know they are not adequate enough, but we need a definite sample for correct answers. How would we mark answers if we don't have this?

ELT-U5, who is also an ELT professional, acknowledged that there are other techniques which are better than TOEFL and IELTS techniques, but she still prefers them because they require fewer resources (e.g., money) than other techniques:

ELT-U5: I know they aren't the best techniques. Let's think in a realistic and practical way. Interactive evaluation techniques need more money, human resources, equipment, and places.

Another ELT professional, ELT-S4, sees that language evaluation depends on the context (e.g., resources and number of the test takers):

ELT-S4: It depends on the context of the tests. The nature of TOEFL and IELTS tests makes it difficult to integrate communication skills because of the large number of test takers... I think in school and university courses it's possible to do that.

ELT-U1, who is an ELT professional and had taken an ELF course, sees that changes in needs influence changes in preferences and practices:

ELT-U1: Assessment techniques should match contextual purposes. TOEFL measures one's American English and knowledge of American culture because it is designed for people who want to study, work, or live in the American community. IELTS measures one's British English and knowledge of British culture because it is designed for people who want to study, work, or live in the British community. They are not biased. They are doing their jobs. Some work and educational organisations request TOEFL and IELTS from potential employees or students. This request doesn't make sense if organisations are not in America or Britain. An international assessment should be designed to measure communication skills and knowledge of worldwide cultures because employers or students will communicate with people from different backgrounds. I'm not quite sure how to do this, but I'm sure people should take the test which suits their purposes... For this, I think people should be aware of ELF.

This observation reveals that language is not just an abstract entity unconnected with its actual use. When it comes into the workplace, English may work as a gatekeeper for those who can get a job or gain a promotion. Another participant expressed this idea:

NON-ELT-P1: Some workplaces in Saudi Arabia request a high score in TOEFL or IELTS for having jobs or sometimes promotions. This is ridiculous because people don't need to use American or British English at work here. They just need good English for communication, not necessarily American or British.

Thus, such gatekeeping in some workplaces reflect language ideologies that conflict with actual needs and practices.

6.4   Overall findings of the interviews

The interviews allowed me to build on the survey results, broaden the inquiry, and find explanations for the deviant and typical cases of the statistical tests. The interview findings aligned well with the survey findings and explored in depth what the survey study could not discover. Participants' reactions to written and spoken language demonstrate how users know about language, but can be treated in some investigations as though they do not, and their responses are measured in a way that suggests a lack of knowledge. The interview findings revealed that participants' positive beliefs and attitudes towards English are enhanced by their interest in international communication with anyone who uses English and by their Islamic values that support multilingualism and multicultural interactions. Participants displayed a contextual(ised) tolerance towards ELF variants, which have sociolinguistic, sociocultural, or religious justifications. Participants' awareness of LF functions has been developed by their experiences with both ALF and ELF.

According to Ammon's (2001) grouping of reactions to the worldwide use of English based on the position of their L1, the strongest resisting reactions come from countries whose L1 have been lingua francas of knowledge and science (e.g., Arabic, French, and German) and their position comes in favour of protecting their L1. This position aligns with the present study's findings as participants demonstrated their willingness to protect Arabic and its status as a LF. Ebrahim and Awan (2015) conducted experimental methods to explore how different teaching methods influence Saudis' English acquisition. Their experiments revealed that Arabic always intertwines with English as a subconscious effect of multilingualism to prioritise Arabic over English, despite considering all kinds of pedagogical issues. This finding aligns with the present study's findings as participants tended to prioritise Arabic and its value as the language of Quraan/Islam.

In the present study, participants acknowledged the roles of timescales (e.g., temporal motives and goals), contextual dimensions, and dynamism of identity negotiation/management in modifying the way they perceive and practise the language (English and Arabic). In other words, what constitutes 'appropriate' English for them depends heavily on the context. In formal and pedagogical settings, participants showed a preference for standard language models, particularly the modern standards of Saudi/Gulf Arabic and American/British English without. In informal and non-pedagogical settings, participants showed a preference for non-standard Arabic and non-standard English usages. In some cases, when participants have a specific impression about the ALF that is used by a particular nation, they tended to transfer that same impression to the ELF that is used by that nation. In international settings, some participants noted that they prefer to avoid, or at least minimise, the use of Arabic ready-made expressions in with non-Arabs, and to avoid, or at least minimise, the use of Islamic expressions with non-Muslims. The participants explained this as a willingness to play the role of transcultural mediators, but not at the expense of the priority of Islamic values. Their Islamic identification, they argued, is non-negotiable in all settings. This finding aligns with Elyas's (2011, 2014) findings which revealed the top-priority of Islamic identification for Saudi users of English. ELT professionals, it appears, give priority, after their Islamic identification, to the projection of the professional identity, which means, to them, the use of native-like English.

Furthermore, participants showed an awareness of, and sometimes a preference for, Saudis' shared usages, and justified their misalignment as an (un)conscious projection of L1 linguacultural or Islamic identifications, or as the result of some other sociolinguistic factors, such as late exposure to English, influence of Arabic, and contact with different Englishes. Interestingly, I did not expect to find that participants' actual use of English in their written comments on the survey and their reported and observed use of English during the interviews would match the description of so-called 'Saudi English'. However, the empirical evidence of the present study revealed that 'Saudi English' language patterns can be identified, as previous studies have reported. However, the present study found that these pattern are highly sensitive to changes in order to co-adapt to contextual factors and interlocutors' backgrounds. Also, the empirical evidence indicates that the regularity of these patterns is not a product of random sedimentation (i.e., haphazard repeated practices); the regularity of these patterns a by-product of sedimentation (i.e., repeated practices) with translingual, religious, sociocultural, sociolinguistic, and transcultural justifications. Participants reported certain categories of repetitions, justified their reasons, and limited their uses and acceptance to non-pedagogical oral communications among Saudis, Muslims, and/or Arabs. In addition, participants acknowledged the tendency of ELF variants towards negotiation and their sensitivity to change. The openness to negotiation and contextual co-adaptation suggests a need to go beyond variationist approaches to understand and account for language use and perceptions in the region.

Chapter 7:   Conclusion

7.1   Introduction

In summarising the study, this chapter revisits briefly the rationale of this thesis, its theoretical framework, and its methodology. The chapter then presents the findings in a format that responds to each research question respectively. The chapter next discusses the limitations of the study to suggest potential avenues for future research. It concludes by discussing the implications and possible implementations in pedagogy.

7.2   Research rational

Some previous studies have documented, to some extent, how the use of English in Saudi Arabia: has varied usages in intranational settings; reflects the sociolinguistic realities of Saudi Arabia; contains intensity and depth in its formal, informal, and contextual features; and possesses a body of nativised/localised registers and styles (see Sections 1.2 and 2.4.2). However, previous studies on the linguistic dimension have underestimated how English in the Saudi context is loaded with historically complicated, politically problematic, religiously sensitive, culturally conflicted, and ideologically contradictory issues. These factors affect Saudis' symbolic relationships, identity positioning, and idea formations across gender, ethnic/tribal, regional, and many other fault lines. Because Saudis did not accept English smoothly, Saudi government policies of foreign languages and ELT have been amended several times between 1925 and today (Elyas, 2011; Elyas and Picard, 2012a, 2012b; Faruk, 2014). Despite the efforts of the Saudi government, ELT reforms, and Saudis themselves to improve Saudis' English, the existing literature still reports that Saudis' English suffers from 'frustrating errors' in the four language skills (see Section 1.2.2). This judgment was concluded based on Saudis' scores in StE-based tests. Reports of previous studies, articles, and newspapers suggest that the majority of Saudis are aware of their misalignment with StE and ENL usages but still insist on repeating the same variations.

It is within the interest of this study to explore how Saudi language users view their misalignments and what intentions, influences, and implications exist behind their repetitions. I, as an applied linguist, use language users' views as a valuable source in identifying language-related issues. Identifying these issues can represent a starting point for research into language theory and help in developing a theoretical framework of linguistics and applied linguistics. Developing this theoretical framework is key in establishing recommendations that help in bridging the gap between theory and practice.

While reviewing literature on Saudis' misalignment, I have noticed that there is a circle of blame. There is a tendency for ELT Saudi stakeholders to blame one another, and sometimes themselves, for transferring the same variants from one generation to another. All other ELT-related issues are also blamed, such as delayed introduction of English, policies, management systems, materials, teaching methods, assessment techniques, and teacher education/development programmes (see Section 1.2.2). To explore what can be implemented to improve Saudis' English, Ebrahim and Awan (2015) investigated whether there was a specific 'Saudi way' of acquiring a second or foreign language. The findings of their experiments suggest that Arabic always intertwines with English in a subconscious effect of multilingualism and prioritising Arabic over English. As discussed in Section 1.2.1, previous studies reported that Saudis do not abandon Arabic, or at least Islamic expressions, despite their extensive use of English, even when communicating with non-Arabs. When Saudis communicate with non-Arabs in the KSA, Saudis use ELF and ALF, which is different from Quranic, standard, and all native Arabic varieties. This note indicates that Saudis experience different lingua francas, different kinds of English, and different kinds of Arabic. These experiences widen the scope of the present study as studies into perceptions of English have rarely considered people's relationships with their L1 practices or whether they habitually use another LF.

In this study, Saudi users of both English and Arabic are positioned to shed new light on how English in LF contexts is perceived by those expected to be aware of LF communications in their L1. I aim to explore whether Saudis' perceptions and experiences of Arabic relate to their perceptions of and practices in English. This study may offer insights for future research from those in multilingua franca contexts, displaying how accounts can be informed by a wider approach such as complexity theory. In the field of ELF, scholars have investigated the relationship between perception and practice, though most have approached this area with different orientations other than complexity theory and emergentist approaches (see Chapter 2). As noted by recent ELF studies (e.g., Baird and Baird, 2018), complexity theory and emergentism have not been employed in any depth in ELF research to date. Drawing and building on theoretical advances, this study applies a new conceptual framework to an area of enquiry where its application encourages appreciation of communication practices and the complexity of people's lives, experiences, and ideas of their perceptions of English.

7.3   Theoretical framework

Though previous studies have described the linguistic features of so-called 'Saudi English' by observing actual use, they have not taken into account how conscious introspection interacts with other parts of language use (see Section 2.4.2). Viewing the language as a social practice, not just mere performance, I view perception and context as intrinsic parts of language use in a process of co-adaptation (see Section 1.1.3). With this complexity lens, the present study investigates how Saudis' perceptions interact with their consciously reported use in relation to context, and how their perceptions and reported use relate to 'Saudi English' discourse (see Section 1.4). To add cognitive, affective, conative, social, time, and contextual dimensions to the traditional approaches, this study employs the transdisciplinary approaches of complexity theory (see Section 1.1.3). Adaptation of complexity theory aims to explore holistically Saudis' voices to reveal how far, why, and when they are (in)tolerant of misalignment with StE and ENL usages, how their views relate to their perceptions of ALF, motives, and identity management, and how their perceptions and reported use relate to 'Saudi English' corpora and natural discourse. This aim implies that the unit of study of this research is a nested web of interconnected parts (beliefs, attitudes, ideologies, common sense, ways of thinking, motivations, identity management, and reported use of English in relation to context). Instead of studying one part (e.g., language patterns) or grouping people into an Arabic L1 or religious groups, the growth of English and various interactions with the Arabic-speaking world mean that counter narratives to this trend are important, both socially and in accurately understanding how people interact with and perceive language, as the language exists and as the people exist in real-life situations. A holistic investigation is important in the Saudi Arabian context to understand perceptual and language outcomes of interactions in terms of context.

Using this useful heuristic, as suggested by Baird et al. (2014), I conceptualise language use, including ELF, as dynamic communication involving a number of interconnected complex systems that include an individual's mental representations of language, language as a social practice, and English itself (see Chapter 2). As discussed in Chapter 3, this study conceptualises perception as a dynamic contextualised process of interactions among beliefs, attitudes, ideologies, motives, identities, and experiences to form ways of thinking and representations of understandings. Based on the complexity theory-inspired lens, all of these parts are conceptualised as processes in motion and flux with overlaps. This framework suggests that language practices and perceptions are interrelated in a process of co-adaptation with one another and with other cognitive, affective, social, and contextual parts. The framework also suggests that ELF shows diversity but is not unique in this diversity because the diversity, accommodation, convergence, divergence, and innovation exist in any communication. But, ELF and any LF show diversity more clearly because a LF contains more variations than monolingual and monocultural settings. As inspired by Larsen-Freeman's work on language as a complex adaptive system, this framework suggests that language patterns of a LF are highly sensitive to change of the linguistic, cultural, functional, and contextual (super) diversities of a LF (see Section 2.4.3). If participants' perception and reported use of English display high sensitivity to context and timescales, the idea of 'Saudi English' is rejected.

As acknowledged by scholars who have investigated English in relation to globalisation, English lives within 'explosive situation' in the complexity of the Saudi Arabian context (Elyas and Badawood, 2017). Saudi English users struggle to play the role of guardians of the Islamic identification, Saudi cultural values, and Arabic language because this role contradict sometimes with the demands of globalisation, intercultural settings, and non-Muslim lifestyles. Therefore, I employ complexity theory to explore holistically where this struggle exists. Where this struggle does exist, I explore related issues and consider how Saudis manage the struggle and negotiate their identification in relation to English use and contextual dimensions. This empirical study reveals these issues through the practical application of complexity theory-informed theoretical framework, as this framework adds new insights to an under-researched area. Analysing relationships between theory and practice allows this study to expand on the conceptual foundations of English in the field of ELF and in the Saudi Arabian context.

7.4 The study

7.4.1 Research questions

This thesis aims to offer a complex description of how linguistics interact with cognitive, affective, conative, social, contextual, and time dimensions of language use in terms of the experiences and perceptions of Saudi English users in the global variations of English as they experience various forms and speakers of English, as well as constructs of language and communicative behaviours. To achieve this aim, this project adapts holism, emergentism, and complexity theory-inspired approaches to answer the following nested questions:

RQ1. How, and to what extent, do Saudis report (in)tolerance towards misalignment with StE models?

RQ2. How, and to what extent, do Saudis' judgements of (in)tolerance relate to their:

   a. beliefs and attitudes towards their own English, the global spread of English, and English associations with natives and non-natives;
   b. motives for using/learning English;
   c. identifications and feelings of belongings;
   d. contextual factors?

7.4.2 Methodology

The philosophical orientation of this study follows complexity theory-inspired research paradigm (see Chapter 4). Based on this orientation, the present study avoids research methodologies or analytic tools that apply, frame, or pre-construct universal generalisations, restriction to either induction or deduction, and/or restrictive variables, models, or influences. In the first stage of data collection, I designed a mixed-method survey on a wide range of ELF issues and integrated data from 'Saudi English' corpora within the survey items. I distributed the survey on a relatively large scale in the different regions of the KSA to enable complexity theory-inspired statistical interrelationships tests and examine patterns of responses and degrees of regularities, correlations, and dependence. I used 765 questionnaires in the present study. The survey study was able to answer RQ1 and RQ2 on a preliminary level, display (highly) significant relationships, and produce data that assist in the analysis of the interviews.

The individual semi-structured interviews, conducted among 30 survey respondents, expanded on the results of the survey, broadened inquiries, gave space for data-driven relevant issues, compared between what participants evaluated in quantitative terms and what they expressed in qualitative terms, investigated contextual reflections on language use and 'Saudi English' variants, and explored perceptions in relation to time dimensions (e.g., temporal motives), contextual dimensions, and identity negotiation/management. The field work took place in Saudi Arabia over four months. Viewing diversity and flexibility as parts of behaviours of complex adaptive systems and complexity theory-informed research paradigm, I did not try to soften diversity (e.g., variability of survey items and participants) or reduce flexibility (e.g., interview language and length) to ensure that I did not lose the information that may shed light on emergence. This orientation aimed at building a larger, more complex, understanding of perceptions and reported practices of English. In addition, I observed and commented on the differences and similarities between what participants had said/written and how they had actually used the language in the survey and the interviews. This approach aided in collecting more in-depth data on how English lives different lives through people who experience, value, and use English in different domains, roles, and identities. This holistic picture of an integrated whole may guide future research.

7.4.3 Research findings in relation to research questions

In answer to RQ1, the survey findings reveal that the overall tolerance towards ELF variants, which have sociolinguistic/sociocultural explanations in previous research, is acceptable (mean = 3.81, Std. Deviation = 0.80). However, this outcome is not fixed as statistical tests display that tolerance is in (highly) significant interrelationships with other cognitive, affective, social, and contextual dimensions, none of which are stable. Participants' reactions to written and spoken language suggest that participants have contextual(ised) tolerance towards ELF variants as participants acknowledged the roles of time dimensions (e.g., temporal motives), contextual dimensions (e.g., contextual purposes and interlocutors), and identity negotiation in the way that they use and judge English. Participants displayed awareness (and sometimes preference) of 'Saudi English' shared usages, justified their usages as (un)intentional promotion of L1 linguacultural identity, and limited their use and acceptance to locally informal settings. On one hand, participants' reported use of English in locally informal settings matched descriptions of 'Saudi English' variants. On the other hand, participants' reported use of English in international, intercultural, and multi-religion settings suggests an openness to negotiation depending on contextual functions. The absence of fully-determined rules for the change in language patterns indicates that the language patterns belong to a LF. Participants' reported use of English enjoys the logic of freedom in LF communications. In other words, they use ELF; they do not use a Saudi identifiable variety of English.

In answer to RQ2, statistical tests display (highly) significant interrelationships among tolerance towards ELF variants, beliefs, attitudes, motives, identity management/negotiation, and context. In conclusion, self-description of one's own English relates to both one's identity projection on English (χ^2 = 106.717, p-values = 0.000) and one's (in)tolerance towards ELF variants (χ^2 = 139.496, p-values = 0.000). One's implicit (in) tolerance to ELF variants relates to both one's explicit position towards language standardisation (χ^2 = 113.904, p-values = 0.000) and one's identity projection on English (χ^2 = 51.476, p-values = 0.000). The extent of one's (in)tolerance towards ELF variants relates to one's motives (χ^2 =11.647, p-values = 0.020). One's identity projection on English relates to one's motives for using English (χ^2 = 74.729, p-values = 0.000), one's perception of native-like English (χ^2 = 88.553, p-values = 0.000), and one's perception/target of proficiency in English (χ^2 = 60.667, p-values = 0.000). In the typical cases of the present study's statistical analysis, the lack of a target (ENL) nation relates to ELF-oriented perceptions (χ^2 = 11.647, p-values = 0.020) and tolerance to misalignment with StE and ENL linguistic usages (χ^2 = 56.279, p-values = 0.000), which, in turn, relates to devaluing ENL cultural-bound usages (χ^2 =41.938, p-values = 0.000). These statistical interrelationships suggest that the outcome of the typical cases is not fixed as it depends on co-adaptations and self-organisations in response to any perceptual, temporal, or contextual change. The interview findings suggest that participants' reported use of English and their perception of acceptable/appropriate English are sensitive to changes in response to change in motives, identity management/negotiation, and contextual factors.

In answer to RQ2.a, the quantitative findings reveal that participants have positive perceptions of the use and spread of English for international aspirations. The qualitative findings suggest that Islamic values play the role of a permanent or long-lasting drive for the positive beliefs and attitudes towards English as they enhance multilingual and multicultural communications. Participants' accounts imply that their understanding of LF functions is developed by their experiences with both ELF and ALF. Participants equalised standard British English with standard Saudi/Gulf Arabic in their prestigious status and compared non-standard American English with Egyptian Arabic due to media popularity. When participants had a specific impression about ALF used by a particular nation, they transferred the same specific impression about the ELF also used by this particular nation. ENL varieties map onto participants' experiences, associations (negative and positive), and identities, as they have engaged with labelled English 'varieties' through their learning, leisure, work, and travel experiences, and have therefore developed associations with these as well as localised English and Arabic classifications.

In answer to RQ2.b, the quantitative findings reveal that participants value the educational and international purposes of English use. Among 86% of respondents, the lack of a target (ENL) nation is accompanied by ELF-oriented perceptions (e.g., tolerance to ELF variants, lack of or neutral interest in native-like English, and promotion of both L1 linguacultural and transcultural identity). However, this outcome is not fixed because statistical tests reveal that motives, goals, and purposes are in (highly) significant interrelationships with other cognitive, affective, social, and contextual dimensions, none of which are stable. Qualitative findings suggest that participants prioritise Arabic over English and have a strong desire to protect Arabic, its status as a LF, and Islamic values. In addition, participants acknowledged the role of temporal drives and contextual(ised) motives to negotiating their use and judgments of English.

In answer to RQ2.c, the survey findings reveal that the acceptance of ELF variants in most cases is accompanied by one's orientation towards projection of L1 linguacultural and transcultural identity. Interview findings reveal that participants view themselves as global Muslim Saudi users of English. Participants expressed being aware of the complexity of their identity management/negotiation in ELF settings and indicated that they use English differently in international settings, particularly with non-Muslims. Participants expressed that they often avoided Islamic expressions that may remind non-Muslims of terrorism. In addition, participants communicated a willingness to play the role of a transcultural mediator, but not at the expense of their non-negotiable Islamic values.

ELT professionals prioritised, after Islamic identification, professional identity, which means, to them, the use of native-like English in professional settings.

In answer to RQ2.d, the survey findings reveal that what makes good/acceptable/appropriate English depends heavily on context. For instance, the same respondent group that displayed ELF-oriented perceptions (e.g., tolerance and tendency to misalignment with StE and ENL usages) in non-pedagogical settings shifted towards preference of StE linguistic models and nativespeakerism discourses in pedagogical settings. On one hand, interview findings reveal that tolerance and tendency to misalignment with StE and ENL usages in non-pedagogical settings is enhanced by experiences with ELF and ALF and preference for non-standard Arabic in non-pedagogical settings. On the other hand, preference for StE linguistic models and nativespeakerism discourses (without its ENL cultural packages) in pedagogical settings is enhanced by preference for standard Arabic in pedagogical settings. Participants acknowledged that the extent of their tolerance and tendency towards misalignment with StE linguistic models depended on the purposes and functions of the context.

7.5 Limitations and avenues for future research

Similar to any self-reported data, one issue in this study surrounds whether the responses represent what I hoped they would represent or demonstrate useful answers to the formulated questions. I understand that survey responses and interview accounts may not accurately reflect participants' perceptions, perspectives, experiences, and practices because participants may reply with what they deem appropriate. The articulated views may not reflect the exact beliefs, attitudes, and representations that the participants hold (due to their implicit characteristics). However, verbalised opinions and ideas may offer insights into the motives employed by participants to position themselves on a certain issue (Preston, 1989, 1994, 2004, 2011). Therefore, responses are not taken as the absolute truth of their actual relationships with the outside world, but rather as indicators of reality, which in itself is fluid, dynamic, and complex (Baird, 2013). People's responses may represent what they think are appropriate to answer a particular question about a particular topic in a particular context with a particular interviewer (Baird, 2013). I, therefore, was aware of how I enquired, analysed, and reported the data with the idea that the data emerged from different stimuli, at different times, for different people, and in different contexts. I had to allow this awareness to influence my reporting, though I cannot entirely rule out miscommunication of data or issues with expressing interpretations as I intend them to be understood.

Another limitation of the present study is its reliance on reported (not observed) usages of English. From a complexity theory lens, studies that rely solely on observed use (e.g., corpora and natural discourse studies) may be criticised for not taking into consideration users' views of language. In alignment with Larsen-Freeman and Cameron (2012), I approach conscious introspection as inseparable from other constitutive parts of language use. As I believe that direct and indirect approaches complement one another, I used some data from 'Saudi English' corpora in the survey and interview questions. However, I am aware that these extracts are not language in terms of performed contextual communication. Instead, these extracts are linguistic parts of the language, though they serve as a useful access point to social dimensions of language in participants' minds. Participants' responses in terms of language yield evidence of patterns of meanings in terms of what is considered appropriate use that has an effect on language practices. Motschenbacher (2013) offered an important insight:

'If the code choice practices reported on by the participants do not conform to their actual practices, such comments can still be taken as indexes of what is deemed appropriate' (Motschenbacher, 2013; 79).

Metalinguistic comments (i.e., language about language) and their mismatches with real-life language practices may reflect ideological dimensions that influence respondents' comments on language (Jaworski, Coupland, and Galasinski, 2004; Motschenbacher, 2013; Preston, 1989, 1994, 2004, 2011). Although observing participants' discourse in interviews can reveal how they use English to some extent, it may not provide comprehensive 'direct' knowledge of their real-life language practices (Kitazawa, 2013). From a phenomenological perspective, Kitazawa (2013) argues that observation alone is not considered a direct observation because it cannot access the emic perceptions (i.e., personal and social meanings) of the observed practices from the perspectives of the subjects.

This study attempts to foreground the complexity of the social landscape in the KSA by widening the scope of the investigation and developing insights into a range of areas of people's ideas and experiences. However, the width of the scope was expanded, but at the expense of the depth of the investigation. Future research may develop deeper insights into people's ideas and language than I have been able to in this project. For instance, ethnography and (longitudinal) case study approaches may be employed to develop deeper insights into a range of areas of people's practices and/or perceptions. The value of this study is in achieving insight into participants' perceptions of their practices and experiences (their own realities) in their own words and on their own terms. The findings of the present study offer awareness from those in ELF contexts for future research on how ELF users may perceive ELF use and users, and what accounts can be informed by wider theory and practice. However, ongoing or future research may enhance our awareness of a range of contextual uses of English (e.g., local, international, and pedagogical, etc.). This study provides avenues for future research on ELF and pedagogy by exploring Saudis' perceptions of ELF issues.

Future studies in other contexts can use the present study as a reference and broaden the understanding of perceived use of English from users of other L1 and cultural backgrounds. In addition, language policy may be an interesting area for future research in achieving a comprehensive understanding of the influences on use and perception.

7.6 Implications and implementations

This thesis poses a challenge to the partialist approaches to language and perception. This research is different from variationist studies on ELF as I conceptualise the language in general, and ELF in particular, as a complex adaptive system within other complex adaptive systems. As reported by the present study's participants, use of English is (re)perceived, (re)judged, (re)developed, (re)valued, (re)adjusted, and (re) negotiated by ongoing contextual(ised) dimensions. The empirical evidence of the present study demonstrates that the regularity of 'Saudi English' language patterns is an outcome of repeated engagements with purposefully shared practices in flux. However, the present study finds that this regularity is highly sensitive to changes in response to timescale and contextual changes. Therefore, I reject the label 'Saudi English' as the present study demonstrates that the English used and perceived by Saudis is a LF and not a geographically confined 'variety'. The fluidity and interconnectivity of language use and perception imply a need to explore beyond partialist and varationist approaches when seeking to account for language and perception.

This study has also offered a profile of Saudis' beliefs, attitudes, motives, identities, and experiences in terms of their English use. The findings inform of the dynamic interrelationships of these parts with timescales (e.g., temporal goals) and contextual functions. Beliefs, attitudes, motives, and identity management are (re)developed and (re)negotiated differently in different contexts. Participants reported that their use, (in) tolerance towards misalignment with StE and ENL usages, and judgment of appropriateness of English use in local settings differed from those that they had in international settings. Participants tended to project L1 linguacultural identity in local settings and transcultural identity in international settings. In addition, participants expressed a preference for non-standard language use in non-pedagogical settings and standard language use in pedagogical settings. These emergences suggest undercurrents towards developing more profound insights into individuals' perceptions and experiences in different areas of their lives. Participants' accounts in this study demonstrate that language users know more about distinctions between false constructs/practices and real-life language use than many researchers give them credit for. This finding suggests that language uses need to be understood in terms of contexts and speakers with open questions.

Furthermore, the research findings provide insightful implications for ELT in the KSA, calling for the provision of a pedagogical space to address today's linguistic, cultural, and contextual diversity and the dynamism of ELF settings. Non-ELT professionals, students, and ELT professionals expressed their dissatisfaction with ELT's focus on formulaic conformity to StE and ENL usages, with the limitations of the cultural components of ELT in the KSA, and with StE-based evaluation systems. Therefore, this study supports giving ELF-related topics a pedagogical space. Specifically, this space should offer exposure to ELF use, allow for practice of communication and accommodation skills, emphasise development of transcultural awareness, and contextually evaluate how English underscores the ability to exploit multiple resources and achieve contextual purposes. As the study demonstrates how ELT professionals seemed reluctant to put this space into practice, I suggest inclusion of ELF critical awareness within ELT teacher education and development programmes to expand teachers' visions beyond apprehending StE and ENL usages. The critical awareness of ELF use can be increased by facilitating self-reflections on alternative usages including StE models, ENL usages, and ELF communications. This proposal aims to let users (re)develop their understanding and use of English alone. When individuals become ELF-aware, they can play a role in making critical decisions about future treatments of ELT education, research, and polices in the KSA.

Appendices

Appendix 1: The survey

Saudis' Perceptions of English in relation to Globalisation

Section (A): Background information

1. **Gender**: Male / Female

2. **Age:** 18-23 24-29 30-35 36-40 40+

3. **Occupation:**

    ○ Undergraduate/postgraduate student (please specify which major) ....

    ○ Working in the field of English Language Teaching (please specify) ....

    ○ Working in a field other than English Language Teaching (please specify).......

4. **Last academic degree:**

    ○ Still an undergraduate (please write which level)

    _____

    ○ Bachelor Degree in _____

    ○ Master Degree in _____

    ○ PhD Degree in _____

5. **Working experience:**

   ○ From 0 to less than 5 years

   ○ From 5 years to 10 years

   ○ More than 10 years but less than 16 years

   ○ 16 years or more

6. **Have you ever received formally a course or training on the field of English as a Lingua Franca?** Yes No

   _____

   _____

   _____

   _____

If your answer to the previous question (Q6) is 'yes', please write about this experience briefly (e.g. its location, its duration, its purposes, its main topics, and your impressions of it).

Section (B): Use of English

7. **How often do you use English? (Choose only one)**

   ○ Never

   ○ Rarely

   ○ Sometimes

   ○ Often

   ○ Always

8. **What are your purposes for using English? (More than one option can be chosen)**

   ○ Education

   ○ Work

   ○ Tourism

   ○ Friends and family

   ○ Social networks (e.g. WhatsApp, Facebook, Twitter, LinkedIn, professional Forums….etc.)

   ○ Integration with native English users (e.g. Americans, British, Canadians, Australians, New Zealanders)

   ○ Other (please specify) _____

9. **You may use English with different interlocutors for different purposes. In most cases, you use English to communicate with ……… (Choose only one)**

   ○ Native English users (e.g. Americans, British, Canadians, Australians, New Zealanders)

   ○ Non-native English users (e.g. French, Italians, Indians, Chinese, Japanese, Philippines, Arabs … etc)

   ○ Saudi users of English

10. **Describe the English you use. (Choose only one)**

   ○ American English

   ○ British English

   ○ Mixture of American English and British English

   ○ English with Saudi/Arabic imprints

   ○ Other (please specify) _____

11. **Circle the statement that best describes you. (Choose only one)**

○ Most of the time, I want my own English to represent my Saudi identity when I use it (e.g. using my accent, local expressions, and communicative styles in English)

○ Most of the time, I want the English I use to be recognised as native English (e.g. American, British, Canadian, Australian, and New Zealand English).

12. **Please mark the number that matches the way you think of English.**

1-Strongly disagree 2-Disagree 3- Neutral 4-Agree 5-Strongly agree

Opinions	1	2	3	4	5
12.1. English is today's worldwide lingua franca.					
12.2. English is a threat to my cultural values and Arabic language.					
12.3. English enriches our linguistic skills.					
12.4. English is a trend which we are forced to follow.					

13. **Please mark the number that represents your personal opinion about the <u>linguistic structures/elements</u> of the following sentences.**

1-Completely unacceptable 2-Unacceptable 3- Neutral

4-Acceptable 5-Completely acceptable

Sentences	1	2	3	4	5
13.1. Mashallah, she is successful.					
13.2. She is wearing her Abaya and Niqaab.					
13.3. We love the talented children.					
13.4. I ran to you as a friend more than as a mother.					

13.5. It is a very very interesting story.					
13.6. Riyadh is the city which she lives in it all her life.					
13.7. I sometimes go to Jeddah for shopping with my family.					
13.8. What a good luck.					
13.9. Let's go to one of the hypermarkets.					
13.10. Don't open the computer.					
13.11. A good teacher is flexible with his students.					
13.12. This is my favorite colour.					
13.13. He is facing difficulty solving the problem.					
13.14. They should set up natural settings with authentic data.					
13.15. May God give you a long life.					
13.16. My mother always gives me advices.					
13.17. The Saudi government supports Saudization.					

14. **Based on your experiences, how do you rank the necessity of the following skills for success of international communications in English?** Please start with 0 to represent the unnecessary skill, then 1 to represent the least necessary skill, then 2, then 3, then 4, then 5, and finally 6 to represent the most necessary skill.

	14.1. Accuracy of grammar and conformity to standard English
	14.2. Sounding like native English accents
	14.3. Use of native English idioms
	14.4. Fulfilling contextual functions (e.g. achieving mutual understanding or building relations)
	14.5. Communication skills (e.g. clarity, resolution conflict, adjustment depending on audiences and situations)
	14.6. Familiarity with native English cultures/societies
	14.7. Accommodating responses to cultural diversities

Section (C): Teaching and learning English

15. Which of the following teacher groups do you prefer for teaching English in Saudi Arabia? (Choose only one)

- ○ Native English users

- ○ Non-native English users with good command of English and specialised in teaching English.

- ○ Saudis with good command of English and specialised in teaching English.

16. Would you please justify your preference for the previous question (Q15). If you have any additional comment, you can write it.

_____

_____

_____

_____

_____

17. Please mark the number that represents your opinion about the importance of each of the following activities for development of English using skills.

1-Very unimportant 2-Unimportant 3- Neutral 4-Important 5-Very important

Activities on	1	2	3	4	5
17.1. American English usages					
17.2. British English usages					
17.3. All/any native English usages					

	1	2	3	4	5
17.4. Non-native English usages					
17.5. English usages in international domains					

18. **Please mark the number that matches your opinion about the truth of each statement.**

1-Very false 2-False 3- Neutral 4-True 5-Very true

Goals	1	2	3	4	5
18.1. One of my primary motives for learning/ using English is to interact with native English users.					
18.2. One of my primary motives for learning/ using English is to communicate with anyone who can use English (native and non-native English users).					
18.3. One of my ultimate goals for learning/ using English is to produce native or native-like English.					
18.4. One of my ultimate goals for learning/ using English is to produce understandable English, and I don't mind if it seems different from standard and native English usages.					
18.5. It is important to stick to a single standard English model (e.g. only standard British model).					
18.6. Today, it is important to be familiar with non-standard and non-native English usages.					

19. **If we plan to enrich English language subjects/courses with cultural/social topics, which of the following sources do you suggest for this supplementation? (Choose only one)**

   ○ American sources

   ○ British sources

   ○ All/any native English sources

○ Learners' local sources

○ Different worldwide sources including the learners' local sources

20. **Which of the following options should be obtained/mastered in order to build/develop English communication expertise? (Choose only one)**

○ Correct grammar and accurate usages based on standard English models.

○ Communicative styles of native English users

○ Communicative styles of students' own locale

○ Communicative skills required for global use of English

○ Other (please specify)_____

21. **In teaching/learning settings, how should teachers/learners prioritise the following English using skills/capabilities?**

Please start with 0 to represent non-priority, then 1 to represent the last priority, then 2, then 3, then 4, then 5, and finally 6 to represent the first priority.

	21.1. Accuracy of grammar and conformity to standard English.
	21.2. Sounding like native English accents
	21.3. Writing in native English styles
	21.4. Use of native English idioms
	21.5. Appropriateness to discourse (e.g. formal or informal, written or spoken, friendly or business)
	21.6. Familiarity with native English cultures/societies
	21.8. International communication skills (e.g. clarity, resolution conflict, adjustment depending on audiences and situations)

22. **Circle the choice(s) which reflect(s) your opinion(s) about internationally standard-based English tests (e.g TOEFL and IELTS). (More than one option can be chosen)**

- ○ They use accurate measurements of English language proficiency.

- ○ They are based on outdated methods.

- ○ They use the right benchmark.

- ○ They should display some sort of flexibility with non-standard and non-native English usages.

- ○ I agree with the idea of focusing on the basic skills and breaking them into sections (e.g. listening, speaking, vocabulary, grammar, reading, and writing).

- ○ They should integrate some assessment techniques that consider international communication skills.

- ○ Other opinions (please specify) _____

Section (D): Additional participation (optional)

If you would like to add any comments on relevant issues to this questionnaire, feel free to write them or contact me.

_____

_____

_____

_____

_____

If you are happy for me to contact you or willing to participate in the individual interviews, please provide your contact information.

_____

_____

_____

_____

Thanks

Appendix 2: Information and consent forms

Appendix 2.1: Information and consent form of the survey questionnaire

Saudis' Perceptions of English in relation to Globalisation

Dear Saudis,

I am an iPhD student in applied linguistics and English language teaching at the University of Southampton, Britain. My PhD project aims to explore Saudis' views about using and teaching English in relation to globalisation. If you are a Saudi who graduated at least from high school, you are invited to complete this survey according to your own personal experiences and opinions. Completion of the questionnaire may need from 30 to 40 minutes. Your participation is voluntary. Your responses will be saved confidential and anonymous, and they will be used for research purposes only.

If you have any question, you can contact me at sab2g14@soton.ac.uk/ sbukhary@kau.edu.sa. If you are willing to participate, please tick all the following boxes to indicate that you agree with their statements:

I have read and understood the information above. Also, I have had the opportunity to ask questions about the study.

I agree to take part in this research project and agree for my data to be used for this project and any future research purposes.

I understand my participation is voluntary and I may withdraw during data collection period without my legal rights being affected.

Name of participant _____

Signature _____

Date _____

Thank you very much for your cooperation.
Shahinaz Bukhari. February, 2017

Appendix 2.2: Information and consent form of the interview

Saudis' Perceptions of English in relation to Globalisation

Dear Saudis,

I am an iPhD student in applied linguistics and English language teaching at the University of Southampton, Britain. My PhD project aims to explore Saudis' views about using and teaching English in relation to globalisation.

The discussion of the interview will be audio-recorded. Your participation is absolutely voluntary. Your responses will be kept confidential and anonymous, and they will be used only for research purposes. If you have any question, you can contact me at sab2g14@soton.ac.uk/sbukhary@kau.edu.sa, or you can ask me directly face-to-face when we meet.

If you are willing to participate, please tick all the following boxes to indicate that you agree with their statements:

I have read and understood the above information and have had the opportunity to ask questions about the study.

I agree to take part in this research project and agree for my data to be used for the purpose of this study.

I understand my participation is voluntary and I may withdraw at any time without my legal rights being affected.

Name of participant (print name)_____

Signature of participant_____

Date_____

Thank you very much for your cooperation.
Shahinaz Bukhari
February, 2017

Appendix 2.3: Information and consent form of the focus group

Saudis' Perceptions of English in relation to Globalisation

Dear Saudis,

I am an iPhD student in applied linguistics and English language teaching at the University of Southampton, Britain. My PhD project aims to explore Saudis' views about using and teaching English in relation to globalisation.

The discussion of the focus grtoups will be audio-recorded. Your participation is absolutely voluntary. Your responses will be kept confidential and anonymous, and they will be used only for research purposes. If you have any question, you can contact me at sab2g14@ soton.ac.uk/sbukhary@kau.edu.sa, or you can ask me directly face-to-face when we meet.

If you are willing to participate, please tick all the following boxes to indicate that you agree with their statements:

I have read and understood the above information and have had the opportunity to ask questions about the study.

I agree to take part in this research project and agree for my data. to be used for the purpose of this study

I understand my participation is voluntary and I may withdraw at any time without my legal rights being affected.

Name: _____

Signature: _____

Date: _____

Thank you very much for your cooperation.
February, 2017, Shahinaz Bukhari

Appendix 3: Background characteristics of the interview participants

Participant Number	Participant Code	Gender	Age	Occupation	Last academic degree	Working Experiences
1	NON-ELT-P1	Female	+40	Employer/ Government sector	Bachelor degree in English Literature	More than 10 years but less than 16 years
2	NON-ELT-P2	Male	+40	Engineer and Project Manager/ Private sector	Bachelor degree in Mechanical Engineering	16 years or more than 16 years
3	NON-ELT-P3	Male	30-35	Dentist	PhD in Dentistry	From 5 years to less than 10 years
4	NON-ELT-P4	Female	24-29	Physician	Bachelor degree in Medicine	From 5 years to less than 10 years
5	NON-ELT-P5	Male	40+	Businessman	Bachelor degree in Business	16 years or more than 16 years
6	NON-ELT-P6	Male	30-35	Flight attendant	High School and Diploma of Flight Attendance	More than 10 years but less than 16 years
7	NON-ELT-P7	Male	40+	Associate professor	PhD in Islamic Studies	16 years or more than 16 years
8	NON-ELT-P8	Male	40+	Employer/Private sector	Bachelor degree in Business	16 years or more than 16 years
9	NON-ELT-P9	Female	24-29	Physician	Bachelor degree in Medicine	From 0 to less than 5 years

10	NON-ELT-P10	Female	30-35	Businesswoman	Bachelor degree in Tourism	From 5 years to less than 10 years
11	S1	Female	18-23	University student	Preparation Year	From 0 to less than 5 years
12	S2	Male	18-23	University student	Preparation Year	From 0 to less than 5 years
13	S3	Female	18-23	University student	3rd year Medicine	From 0 to less than 5 years
14	S4	Male	18-23	University student	4th year Accounting	From 0 to less than 5 years
15	S5	Female	30-35	Postgraduate student	MBA student	From 0 to less than 5 years
16	S6	Female	18-23	University student	3rd year English	From 0 to less than 5 years
17	S7	Female	24-29	University student	2nd year Nutrition	From 0 to less than 5 years
18	S8	Female	24-29	Postgraduate student	Master student in Arabic	From 5 years to less than 10 years
19	S9	Female	18-23	University student	Preparation Year	From 5 years to less than 10 years
20	S10	Male	18-23	University student	3rd year Business	From 5 years to less than 10 years
21	ELT-U1	Female	30-35	Assistant Professor	PhD in Applied Linguistics	More than 10 years but less than 16 years

22	ELT-U2	Male	36-40	Associate Professor	PhD in Applied Linguistics	From 5 years to less than 10 years
23	ELT-U3	Male	40+	Associate professor	PhD in Linguistics	More than 10 years but less than 16 years
24	ELT-U4	Female	30-35	Lecture	Master in ELT	More than 10 years but less than 16 years
25	ELT-U5	Female	30-35	Assistant Professor	PhD in Applied Linguistics	From 5 years to less than 10 years
26	ELT-S1	Male	36-40	Teacher supervisor	Master degree in Linguistics	More than 10 years but less than 16 years
27	ELT-S2	Male	40+	Teacher supervisor and trainer	Master degree in Applied Linguistics	16 years or more than 16 years
28	ELT-S3	Female	40+	Schoolteacher	Bachelor degree in English	16 years or more than 16 years
29	ELT-S4	Female	24-29	Schoolteacher	Bachelor degree in English	From 0 to less than 5 years
30	ELT-S5	Female	36-40	Schoolteacher	Bachelor degree in English	More than 10 years but less than 16 years

Appendix 4: Examples of the analytical processes

Abbreviation	Code	Brief explanation	Examples
First-level descriptive codes			
At.	Attitude	The evaluative and judgmental functions of beliefs	*ELT-S3: When an Italian person: speaks Arabic, it seems different, but (5) alluring...Their English is (2) alluring, too.*
Mv.	Motive	The willingness to take actions to satisfy desires	*NON-ELT-P2: English is just a communication language for work, education, and (3) tourism.*
Second-level analytic codes			
Arabic	The role of Arabic language	How perceptions and experiences of Arabic relate to perceptions and reported practices of English	*NON-ELT-P5: It seems weird @@@ when non-Arabs try to use standard Arabic with us because we use it only in Arabic and Religion... We don't use it elsewhere... It would be weird @@@ to use standard English in UK and USA streets.*
Context	The role of context	How perceptions and reported practices of English relate to contextual factors.	*S1: I don't use any Islamic expressions with non-Muslims...I don't want to terrify them.* Umm: *They may think I am a terrorist.*

Data transcription conventions

... shows omitted utterances for reasons of clarity or anonymity.

@@@ indicates laughter.

(1) pauses are timed in seconds.

: lengthened sounds are marked with a colon.

Appendix 5: Translation samples

Utterances before translation	Utterances after translation
S3:ماعجبني تحيزها مع الاطفال الموهوبين I love the children, all the kids, not only the talented ones.	S3: I didn't like its bias towards the talented kids. I love the children, all the kids, not only the talented ones.
S9: زي أي كلمة انجليزية الي توصف الملابس الكلمات 'Abaya' and 'Niqab' should not be capitalised. Do we capitalise nuns' clothes? Why do you capitalise Muslim females' clothes?	S9: Like any English word that describes clothes, the words 'Abaya' and 'Niqab' should not be capitalised. Do we capitalise nuns' clothes? Why do you capitalise Muslim females' clothes?
NON-ELT-P3: أعتقد الكلمة 'Sauditization' is better than 'Saudization'.	NON-ELT-P3: I think the word 'Sauditization' is better than 'Saudization'.
NON-ELT-P1:أحيانا نتكلم عربي وبعدين فجأة ندخل one of the widely shared invented English words in the middle of an Arabic sentence زي ‹كنسلت›، عشان نعرب و نختصر Arabitise and summaries the expression I have cancelled	NON-ELT-P1: Sometimes, we speak Arabic, and then suddenly, we insert one of the widely shared invented English words in the middle of an Arabic sentence like 'kansalt' to Arabitise and summarise the expression 'I have cancelled'.
ELT-S2: Some people say this is right. Some people say this is خطأ. I don't know who is right. Native English speakers themselves don't agree on what is right and what is wrong. I saw them arguing in social networks about this. Anyway, في النهاية, I choose what I remember, what I like, or what I think it suits the situation.	ELT-S2: Some people say this is right. Some people say this is wrong. I don't know who is right. Native English speakers themselves don't agree on what is right and what is wrong. I saw them arguing in social networks about this. Anyway, at the end, I choose what I remember, what I like, or what I think it suits the situation.
ELT-U2: I don't see anything wrong in this sentence, but I rejected it because I didn't agree with its meaning. My mother doesn't give me always advices. Sometimes, مو دايما	ELT-U2: I don't see anything wrong in this sentence (13.16: My mother always gives me advices.), but I rejected it because I didn't agree with its meaning. My mother doesn't give me always advices. Sometimes, not always.

Appendix 6: Additional comparisons between ELT groups and non-ELT groups

Q20. Which of the following options should be obtained/ masterd in order to build/develop English communication expertise? (Choose only one)

Occupation	Options	Frequency	%
Student	Correct grammar and accurate usages based on standard English models	85	37.4
	Communicative styles of native English users	17	7.5
	Communicative styles of students' own locale	5	2.2
	Communicative skills required for global use of English	88	38.8
	Other (please specify)	32	14.1
	Total	227	100.0
ELT schoolteacher	Correct grammar and accurate usages based on standard English models	53	44.9
	Communicative styles of native English users	7	5.9
	Communicative styles of students' own locale	3	2.5
	Communicative skills required for global use of English	53	44.9
	Other (please specify)	2	1.7
	Total	118	100.0

ELT university instructor	Correct grammar and accurate usages based on standard English models	24	22.2
	Communicative styles of native English users	8	7.4
	Communicative styles of students' own locale	3	2.8
	Communicative skills required for global use of English	58	53.7
	Other (please specify)	15	13.9
	Total	108	100.0
Non-ELT professional	Correct grammar and accurate usages based on standard English models	102	32.7
	Communicative styles of native English users	35	11.2
	Communicative styles of students' own locale	8	2.6
	Communicative skills required for global use of English	148	47.4
	Other (please specify)	19	6.1
	Total	312	100.0

Q17. Please mark the number that represents your opinion about the importance of each of the following activities for development of English using skills.

Occupation	Activities on	Very unimportant		Unimportant		Neutral		Important		Very important		Weighted Mean	Std. Deviation	Overall Response (in Mean)	Rank
		f	%	f	%	f	%	f	%	f	%				
Student	17.1. American English usages	16	7.0	29	12.8	79	34.8	52	22.9	51	22.5	3.41	1.17	Important	2
	17.2. British English usages	18	7.9	32	14.1	89	39.2	47	20.7	41	18.1	3.27	1.15	Neutral	3
	17.3. All/any native English usages	66	29.1	33	14.5	72	31.7	37	16.3	19	8.4	2.60	1.29	Unimportant	4
	17.4. Non-native English usages	79	34.8	39	17.2	57	25.1	34	15.0	18	7.9	2.44	1.31	Unimportant	5
	17.5. English usages in international domains	18	7.9	17	7.5	54	23.8	29	12.8	109	48.0	3.85	1.31	Important	1
	Total	197	17.36	150	13.22	351	30.93	199	17.53	238	20.97	3.12	0.66	Neutral	

Occupation	Activities on	Very unimportant		Unimportant		Neutral		Important		Very important		Weighted Mean	Std. Deviation	Overall Response (in Mean)	Rank
		f	%	f	%	f	%	f	%	f	%				
ELT Schoolteacher	17.1. American English usages	6	5.1	10	8.5	37	31.4	35	29.7	30	25.4	3.62	1.11	Important	3
	17.2. British English usages	3	2.5	6	5.1	29	24.6	30	25.4	50	42.4	4.00	1.05	Important	1
	17.3. All/any native English usages	30	25.4	20	16.9	48	40.7	8	6.8	12	10.2	2.59	1.23	Unimportant	4
	17.4. Non-native English usages	52	44.1	15	12.7	30	25.4	10	8.5	11	9.3	2.26	1.35	Unimportant	5
	17.5. English usages in international domains	13	11.0	9	7.6	20	16.9	16	13.6	60	50.8	3.86	1.40	Important	2
	Total	104	17.63	60	10.17	164	27.80	99	16.78	163	27.63	3.27	0.61	Neutral	

Occupation	Activities on	Very unimportant		Unimportant		Neutral		Important		Very important		Weighted Mean	Std. Deviation	Overall Response (in Mean)	Rank
		f	%	f	%	f	%	f	%	f	%				
ELT university instructor	17.1. American English usages	2	1.9	8	7.4	42	38.9	26	24.1	30	27.8	3.69	1.02	Important	2
	17.2. British English usages	1	0.9	8	7.4	35	32.4	20	18.5	44	40.7	3.91	1.05	Important	1
	17.3. All/any native English usages	19	17.6	10	9.3	61	56.5	15	13.9	3	2.8	2.75	1.00	Neutral	4
	17.4. Non-native English usages	32	29.6	12	11.1	50	46.3	9	8.3	5	4.6	2.47	1.14	Unimportant	5
	17.5. English usages in international domains	20	18.5	2	1.9	30	27.8	11	10.2	45	41.7	3.55	1.50	Important	3
	Total	74	13.70	40	7.41	218	40.37	81	15.00	127	23.52	3.27	0.57	Neutral	

Occupation	Activities on	Very unimportant		Unimportant		Neutral		Important		Very important		Weighted Mean	Std. Deviation	Overall Response (in Mean)	Rank
		f	%	f	%	f	%	f	%	f	%				
Non-ELT professional	17.1. American English usages	19	6.1	25	8.0	83	26.6	96	30.8	89	28.5	3.68	1.15	Important	2
	17.2. British English usages	18	5.8	30	9.6	101	32.4	94	30.1	69	22.1	3.53	1.11	Important	3
	17.3. All/any native English usages	50	16.0	32	10.3	117	37.5	72	23.1	41	13.1	3.07	1.22	Neutral	4
	17.4. Non-native English usages	67	21.5	59	18.9	100	32.1	55	17.6	31	9.9	2.76	1.25	Neutral	5
	17.5. English usages in international domains	33	10.6	20	6.4	87	27.9	44	14.1	128	41.0	3.69	1.34	Important	1
	Total	187	11.99	166	10.64	488	31.28	361	23.14	358	22.95	3.34	0.68	Neutral	

Appendix 7: Sample of survey responses

13. **Please mark the number that represents your personal opinion about the linguistic structures/elements of the following sentences.**

1-Completely unacceptable   2-Unacceptable   3- Neutral

4-Acceptable   5-Completely acceptable

Sentences	1	2	3	4	5
13.1. Mashallah, she is successful.					✓
13.2. She is wearing her Abaya and Niqaab.			✓	✓	
13.3. We love the talented children.			✓		
13.4. I ran to you as a friend more than as a mother.			✓		
13.5. It is a very very interesting story.		✓			✓
13.6. Riyadh is the city which she lives in it all her life.		✓	✓		
13.7. I sometimes go to Jeddah for shopping with my family.				✓	
13.8. What a good luck.		✓			
13.9. Let's go to one of the hypermarkets.				✓	
13.10. Don't open the computer.		✓	✓		
13.11. A good teacher is flexible with his students.					✓
13.12. This is my favorite colour.					✓
13.13. He is facing difficulty solving the problem.					✓
13.14. They should set up natural settings with authentic data.	✓	✓			
13.15. May God give you a long life.			✓		
13.16. My mother always gives me advices.	✓				
13.17. The Saudi government supports Saudization.				✓	

List of references

Abdalla, A. (2008). On the study of English as a world lingua franca: Some implications for training in EFL contexts. [pdf] Available at: https://www.researchgate.net/ [Accessed 26 March 2016].

Ahmad, H. and Shah, S. (2014). EFL textbooks: Exploring the suitability of textbook contents from EFL teachers' perspective. *VFAST Transactions on Education and Social Sciences*, 5(1), pp. 10–18.

Ahmad, S. and Ahmad, N. (2015). Fostering inter-cultural communication skills among learners through teaching English as an international language. *International Journal of Applied Linguistics and English Literature*, 4(6), pp. 52–57.

Al Asmari, A. (2014). Redefining pedagogical priorities: An investigation of EFL teachers' perceptions towards teaching English as a lingua franca in the Saudi higher education context. *Journal of Education and Practice*, 5(28), pp. 81–93.

Al Khateeb, A. (2015). The impact of English language on the public education system in Saudi Arabia in the globalisation era: A critical analysis of the situation. *International Journal of Research and Reviews in Education*, 2, pp. 1–5.

Al-Asmari, A. and Khan, M. (2014). World Englishes in the EFL teaching in Saudi Arabia. *Arab World English Journal*, 5(1), pp. 316–325.

Alfahadi, A. (2012). Saudi teachers' views on appropriate cultural models for EFL textbooks: Insights into TESOL teachers' management of global cultural flows and local realities in their teaching worlds. [pdf] Available at: https://ore.exeter.ac.uk/ [Accessed 24 March 2016].

Alharbi, N. (2016). *Business English as a Lingua Franca in Saudi Multinational Corporations: A Qualitative Investigation of*

Communicative Strategies and Orientations to Use in International Workplaces. PhD. King's College.

Alhawsawi, S. (2014). *Investigating Student Experiences of Learning English as a Foreign Language in a Preparatory Programme in a Saudi University.* PhD. University of Sussex.

Al-Johani, H. (2009). *Finding a Way Forward: The Impact of Teachers' Strategies, Beliefs and Knowledge on Teaching English as a Foreign Language in Saudi Arabia.* PhD. University of Strathclyde.

Alrashidi, O. and Phan, H. (2015). Education context and English teaching and learning in the Kingdom of Saudi Arabia: An overview. *English Language Teaching,* 8(5), p. 33–44.

Al-Rawi, M. (2012). Four grammatical features of Saudi English. *English Today,* 28(2), pp. 32–38.

Al-Seghayer, K. (2014). The four most common constraints affecting English teaching in Saudi Arabia. *International Journal of English Linguistics,* 4(5), pp. 17–26.

Alseweed, M. (2012). University students' perceptions of the influence of native and non-native teachers. *English Language Teaching,* 5(12), pp. 42–53.

Alshahrani, K. and Al-Shehri, S. (2012). Conceptions and responses to e-learning: The case of EFL teachers and students in a Saudi Arabian university. *Monash University Linguistics Papers,* 8(1), pp. 21–31.

Al-Shurafa, N. (2009). Linguistic variations and use of the 21st Century Arabicisation of English. [online] Available at: http://www. education.ox.ac.uk/wordpress/wp-content/uploads/2010/08/ Nuha-Al-Shurafa.doc [Accessed 17/07/2016].

Alzayid, A. (2012). *The Role of Motivation in the L2 Acquisition of English by Saudi Students: A Dynamic Perspective.* MFA. Southern Illinois University Carbondale.

Ammon, U. (2001). English as a future language of teaching at German universities? A question of difficult consequences, posed by the decline of German as a language of science. *Contributions to the Sociology of Language*, 84, pp. 343–362.

Archibald, A., Cogo, A., and Jenkins, J. eds. (2011). *Latest trends in ELF research*. Cambridge Scholars Publishing.

Azuaga, L. and Cavalheiro, L. (2012). Three continents, one language: Studying English in a Portuguese landscape (Brazil, Cape Verde and Portugal). *Revista Anglo Saxonica*, 3(4), 35–51.

Baird, R. (2012). English as a lingua franca: The study of language practices. *Englishes in Practice*, 1, pp. 3–17.

Baird, R. (2013). *Investigating Perceptions of Master's Students on English-as-a-medium-of-instruction Programmes in East Asia*. PhD. University of Southampton.

Baird, R. and Baird, M. (2018). English as a lingua franca: Changing 'attitudes'. In: Jenkins, J., Baker, W., and Dewey, M., eds., *The Routledge Handbook of English as a Lingua Franca*. London: Routledge, pp. 531–543.

Baird, R., Baker, W., and Kitazawa, M. (2014). The complexity of ELF. *Journal of English as a Lingua Franca*, 3(1), p. 171–196.

Baker, W. (2009). *Intercultural Awareness and Intercultural Communication Through English: An Investigation of Thai English Language Users in Higher Education*. PhD. University of Southampton.

Baker, W. (2011). Intercultural awareness: Modelling an understanding of cultures in intercultural communication through English as a lingua franca. *Language and Intercultural Communication*, 11(3), pp. 197–214.

Baker, W. (2012a). *Using Online Learning Objects to Develop Intercultural Awareness in ELT: A Critical Examination in a Thai Higher Education Setting*. PhD. University of Southampton.

Baker, W. (2012b). From cultural awareness to intercultural awareness: Culture in ELT. *ELT Journal*, 66(1), pp. 62–70.

Baker, W. (2015a). *Culture and identity through English as a lingua franca: Rethinking concepts and goals in intercultural communication.* Vol. 8. Berlin: Walter de Gruyter.

Baker, W. (2015b). Culture and complexity through English as a lingua franca: Rethinking competences and pedagogy in ELT. *Journal of English as a Lingua Franca*, 4(1), pp. 9–30.

Baker, W. and Jenkins, J. (2015). Criticising ELF. *Journal of English as a Lingua Franca*, 4(1), p. 191–198.

Baker, W., Jenkins, J., and Baird, R. (2014). ELF researchers take issue with 'English as a lingua franca: An immanent critique'. *Applied Linguistics*, 36(1), pp. 121–123.

Barcelos A. (2003). Researching beliefs about SLA: A critical review. In: Kalaja P., Barcelos A. M. F., eds., *Beliefs about SLA*. Vol 2. Dordrecht: Springer, pp. 7–33.

Bayyurt, Y. and Altinmakas, D. (2012). A WE-based English communication skills course at a Turkish university. In: Matsuda, A., ed., *Principles and Practices of Teaching English as an International Language*. 25th ed. Bristol: Multilingual Matters, p. 169–179.

Bayyurt, Y. and Akcan, S. (2015). *Current Perspectives on Pedagogy for English as a Lingua Franca*. Berlin/Boston: De Gruyter.

Beckner, C., Blythe, R., Bybee, J., Christiansen, M. H., Croft, W., Ellis, N. C., Holland, J., Ke, J., Larsen-Freeman, D. and Schoenemann, T. (2009). Language is a complex adaptive system: Position paper. *Language Learning*, 59(s1), pp.1–26.

Björkman, B. (2008a). English as the lingua franca of engineering: The morphosyntax of academic speech events. *Nordic Journal of English Studies*, 7(3), pp.103–122.

Björkman, B. (2008b). 'So where we are?' Spoken lingua franca English at a technical university in Sweden. *English Today*, 24(2), pp. 35–41.

Björkman, B. (2013). *English as an academic lingua franca: an investigation of form and communicative effectiveness.* Vol. 3. Berlin: Walter de Gruyter.

Blommaert, J. (2010). *The sociolinguistics of globalization.* Cambridge: Cambridge University Press.

Blommaert, J. (2013). *Ethnography, superdiversity and linguistic landscapes: Chronicles of complexity.* Vol. 18. Bristol: Multilingual Matters.

Bolton, K. (2008). English in Asia, Asian Englishes, and the issue of proficiency. *English Today*, 24(02).

Brumfit, C. (2001). *Individual Freedom in Language Teaching.* Oxford: Oxford University Press.

Bryman, A. (2006). Integrating quantitative and qualitative research: how is it done?. *Qualitative Research*, 6(1), pp.97-113.

Bukhary, S. and Bahanshal, D. (2013). Motivation and learning strategies in a foreign language classroom: A look at learners of Saudi Arabia. *International Journal of Applied Linguistics and English Literature*, 2(5), pp. 192–200.

Byram, M. (1997). *Teaching and assessing intercultural communicative competence.* Bristol: Multilingual Matters.

Canagarajah, A. (2007). Lingua franca English, multilingual communities, and language acquisition. *The Modern Language Journal*, 91(s1), pp. 923–939.

Canagarajah, A. (2009). The plurilingual tradition and the English language in South Asia. *AILA Review*, 22(1), pp. 5–22.

Canagarajah, A. (2012). *Translingual practice: Global Englishes and cosmopolitan relations.* Oxon: Routledge.

Canagarajah, A., ed. (2015). *Reclaiming the local in language policy and practice*. New York: Routledge.

Canale, M. (1983). From communicative competence to communicative language pedagogy. *Language and Communication*, 1(1), pp. 1–47.

Canale, M. and Swain, M. (1980). Theoretical bases of communicative approaches to second language teaching and testing. *Applied Linguistics*, 1(1), pp. 1–47.

Cavalheiro, L. (2015). *English as a Lingua Franca: Bridging the Gap Between Theory and Practice in English Language Teaching*. PhD. University of Lisbon.

Cogo, A. (2010). Strategic use and perceptions of English as a lingua franca. *Poznań Studies in Contemporary Linguistics*, 46(3), pp. 295–312.

Cogo, A. (2015). English as a lingua franca: Descriptions, domains and applications. In: Bowles H. and Cogo A., eds., *International Perspectives on English as a Lingua Franca*. London: Palgrave Macmillan, pp. 1–12.

Cogo, A. and Dewey, M. (2012). *Analysing English as a lingua franca: A corpus-driven investigation*. London: Continuum.

Cohen, L., Manion, L. and Morrison, K. (2013). *Research methods in education*. Hoboken: Taylor and Francis.

Cook, V. (1992). Evidence for multicompetence. *Language Learning*, 42(4), pp. 557–591.

Cook, V. (2008). Multi-competence: Black hole or wormhole for second language acquisition research. In: Han, Z. and Park, E. S., eds., *Understanding Second Language Process*. Clevedon: Multilingual Matters, pp. 16–26.

Cooper, R. and Fishman, J. (1977). A study of language attitudes. *Bilingual Review/La Revista Bilingüe*, 4(1/2), pp. 7–34.

Crystal, D. (1998). English as a global language. *European Review-Chichester*, 6, pp. 371–373.

Davies, A. (2003). *The native speaker: Myth and reality.* Vol. 38. Clevedon: Multilingual Matters.

Dewey, M. (2011). Accommodative ELF talk and teacher knowledge. In: Archibald, A., Cogo A., and Jenkins, J., eds., *Latest Trends in ELF Research.* Newcastle upon Tyne: Cambridge Scholars Publishing, pp. 205–227.

Dewey, M. (2012). Towards a post-normative approach: Learning the pedagogy of ELF. *Journal of English as a Lingua Franca*, 1(1), pp. 141–170.

Dewey, M. (2014). Pedagogic criticality and English as a lingua franca. *Atlantis*, 36(2), pp. 11–30.

Dörnyei, Z. (2000). Motivation in action: Towards a process-oriented conceptualisation of student motivation. *British Journal of Educational Psychology*, 70(4), pp. 519–538.

Dörnyei, Z. (2001). *Motivational strategies in the language classroom.* Cambridge: Cambridge University Press, pp. 43–50.

Dörnyei, Z. (2014). *Research methods in applied linguistics.* 12th ed. Oxford: Oxford University Press.

Dow, J., Niedzielski, N. and Preston, D. (2001). Folk Linguistics. *The Journal of American Folklore*, 114(454), p.504.

Ebrahim, M. and Awan, N. (2015). Second language acquisition in Arab learners: A paradigm shift. *International Journal of Languages, Literature and Linguistics*, 1(3), pp. 193–197.

Elyas, T. (2011). *Diverging Identities: a 'Contextualised' Exploration of the Interplay of Competing Discourses in Two Saudi University Classrooms.* PhD. University of Adelaide.

Elyas, T. (2014). Exploring Saudi Arabia's EFL student identity: A narrative critical approach. *International Journal of Applied Linguistics and English Literature*, 3(5), pp. 28–38.

Elyas, T. (2015). Teaching and learning English in the Arabic-speaking world. *ELT Journal*, 69(4), pp. 463–466.

Elyas, T. and Badawood, O. (2017). English language educational policy in Saudi Arabia post 21st Century: Enacted curriculum, identity, and modernisation: A critical discourse analysis approach. *FIRE: Forum for International Research in Education*, 3(3), pp. 70–81.

Elyas, T. and Picard, M. (2012a). Teaching and moral tradition in Saudi Arabia: A paradigm of struggle or pathway towards globalization? *Procedia—Social and Behavioral Sciences*, 47, pp. 1083–1086.

Elyas, T. and Picard, M. (2012b). Towards a globalized notion of English language teaching in Saudi Arabia: A case study. *The Asian EFL Journal Quarterly*, 14(2), p. 99–124.

Evans, V. (2007). *Glossary of cognitive linguistics*. Edinburgh: Edinburgh University Press.

Faruk, S. (2014). Chinese and Saudi English language education policies: A world system perspective. *Romanian Journal of English Studies*, 11(1), pp. 264–271.

Firth, A. (1996). The discursive accomplishment of normality: On 'lingua franca' English and conversation analysis. *Journal of Pragmatics*, 26(2), pp. 237–259.

Fussell, B. (2011). The local flavour of English in the Gulf. *English Today*, 108, pp. 26–32.

Galloway, N. (2013). Global Englishes and English language teaching (ELT)–Bridging the gap between theory and practice in a Japanese context. *System*, 41(3), pp. 786–803.

Galloway, N. and Rose, H. (2013). "They envision going to New York, not Jakarta": The differing attitudes toward ELF of students, teaching assistants, and instructors in an English-medium business program in Japan. *Journal of English as a Lingua Franca*, 2(2), pp. 229–253.

Galloway, N. and Rose, H. (2014). Using listening journals to raise awareness of global Englishes in ELT. *ELT Journal*, 68(4), pp. 386–396.

Galloway, N. and Rose, H. (2015). *Introducing Global Englishes*. Oxon: Routledge.

Gardner, R. (1983). Learning another language: A true social psychological experiment. *Journal of Language and Social Psychology*, 2(2-3-4), pp. 219–239.

Gardner, R. (2006). The socio-educational model of second language acquisition: A research paradigm. *Eurosla Yearbook*, 6(1), pp.237–260.

Garrett, P., Coupland, N. and Williams, A., eds. (2003). *Investigating language attitudes: Social meanings of dialect, ethnicity and performance*. Cardiff: University of Wales Press.

Giles, H. (2009). The process of communication accommodation. In: Coupland, N. and Jaworski, A., *The New Sociolinguistics Reader*. London: Macmillan Education, pp. 276–286.

Goebl, H. ed. (1997). *Kontaktlinguistik/Contact Linguistics/Linguistique de contact*. Berlin: Walter de Gruyter.

Grami, G. (2012). Are learner-centred approaches the answer to Saudi language classes? *Annual Review of Education, Communication & Language Sciences*, 9, pp. 1–14.

Greene, J., Caracelli, V. and Graham, W. (1989). Toward a Conceptual Framework for Mixed-Method Evaluation Designs. *Educational Evaluation and Policy Analysis*, 11(3), pp.255-274.

Grill, J. (2010). Whose English counts? Native speakers as English language learners. *TESOL Journal*, 1(3), pp. 358–367.

Grix, J. (2010). *The foundations of research*. 2ⁿᵈ ed. Hampshire: Palgrave Macmillan.

Guerra, L. (2005). *Teaching and Learning English as an International Language in Portugal: Policy, Practice and Perceptions*. PhD. University of Warwick.

Halliday, M. (1975). *Learning how to mean: Explorations in the development of language*. London: Edward Arnold.

Halliday M. (1997) Language in a social perspective. In: Coupland N. and Jaworski A., eds., *Sociolinguistics*. London: Macmillan Publishers Limited, pp. 31– 38.

Hassan, B. (2009). *Ideology, Identity, and Linguistic Capital: A Sociolinguistic Investigation of Language Shift Among the Ajam of Kuwait*. PhD. University of Essex.

Herdina, P. and Jessner, U. (2002). *A dynamic model of multilingualism: Perspectives of change in psycholinguistics*. Vol. 121. Clevedon: Multilingual Matters.

Holliday, A. (2006). Native-speakerism. *ELT Journal*, 60(4), pp. 385–387.

Hopper, P. (1988). Emergent grammar and the a priori grammar postulate. In: Tannen, D., ed., *Linguistics in Context— Connecting Observation and Understanding*. Ablex Publishing Corporation, pp. 117–134.

House, J. (2002). Communicating in English as a lingua franca. *Eurosla Yearbook*, 2(1), pp. 243–261.

House, J. (2003). English as a lingua franca: A threat to multilingualism? *Journal of Sociolinguistics*, 7(4), pp. 556–578.

House, J. (2010). English as a global lingua franca: A threat to multilingualism? In: Shiyab, S. M., Rose, M. G. and House, J., eds., *Globalization and Aspects of Translation*. Newcastle upon Tyne, Cambridge Scholars Publications, pp. 11-35.

House, J. (2014). English as a global lingua franca: A threat to multilingual communication and translation? *Language Teaching*, 47(3), pp. 363–376.

Hudson, P. (2011). *Beef and Lamb, Chicken and H**: Censorship and Vocabulary Teaching in Arabia*. PhD. Canterbury Christ Church University.

Hurley, S. (2002). *Consciousness in action*. Cambridge, Mass.: Harvard University Press.

İnal, D. and Özdemir, E. (2015). Reconsidering the English language teacher education programs in Turkey from an ELF standpoint: What do the academia, pre-service and in-service teachers think? *Current Perspectives on Pedagogy for English as a Lingua Franca*, 6, p.135–152.

Ishikawa, T. (2015). Academic rigour in criticising English as a lingua franca. *Englishes in Practice*, 2(2), pp. 39–48.

Ishikawa, T. (2017). Conceptualising English as a global contact language. *Englishes in Practice* 4(2), pp. 31–49.

Javid, C., Farooq, U. and Gulzar, M. (2012). Saudi English-major undergraduates and English teachers' perceptions regarding effective ELT in the KSA: A comparative study. *European Journal of Scientific Research*, 85(1), pp. 55–70.

Jaworski, A., Coupland, N. and Galasinski, D., eds. (2004). *Metalanguage: Social and ideological perspectives*. Vol. 11. Berlin: Walter de Gruyter.

Jenkins, J. (2006a). Global intelligibility and local diversity: Possibility or paradox. In: Rubdy, R. and Saraceni, M., eds., *English in the World: Global Rules, Global Roles*. London: Continuum, pp. 32–39.

Jenkins, J. (2006b). Current perspectives on teaching world Englishes and English as a lingua franca. *TESOL Quarterly*, 40(1), pp.157–181.

Jenkins, J. (2006c). Points of view and blind spots: ELF and SLA. *International Journal of Applied Linguistics*, 16(2), p. 137–162.

Jenkins, J. (2007). *English as a lingua franca: Attitude and identity.* Oxford: Oxford University Press.

Jenkins, J. (2009a). English as a lingua franca: Interpretations and attitudes. *World Englishes*, 28(2), pp. 200–207.

Jenkins, J. (2009b). (Un)pleasant? (In)correct? (Un)intelligible? ELF speakers' perceptions of their accents. In: Mauranen, A. and Ranta, E., eds., *English as a lingua franca: Studies and findings.* Newcastle upon Tyne: Cambridge Scholars Publishing, pp. 10–36.

Jenkins, J. (2011). Accommodating (to) ELF in the international university. *Journal of Pragmatics*, 43(4), pp. 926–936.

Jenkins, J. (2013). *English as a lingua franca in the international university: The politics of academic English language policy.* London: Routledge.

Jenkins, J. (2014). *Global Englishes: A resource book for students.* London: Routledge.

Jenkins, J. (2015a). Repositioning English and multilingualism in English as a lingua franca. *Englishes in Practice*, 2(3), pp. 49–85.

Jenkins, J. (2015b). International tests of English: Are they fit for purpose? [online] Available at: https://www.researchgate.net/publication/275654877_International_tests_of_English_are_they_fit_for_purpose [Accessed 29 March 2016].

Jenkins, J. (2017a). The future of English as a lingua franca? In: Jenkins, J., Baker, W. and Dewey, M. eds., *The Routledge Handbook of English as a Lingua Franca.* London: Routledge, pp.594–605.

Jenkins, J. (2017b). Not English but English-within-multilingualism. In: Coffey, S. and Wingate, U., eds., *New Directions for Research in Foreign Language Education.* New York: Routledge, pp. 63–78.

Jenkins, J., Cogo, A. and Dewey, M. (2011). Review of developments in research into English as a lingua franca. *Language Teaching*, 44(03), pp. 281–315.

Jenks, C. (2012). Doing being reprehensive: Some interactional features of English as a lingua franca in a chat room. *Applied Linguistics*, 33(4), pp. 386–405.

Joseph, J. (2004). *Language and identity: National, ethnic, religious.* Hampshire: Palgrave Macmillan.

Kachru, B. (1986). *The alchemy of English: The spread, functions, and models of non-native Englishes.* Oxford: Pergamon Press.

Kachru, B., ed. (1992). *The other tongue: English across cultures.* 2nd ed. Chicago: University of Illinois Press.

Kahane, H. and Kahane, R. (1976). Lingua franca: The story of a term. *Romance Philology*, 30(1), pp. 25–41.

Källström, R. and Lindberg, I. (2011). *Young urban Swedish: Variation and change in multilingual settings.* Gothenburg: Intellecta Infolog.

Kaur, P. (2014). Attitudes towards English as a Lingua Franca. *Procedia-Social and Behavioral Sciences*, 118, pp. 214–221.

Khan, I. (2011). Learning difficulties in English: Diagnosis and pedagogy in Saudi Arabia. *Educational Research*, 2(7), pp. 1248–1257.

Khan, M. (2015). The myth of reference varieties in English pronunciation across the Subcontinent, Egypt and Kingdom of Saudi Arabia. *International Journal of English Linguistics*, 5(3), p. 19–36.

Kirkpatrick, A. (2007a). English as a lingua franca: Attitude and identity. *Asian Englishes*, 10(2), pp. 106–109.

Kirkpatrick, A. (2007b). Setting attainable and appropriate English language targets in multilingual settings: A case for Hong Kong. *International Journal of Applied Linguistics*, 17(3), pp. 376–391.

Kitazawa, M. (2013). *Approaching Conceptualisations of English in East Asian Contexts: Ideas, Ideology, and Identification* PhD. University of Southampton.

Kramsch, C. (2009). *The multilingual subject: What foreign language learners say about their experience and why it matters.* Oxford: Oxford University Press.

Kronick, L. (2014). *For the Degree of Master of Arts in English as a Second Language.* PhD. University of Minnesota.

Kroskrity, P. (2004). Language ideologies. In: Duranti, A., ed., *A Companion to Linguistic Anthropology.* Malden: Blackwell Publishing, pp. 496–517.

Langacker, R. (1987). *Foundations of cognitive grammar: Theoretical prerequisites.* Vol. 1. Stanford: Stanford University Press.

Larsen-Freeman, D. (2011). A complexity theory approach to second language development/acquisition. In: Atkinson, D., ed., *Alternative Approaches to Second Language Acquisition.* Abingdon: Routledge, pp. 48–72.

Larsen-Freeman, D. and Anderson, M. (2013). *Techniques and principles in language teaching.* 3rd edition. Oxford: Oxford University Press.

Larsen-Freeman, D. and Cameron, L. (2008). Research methodology on language development from a complex systems perspective. *The Modern Language Journal,* 92(2), pp. 200–213.

Larsen-Freeman, D. and Cameron, L. (2012). *Complex systems and applied linguistics.* Oxford: Oxford University Press.

Lenneberg, E. (1967). The biological foundations of language. *Hospital Practice,* 2(12), pp. 59–67.

Lønsmann, D. (2011). *English as a Corporate Language: Language Choice and Language Ideologies in an International Company in Denmark.* PhD. Roskilde University.

MacKenzie, I. (2014). *English as a lingua franca: Theorizing and teaching English*. London: Routledge.

MacKenzie, I. (2015). Will English as a lingua franca impact on native English? [online] Studies in Variation, Contacts and Change in English. Available at: http://www.helsinki.fi/varieng/series/volumes/16/MacKenzie/ [Accessed 05/07/2018].

Mahboob, A. and Elyas, T. (2014). English in the Kingdom of Saudi Arabia. *World Englishes*, 33(1), pp. 128–142.

Mair, C., ed. (2003). *The politics of English as a world language: New horizons in postcolonial cultural studies*. Vol. 65. Amsterdam: Rodopi.

Marotta, V. (2014). The multicultural, intercultural and the transcultural subject. In: Mansouri, F. and de B'béri, B. E., eds., *Global perspectives on the politics of multiculturalism in the 21st century: A case study analysis*. London: Routledge, pp. 106–118.

Matras, Y. (2009). *Language contact*. Cambridge: Cambridge University Press.

Matsuda, A. (2009). Desirable but not necessary? The place of world Englishes and English as an international language in English teacher preparation programs in Japan. In: Sharifian, F., ed., *English as an International Language: Perspectives and Pedagogical Issues*. Bristol: Multilingual Matters, pp. 169–189.

Mauranen, A. (2006). Signaling and preventing misunderstanding in English as lingua franca communication. *International Journal of the Sociology of Language*, 2006(177), pp. 123–150.

Mauranen, A. (2012). *Exploring ELF: Academic English shaped by non-native speakers*. Cambridge: Cambridge University Press.

Mauranen, A. (2013). English as a global lingua franca: changing language in changing global academia. *Waseda working papers in ELF*, 2, pp. 10–27.

McKay, S. (2002). Teaching English as an international language: Rethinking goals and perspectives. *The Electronic Journal for English as a Second Language*, 7(1), pp. 1–5.

McKay, S. (2003). Toward an appropriate EIL pedagogy: Re-examining common ELT assumptions. *International Journal of Applied Linguistics*, 13(1), pp. 1–22.

McKay, S. (2009). Pragmatics and EIL pedagogy. *English as an international language: Perspectives and pedagogical issues*, 11, pp. 227–241.

Medgyes, P. (1994). *The non-native teacher*. London: Macmillan.

Mekheimer, M. and Aldosari, H. (2011). Impediments to cultural teaching in EFL programmes at a Saudi University. *Journal of Intercultural Communication*, 26(3), pp.1404– 1634.

Milroy, J. and Milroy, L. (1985). *Authority in language: Investigating language prescription and standardisation*. London: Routledge.

Milroy, L. (1999). Standard English and language ideology in Britain and the United States. *Standard English: The Widening Debate*, 173, p. 206.

Moran-Ellis, J., Alexander, V. D., Cronin, A., Dickinson, M., Fielding, J., Sleney, J. and Thomas, H. (2006). Triangulation and integration: Processes, claims and implications. *Qualitative Research*, 6(1), pp. 45–59.

Motschenbacher, H. (2013). *New perspectives on English as a European lingua franca*. Amsterdam: John Benjamins Publishing Company.

Nouraldeen, A. and Elyas, T. (2014). Learning English in Saudi Arabia: A socio-cultural perspective. *International Journal of English Language and Linguistics Research*, 2(3), pp. 56–78.

O'Regan, J. (2014). English as a lingua franca: An immanent critique. *Applied Linguistics*, 35(5), pp. 533–552.

Onsman, A. (2012). Distributing the future evenly: English as the lingua franca in the Saudi Arabian higher education sector. *Higher Education Policy*, 25(4), pp. 477– 491.

Osman, H. A. (2015). *Investigating English Teachers' Perceptions of Intercultural Communicative Competence in the Kingdom of Saudi Arabia*. PhD. University of San Francisco.

Pajares, M. (1992). Teachers' beliefs and educational research: Cleaning up a messy construct. *Review of Educational Research*, 62(3), pp. 307–332.

Pennycook, A. (1994). Incommensurable discourses? *Applied Linguistics*, 15(2), pp. 115–138.

Phillipson, R. (2013). *Linguistic imperialism continued*. New York: Routledge.

Pitzl, M. (2009). "We should not wake up any dogs": Idiom and metaphor in ELF. In: Mauranen, A. and Ranta, E., eds., *English as a Lingua Franca: Studies and Findings*. Newcastle upon Tyne: Cambridge Scholars Publishing, pp. 298–322.

Pitzl, M. (2012). Creativity meets convention: Idiom variation and remetaphorization in ELF. Journal of English as a Lingua Franca 1(1), pp. 27–55.

Preston, D. (1989). *Perceptual dialectology: Nonlinguists' views of areal linguistics*. Vol. 7. Dordrecht: Foris Publications Holland.

Preston, D. (1994). Content-oriented discourse analysis and folk linguistics. *Language Sciences*, 16(2), pp. 285–331.

Preston, D. (2004). Folk metalanguage. *Language Power and Social Process*, 11, pp. 75–104.

Preston, D. (2011). Methods in (applied) folk linguistics: Getting into the minds of the folk. *AILA Review*, 24(1), pp.15–39.

Raven, J. (2011). Emiratizing the education sector in the UAE: Contextualisation and challenges. *Education, Business and Society: Contemporary Middle Eastern Issues*, 4(2), pp.134–141.

Saldaña, J. (2013). *The coding manual for qualitative researchers*. Los Angeles: Sage.

Schneider, E. (2007). *Postcolonial English: Varieties around the world*. Cambridge: Cambridge University Press.

Schröder, T., Homer-Dixon, T., Maynard, J., Mildenberger, M., Milkoreit, M., Mock, S., Quilley, S. and Thagard, P. (2013). A Complex Systems Approach to the Study of Ideology: Cognitive-Affective Structures and the Dynamics of Belief Systems. *Journal of Social and Political Psychology*, 1(1), pp.337-363.

Seidlhofer, B. (2001). Closing a conceptual gap: The case for a description of English as a lingua franca. *International Journal of Applied Linguistics*, 11(2), pp.133–158.

Seidlhofer, B. (2002). The shape of things to come? Some basic questions about English as a lingua franca. In: Knapp, K. and Meierkord, C., eds., *Lingua franca communication*. Frankfort: Peter Lang, 269–302.

Seidlhofer, B. (2003). *A concept of International English and related issues: From 'real English' to 'realistic English'?* Strasbourg: Council of Europe.

Seidlhofer, B. (2004). Research perspectives on teaching English as a lingua franca. *Annual Review of Applied Linguistics*, 24, pp.209–239.

Seidlhofer, B. (2006). English as a lingua franca in the expanding circle: What it isn't. In: Rubdy, R. and Saraceni, M., eds., *English in the World: Global Rules, Global Roles*. London: Continuum, pp. 40–50.

Seidlhofer, B. (2009a). Common ground and different realities: World Englishes and English as a lingua franca. *World Englishes*, 28(2), pp.236–245.

Seidlhofer, B. (2009b). Orientations in ELF research: Form and function. In: Mauranen, A. and Ranta, E., eds., *English as a Lingua Franca: Studies and Findings*. Newcastle upon Tyne: Cambridge Scholars Publishing, pp. 37-297.

Seidlhofer, B. (2010). Giving VOICE to English as a lingua franca. In: Facchinetti, R. and Crystal, D., eds., *From International to Local English and Back Again*. Bern: Peter Lang, pp. 132–156.

Seidlhofer, B. (2011). *Understanding English as a lingua franca*. Oxford: Oxford University Press.

Sewell, A. (2013). English as a lingua franca: Ontology and ideology. *ELT journal*, 67(1), pp. 3–10.

Sifakis, N. (2007). The education of teachers of English as a lingua franca: A transformative perspective. *International Journal of Applied Linguistics*, 17(3), pp. 355–375.

Sifakis, N. (2009). Teacher education in the post-modern era: Introducing a transformative dimension in the teaching of English as a lingua franca. *Selected Papers on Theoretical and Applied Linguistics from ISTAL*, 18, pp. 345–353.

Sifakis, N. (2014a). ELF awareness as an opportunity for change: A transformative perspective for ESOL teacher education. *Journal of English as a Lingua Franca*, 3(2), pp. 317–335.

Sifakis, N. (2014b). Teaching pronunciation in the post-EFL era: Lessons from ELF and implications for teacher education. In: de Dios Martínez Agudo, J., ed., *English as a Foreign Language Teacher Education: Current Perspectives and Challenges*. Amsterdam: Rodopi, pp. 127–146.

Sifakis, N. and Bayyurt, Y. (2015). Insights from ELF and WE in teacher training in Greece and Turkey. *World Englishes*, 34(3), pp. 471–484.

Stets, J. and Burke, P. (2000). Identity theory and social identity theory. *Social Psychology Quarterly*, 63(3), pp. 224–237.

Thagard P. (2015) The cognitive–affective structure of political ideologies. In: Martinovsky, B., ed., *Emotion in Group Decision and Negotiation. Advances in Group Decision and Negotiation.* Vol 7. Dordrecht: Springer, pp. 51–71.

Tracy, S. (2013). *Qualitative research methods.* Chichester: Wiley-Blackwell.

Trudgill, P. (2002). *Sociolinguistic Variation and Change.* Georgetown University Press.

Trudgill, P. (2011). *Sociolinguistic typology: Social determinants of linguistic complexity.* Oxford: Oxford University Press.

Ur Rahman, M. and Alhaisoni, E. (2013). Teaching English in Saudi Arabia: Prospects and challenges. *Academic Research International*, 4(1), p. 112.

Van Dijk, T. (1998). *Ideology: A multidisciplinary approach.* London: Sage.

Van Dijk, T. (2006). Ideology and discourse analysis. *Journal of Political Ideologies*, 11(2), pp.115–140.

Verschueren, J. (2012). *Ideology in language use: Pragmatic guidelines for empirical research.* Cambridge: Cambridge University Press.

Wang, Y. (2012). *Chinese Speakers' Perceptions of Their English in Intercultural Communication.* PhD. University of Southampton.

Wang, Y. (2013). Non-conformity to ENL norms: A perspective from Chinese English users. *Journal of English as a Lingua Franca*, 2(2), pp. 255–282.

Wang, Y. (2015a). Native English speakers' authority in English: Do Chinese speakers of English care about native English speakers' judgments? *English Today*, 32(1), pp. 35–40.

Wang, Y. (2015b). Chinese university students' ELF awareness: Impacts of language education in China. *Englishes in Practice*, 2(4), pp. 86–106.

Wang, Y. and Jenkins, J. (2016). "Nativeness" and intelligibility: Impacts of intercultural experience through English as a lingua franca on Chinese speakers' language attitudes. *Chinese Journal of Applied Linguistics*, 39(1), pp. 38–58.

Wei, L. (2017). Translanguaging as a Practical Theory of Language. *Applied Linguistics*, 39(1), pp.9-30.

Wenden, A. (1999). An introduction to Metacognitive Knowledge and Beliefs in Language Learning: beyond the basics. *System*, 27(4), pp.435-441.

Wesely, P. (2012). Learner attitudes, perceptions, and beliefs in language learning. *Foreign Language Annals*, 45(s1), pp. s98-s117.

Widdowson, H. (2012). ELF and the inconvenience of established concepts. *Journal of English as a Lingua Franca* 1(1), 5–26.

Widdowson, H. (2015). Contradiction and conviction: A reaction to O'Regan. *Applied Linguistics*, 36(1), pp. 124–127.

Woods, D. (1996). *Teacher cognition in language teaching: Beliefs, decision-making, and classroom practice*. Cambridge: Cambridge University Press, pp. 3–15.

Woolard, K. (1998). Introduction: Language ideology as a field of inquiry. In: Schieffelin, B. B., Woolard, K. A., and & Kroskity, P. V., eds., *Language ideologies: practice and theory*. New York: Oxford University Press, pp. 3–47.

Printed in the United States
By Bookmasters